D1105328

WILLINGLY TO SCHOOL

WILLINGLY
TO SCHOOL

A History of
Women's Education

by
MARY CATHCART BORER

LUTTERWORTH PRESS
GUILDFORD AND LONDON

First published 1976

ISBN 0 7188 2127 0

COPYRIGHT © 1975 MARY CATHCART BORER

Printed in Great Britain
by Richard Clay (The Chaucer Press) Ltd.,
Bungay, Suffolk

Contents

Acknowledgements

I should like to thank C. J. Long, F.L.A., the Borough Librarian of Hackney, and his archivist Stanley Tongue, for their kind help during my researches on the Hackney Schools, Miss Hilary Claridge for allowing me to see her paper on St. Leonard's Charity School for Boys—1705–1934, and the Francis Holland School for lending me their history of the school and the *Graham Street Memories*.

Thanks are also due to the following organizations and institutions for permission to reproduce the photographs and prints for which they hold the copyright: Christ's Hospital/Hertfordshire Mercury (Plates 2 *top*, 12 *top*); Greater London Council Print Collection (Plates 2 *bottom*, 4, 10, 12 *bottom*); London Borough of Hackney (Plate 6 *bottom*); Kensington and Chelsea Public Libraries (Plate 7 *top*); National Portrait Gallery (Plates 1, 6 *top*, 7 *bottom*); North London Collegiate School (Plates 8 *top left*, 8 *bottom*, 9); Newnham College, Cambridge (Plate 11 *bottom*); Radio Times Hulton Picture Library (Plate 8 *top right*); Red Maids School (Plate 3); Roedean School (Plate 11 *top*); Victoria and Albert Museum, Crown Copyright (Plate 5).

M.C.B.

List of Plates

Chapter One

INTRODUCTION

THE CHILDREN OF the human race are dependent on their parents for a far longer period of time than any other living creatures, and there is a vast sum of knowledge that must be taught them in order that they may become acceptable members of the society into which they have been born. And ever since mankind invented the art of writing, floods of words have poured forth, some wise, some obvious, some plain silly, in regard to the twin problems of what to teach children and the best way of getting the information into their heads so that it has lasting value.

These theories have been argued throughout the centuries with remarkably little variation or conclusion, and for hundreds of years the additional problem of whether girls should receive the same education as boys, or go their own separate ways, has been discussed inconclusively. Nearly every generation has come up with the discovery, heralded on each occasion as new and well-nigh revolutionary, that girls can be as mentally agile as their brothers and as potentially able scholars.

The strongest instinct in any animal is to survive, and that involves the mating of the sexes. As a preliminary, the male and female, however promiscuous, or indeed unadventurous, must, even though for the briefest of periods, please each other, so it would seem that the battle of the sexes began very early in human history. Nevertheless, in prehistoric times, when mankind's principal preoccupation was the eternal quest for food, men and women, recognizing that their natural functions were complementary, shared the work necessary to their survival intelligently.

As civilization and society developed and became more complicated, with the acquisition of property and the establishment of social classes, the relationship between men and women grew more controversial and subject to the vagaries of fashion and economic expediency. And so it has remained ever since. When work is hard to come by and jobs are scarce, woman's place is in the home, well away from the labour market, but when labour is scarce and every hand is needed, then it is woman's duty to take her place gallantly beside her menfolk. All the feminine wiles and graces, so carefully instilled into her during the years of prosperity and peace, must be suddenly shed and replaced by sterner and less glamorous attributes for the duration of the emergency. In fact it is only by being extraordinarily adaptable that she can keep her end up at all.

The social classes were formed, in the first place, by the conquered and the conquerors, and the status of women plumbed its depths in the pagan slave households of the Classical world, where their function in life was 'caring only to serve the pleasure of men', but amongst the upper classes of the free the eternal argument had already been under way for centuries. In order to please themselves, men and women must please each other. To conquer they must pretend to be conquered. To pursue each other successfully they must assume the role of the pursued, and until a stable relationship of marriage, based on love, affection, mutual respect, indifference or plain dislike, has been established, they must play hide and seek with their emotions and their intellects. There is a paradox to be found in every aspect of the game.

While the ancient civilizations of Western Asia waxed and waned before the growing might of the Persians, the civilization of Greece was taking shape—the civilization on which the whole of the western world has been based. 'We are all Greeks,' said Shelley. 'Our laws, our religion, our art, have their roots in Greece.'

Homer, writing about 1000 B.C. gives a picture of Grecian

women during the Heroic Age of Greece, romantic and beautiful creatures, full of grace and charm. The Greeks were monogamous and at this time the family was the important social unit. The married woman, as the mother of the family, was held in high regard, but legally she had no rights. Her only education was in the domestic arts, which she learnt from her mother. Her marriage was arranged by her father, who received a bride-price for her from the bridegroom, and her duties as a wife were to control the household, produce children and care for them.

Gradually the family units united into independent city states. Greece became a man's world, where the state was more important than the individual. Women had no place in this new world of politics and their social position sank disastrously. They had no political rights and their main function in life was to produce worthy young citizens. These were the years of Greek colonization throughout the Mediterranean, but for the women it was a time of increasing seclusion in the home. They were excluded from nearly all the men's interests, including the public games, and as the men's importance in the community rose it was the wife who now brought a dowry to the marriage. She was no longer worth paying for and in most cases her marriage was little more than a political manoeuvre.

By the first half of the sixth century B.C. a group of women had led a minor revolt, asserting a right to recognition as individuals with minds of their own. They were led by the lesbian poetess Sappho, who established her community on the island of Mytilene, and here they devoted themselves to the arts of music, poetry and love, but the impact of Sappho and her cult on the lives of Greek women generally was negligible. The growing menace of the Persians was nurturing a mood of aggressive militarism amongst Greek politicians and men of affairs, and outside the home women had no place at all.

When the Athenian empire was founded in the fifth century B.C. the status of women continued to decline. Until the age of seven a girl was brought up at home with her brothers, under her mother's supervision, and during these few short years she enjoyed the greatest freedom she was ever to know, for afterwards she was kept closely confined to the women's quarters of the house and allowed out only on the rarest occasions, to watch some religious festival, perhaps, or even to take part in it, as a choral dancer.

Her mother taught her to read and write, to spin and weave, and sometimes the rudiments of music, but her most important lesson was to learn the virtue of keeping her mouth shut, both in and out of the house, and conducting herself as unobtrusively as possible.

Her marriage was arranged by her father or nearest male relative and her husband had the right to name his successor, should he die before her. Marriage was a political arrangement and the wife's unquestioned duty was to live at home, take charge of the stores, control the slaves and produce more Athenian citizens.

As in any generation, there were, of course, women of outstanding intellect and character in Greece who came to prominence through the sheer force of their personalities. The Greek legislators recognized two groups of women—the wives, whose duty was to remain secluded and faithful to their husbands, and the courtesans, who themselves had their social grades. And it was from the courtesans that most of the women of intellect emerged. Many were extremely intelligent, delighting, like all Greeks, in debate and mental exercise. Some established salons, comparable with those of France in the eighteenth century. Aspasia, with whom Pericles fell in love, set up a school of philosophy in Athens which Socrates attended. She is said to have taught Pericles the art of rhetoric and to have composed some of his speeches for him. Men ridiculed these women. Euripides, in particular, poured scorn on them, maintaining, like any Victorian paterfamilias, that the only safeguard of a woman's virtue and honesty lay in seclusion in the home and a life of retirement. They were undeterred. Thais was to follow Alexander to Persepolis and far beyond, into more distant parts of Asia. Phyrne, so beautiful that many believed her to be Aphrodite, was the mistress of Praxiteles and inspired some of his greatest work.

An exception to the rigid seclusion and suppression of most Greek women was to be found in Sparta, which was surrounded by hostile states and had living within its boundaries the subject Helots, who were always on the verge of rebellion. Of necessity, the Spartans were a race of warriors and their women were specially trained to produce strong men, the girls being taught to wrestle, throw the quoit and javelin, to box and run races.

As the physical characteristics of the child were thought to be inherited through the mother, Spartan women became socially of great importance and politically powerful. Their dowries were large and they were allowed to share inheritances with their brothers, so that some became immensely rich, and therein lay their undoing. They took to high living, which sadly undermined their physical well-being and moral fibre. And after the battle of Leuctra, in 371 B.C., when Sparta itself was threatened by Epaminondas, they disgraced themselves by fleeing in tears and lamentation to the refuge of the temples.

It was only a few years after this that Plato proclaimed his views on women and their education. In his *Laws*, the Athenian maintains that there must be public teachers in Athens, receiving a stipend from the state, and they must have for their scholars not only boys and men, but the girls and women. 'For so long as the young generation is well brought up, our ship of State will have a fair voyage, while in the contrary case the consequences are better left unspoken . . . ' he said, a sentiment which has been repeated often enough during the ensuing twenty-four centuries.

Girls and women should be subject to the same laws as men and receive the same education, he declared. It was not that Plato had any particular regard for the sex. Far from it, for he felt that they had an 'inherent weakness of the soul' and were mischief makers. The idea of bringing them under control was a purely practical one, for the benefit of the State.

The mind reels at the amount of knowledge which did not

13

exist at this time for the young to assimilate—the continents unexplored, sciences undiscovered, battles unfought and mountains of literature unwritten—but Pythagoras had paved the way for the heartaches and headaches of future generations of school children half a century before Plato was born and Aristophanes, Socrates, Hippocrates and Aristotle were all his contemporaries.

Plato defined education as 'a training in goodness, which inspires the recipient with a passionate and ardent desire to become a perfect citizen, knowing both how to wield and how to submit to righteous rule'. 'It was,' he said, 'the highest blessing bestowed on mankind. . . .'

He advocated a nursery day school in every village for boys and girls from the age of three to six, under the supervision of nurses who were to watch over their behaviour. Then it was time for lessons and the sexes should be segregated. The schools should be public, with resident, salaried masters in the various subjects of the syllabus—dancing, mime and callisthenics, as well as choric art and the playing of the lyre— while for the select few who showed uncommon intellectual powers higher education would be provided which should include ciphering and arithmetic, mensuration and astronomy.

But most important of all was physical training in horsemanship and the use of weapons. 'My law,' said Plato, 'will apply in all respects to girls as well as to boys; the girls must be trained exactly like the boys. And in stating my doctrine, I intend no reservation on any point of horsemanship or physical training, as appropriate for men but not for women.'

The Athenian women may not have been so enthusiastic about these plans for their education as Plato. He admitted that they were 'used to the shady corner' and would 'offer a furious resistance . . . if forced from it', but he argued that it was pure folly not to use their services for the good of the State. And the real sting was in the tail. 'A legislator should be thorough, not half-hearted,' he said. 'He must not, after making regulations for the male sex, leave the other to the enjoyment of an existence of uncontrolled luxury and expense, and so endow his society with a mere half of a thoroughly felicitous life in place of the whole.'

Plato wrote at a time when Athens was dangerously threatened but he also pressed for the training of girls in the arts of peace as well as war and insisted that there must be a complete association of men and women in education as in everything else.

He advocated military service for men from the age of twenty to sixty and for a woman 'whatever military employments it may be thought right to impose on her after she had borne her children', up to the age of fifty.

Plato died in 347 B.C. and only nine years later Philip of Macedon, father of Alexander the Great, marched south to conquer the city states of Greece. The women of Greece remained in their seclusion and during the next two or three hundred years the power of Greece in the Mediterranean rose to its zenith and then sank before the growing might of Rome.

As the Roman republic grew in strength it became increasingly, as Greece had been, a man's world, in which women played a very minor part. Legally they had few rights, even in the home, and the father had absolute power over his wife and children, but natural affection is stronger than any law, and in practice women were, generally speaking, treated well and with respect, while in myth and folk history their virtues were extolled. Romans were grateful for the accommodating good sense of the Sabine women, they praised the morality of Lucretia and mourned the tragedy of Virginia: and they had a profound respect for the vestal virgins, although they were pitiless in their treatment of any who broke their vows of chastity.

There were elementary schools in Rome for the wealthy, where both girls and boys learnt the three R's, but when the boys passed on to a higher education, comprising history, geography, rhetoric, elocution and the study of the Greek and Roman poets, the girls returned home to learn the arts and manifold duties of the household.

The Punic wars of the third century B.C. brought Rome vast

riches and increasing power. By the second century B.C.
Greece had come under Roman sway, and the effect of these
events on the lives of many Roman women was profound.
They found themselves not only with great wealth, but leisure
in which to enjoy it, for they now had an abundance of slaves
to perform the duties which had hitherto absorbed so much of
their time.

Though legally their position was to improve only slowly,
they had always had more social freedom than the women of
Greece, and now it became boundless. Some dealt with the
situation wisely. Others lost all sense of proportion and began
the slide downhill to degradation and depravity.

The women with brains became interested in Greek art,
literature and philosophy, one of the pioneers of the intellectual
movement being Cornelia, the mother of the Gracchi, who
won the admiration of Plutarch by the manner in which she
combined her learning with her care of her family. Aurelia,
mother of Julius Caesar, was another intellectual who devoted
herself to the well-being of her son; and of Cornelia, wife of
Pompey, Plutarch, after describing her youthful beauty and
long list of intellectual attainments, added that she had a
disposition 'free from all affectation and display of pedantry—
blemishes which such acquirements usually breed in women'.

Yet learning did not rest so easily on the shoulders of many
Roman matrons and most men quailed before their recondite
erudition, no less than their impregnable virtue. Of the Elder
Agripinna, courageous though she was and the mother of many
children, Tacitus said that 'her masculine preoccupation left
no place for . . . feminine frailties in this domineering and
ambitious soul'. Quite clearly, most men felt that the subtler
arts of the cultured Greek courtesan made for more comfortable living.

But more numerous than the women of true learning in
Rome were those who, rich and restless and for ever seeking
new diversions and experiences, turned to Hellenic studies as a
fashionable pursuit, in much the same way as they adopted
Greek dress. Yet their way of living was a complete contrast to

that of the secluded women of Greece. During the closing years of the Republic thousands of them, emancipated from the ties of household cares, shed at the same time the moral restrictions of family life. Many became morally depraved and their excesses culminated in the frenzied orgies of the Bacchanalia.

With the days of the Empire, matters grew worse and immorality ever more brazen. The excesses of these times were recorded by Juvenal and Tacitus. They may have been exaggerated, but they certainly existed, and the standards set by the upper classes inevitably seeped down through the social strata.

The supreme examples of viciousness were the Empress Messalina, wife of Claudius, and her successor, Agrippina, mother of Nero. 'They were rivals in their vices no less than in the gifts which fortune had given them,' wrote Tacitus. And of Nero's wife, Poppaea, he said that she 'possessed everything but a sense of decency'.

In contrast to all this evil, the names of a few educated and steadfast wives of the Roman Empire have survived through the centuries. Octavia bore nobly and loyally with Anthony, while he dallied in Egypt with Cleopatra, and Paulina and Seneca were deeply in love all their lives. 'For what is more pleasant than to be so precious to your wife that for that very reason you become more precious to yourself?' he said, in gratitude for her tender devotion.

Yet generally speaking, the Roman world into which Christ was born and the Christian church was eventually established, was as sorry a place as it had ever been, and Roman women, with their learning and social freedom, were doing nothing to improve matters.

Chapter Two

BEFORE THE NORMAN CONQUEST

URING THE PERSECUTION and suffering, the trials
and debates which preceded the establishment of the
Christian Church throughout much of the known
western world, the position and function of women in society
was defined. The legends of the Virgin Mary, which first
appeared during the second century, confirmed that the way
of life ordered for Christian girls was that which the Virgin
had herself followed.

By the end of the century, Clement of Alexandria had
reaffirmed the simple truth that men and women are equal in
the sight of God, subject to the same laws of good and evil and
sharing the same promise of ultimate salvation, but at the same
time he laid down not only the functions which God had
decreed for women in society, but the manner in which they
should at all times comport themselves. Freedom was given
with one hand and taken away with the other. They must be
quiet and modest in demeanour, pure and chaste in their
behaviour. At table their good manners should be an example
to others and they should take no wine. They should never
indulge in immoderate laughter, lest it distort their faces.
Only a gentle smile might be permitted, however comic
the situation in which they found themselves. In general
deportment, they must walk with dignity, head straight,
shoulders back and countenance serene. And more important than all this, Clement decreed that God's plan for
them was that they spend their time, when not at prayer,
in spinning and weaving, the making and embroidering

of garments, the care of the household and the preparation of food.

Later writers of the third and fourth centuries, including St. Jerome, pursued and developed this theme and the life of the ideal Christian woman became even more circumscribed. Extravagance in dress was deplored. Cosmetics were abhorred. She was exhorted to spend ever longer hours in prayer and meditation.

Thus the pattern of behaviour for the good woman was set for centuries to come—modest deportment and the quiet smile, constant prayer, humility and obedience to parents. It was in order for her to be taught to read and write. In fact, precocity in the young was regarded as an admirable quality and a sign of God's special blessing, while handicrafts were a sacred duty. No music or dancing was allowed and a woman's only creative outlet was the toil of endless needlework, with perhaps a study of the healing properties of herbal medicines, to justify the assumption that, in accordance with the legends of the Virgin Mary, she was especially endowed as a healer of bodily ills.

A girl's upbringing was to be so sheltered and secluded that the logical outcome was the establishment of the nunnery, the only safe place for such a refinement of purity: and with a fine disregard for the future of Christendom, or indeed for the propagation of the human race, the virtues of virginity were extolled, girls being told that if they felt the call to the monastic life they should obey it, even if it were against the wishes of their parents.

There was a ready answer for every problem and doubt they may have had, and those who questioned the blessings of virginity, because they felt a natural desire for children, were told: 'If thou desirest children, thou shalt bring forth daughters and sons of spiritual virtues that never can die, but ever play before thee in heaven.'

These exhortations applied only to girls of noble birth, however, who were considered to be closer to God in the first place than the general run of mortal clay.

It was not until A.D. 363 that the Christian faith ultimately prevailed in Rome and the first Bishop of Rome, the Pope, spiritual successor to St. Peter, was enthroned. Roman Britain became a part of Christendom and the first Christian churches were established in this country: but the Roman Empire was already crumbling and less than fifty years later Rome was sacked by the Goths and the great days of the Empire were over.

The barbarians who had been halted on its fringes rushed in to pillage and occupy the undefended countries which had lived under Rome's enlightened influence. Yet on the mainland of Europe, after the first savage onslaughts, much of Roman civilization survived and was preserved. In Gaul the conquering Franks assimilated the high degree of culture they discovered, including the religion of Christianity, and the Roman tradition continued with hardly a break.

In Britain the story was different. The pagan Anglo-Saxon invaders, soon to be followed by the Jutes, needed land and were determined on total conquest, involving nothing less than the dispossession and annihilation of the British. A few stood to fight. King Arthur may have been one who checked the invaders for a while, but nowhere was the British resistance effective for long. Most of the survivors fled to the hills and mountains of Cornwall and Wales, the Lake District or Scotland, and those who remained became slaves in the households of the conquerors.

It was from these three nations, the Angles, Saxons and Jutes, that during the next three hundred years, the English nation evolved, though it was later to receive a fresh injection of blood from the invasions of the Vikings and Normans, who both belonged to the same Nordic race.

The pagan gods of the Angles and Saxons were terrible and ever hungry for propitiation, in stark contrast to the Christian concept of an all-powerful loving Father. The men were savage, rumbustious, flamboyant warriors, who deemed it the highest honour to die in battle, so that they might be chosen by the Valkyries, the virgin attendants of Woden, to join him in his celestial Valhalla. We know little about their womenfolk, but in a community which, despite its warlike propensities, was economically based on farming, they were skilled in the household arts of spinning and weaving wool and fine linen, and a few may have been literate, like their menfolk, who translated their thoughts into letters and words which they believed to have magical properties and were therefore called runes—secret, mysterious things.

While the ancient kingdoms of England, after years of struggle for supremacy, emerged as Northumbria in the north-east, Wessex in the south, Mercia in the heart of the country and East Anglia in the east, elsewhere in Europe the Christian church was gaining strength.

As early as A.D. 393 St. Patrick, the son of a Roman official and grandson of a Christian priest, was born in Scotland. As a youth, he was carried off by slave raiders to Ireland, from where he escaped to Gaul and then to Rome, returning eventually to Ireland, about A.D. 427 as a Christian missionary.

More than a century later, St. Columba sailed from Ireland to the island of Iona, to found a monastery and begin a Christian mission.

South of the border, the English, enjoying a period of comparative peace, established new contacts with the mainland of Europe, which included a trade in British and English slaves.

Then Ethelbert, King of Kent, married Bertha, the daughter of the Frankish king of Paris. Bertha was a Christian and with her to Canterbury, the royal city of Kent, came her Christian bishop. They found there the remains of a Christian church, which had been empty and forsaken for over a hundred and fifty years, and in it they began Christian worship once more. A few years later, in A.D. 598, the Roman abbot, Augustine, and his band of monks, were sent from Rome by Pope Gregory, to visit Queen Bertha and begin a Christian mission in Kent.

Within the space of two generations, the Roman church could claim that Britain was again part of a great cultural empire—the spiritual empire of Christendom. Monasteries and churches were built and the bishops and their priests travelled the lonely countryside, with its widely scattered hamlets and solitary farm houses, explaining to their newly acquired flock the meaning of the Creed and the Lord's Prayer, the significance of the celebration of the Mass and the office of baptism.

Yet the reign of terror of the pagan gods was not easily forgotten. For the poor and humble, these were harsh years, and many must have propitiated them in secret, terrified that their sorrows and afflictions were a punishment imposed by some abandoned and affronted god. Although pagan festivals were endowed with Christian attributes, they nevertheless persisted: and inevitably a new, disreputable priesthood arose, to prey on the credulity of the simple, a strange fraternity of sorcerers and dealers in amulets and talismans, witches and purveyors of black magic.

Queen Bertha had been educated in a French convent and Pope Gregory had applauded her learning. When the first religious houses were founded in England, therefore, there began a long tradition of learning and high intellectual attainment among the nuns. Latin was again introduced and with it the works of the poets, philosophers and historians of Greece and Rome, the Greek writers being mainly in Latin translations. Some of the monasteries were settlements for both monks and nuns, which were ruled by an abbess, one of the earliest being at Wimborne in Dorset, where the abbess gave her orders, which none might question, through a grille. The monks and nuns were strictly segregated, and the nuns' only male visitor was the priest who, accompanied always by the abbess, came to say Mass.

Inevitably there were a few backslidings in such a strangely repressed community, but in the early years of religious fervour and simple piety remarkably few scandals came to light.

In addition to their religious duties and their embroidery and needlework, the nuns spent much of their time in study, many of them proving themselves to be profound and able scholars. They trained nuns to become the heads of new foundations and some of the bishops and other clergy also received their education from the nuns and abbesses. Royal children and a few from the nobility were sometimes sent to the monasteries to be educated, but in the main their pupils were those who intended to enter the monastic life permanently.

The most urgent need was for books, and these both monks and nuns composed or copied, with infinite labour and patience, on to precious parchment.

These first lesson books were Latin grammars and treatises on philosophy, science and mathematics, which the few privileged children who were received as pupils would copy, letter by letter, on to their slates. They began their education at the age of seven or eight and there was little in these early lesson books to lighten their labours. The author of the first children's book in England was Aldhelm, Abbot of Malmesbury, born in the middle of the seventh century, and in a letter to the Bishop of Winchester, describing the difficulties of his profession, is a cry from the heart: 'But what shall I say of arithmetic, whose long and intricate calculations are sufficient to overwhelm the mind and throw it into despair?'

It was Aldhelm who began the method of teaching by question and answer, which some twelve hundred years later was still being used in Victorian seminaries for young ladies, where the teachers leaned heavily on Miss Richmal Mangnall's famous works, *Historical and Miscellaneous Questions* and *Child's Guide to Knowledge*.

Whitby Abbey was another community of both men and women and during the seventh and eighth centuries it was one of the most important of the northern abbeys. The Abbess Hild, a member of the royal house of Northumbria, was born in A.D. 614 and became perhaps the most scholarly woman of her day. She was thirty-three when she took the veil, and Bishop Aidan appointed her first to the monastery at Hartlepool and then to Whitby, where she proved herself to be as able an administrator as scholar. Her nuns loved her, and to novices she gave special instruction before they took their final vows. She prepared some of her monks for the priesthood and encouraged Caedmon, who was a secular attendant at the abbey when he first began to write his poetry, before entering the order as a monk.

Hild died in A.D. 668 and her successor was Aelflaed, daughter of a king of Northumbria who had been placed in Hild's care when she was only twelve months old, bringing with her a valuable dowry of land. She was in many ways as able as Hild, but after her death the importance of Whitby as a seat of learning declined.

It was for Hildelith, Abbess of Barking, that Aldhelm wrote *De Laudibus Virginitatus*, in which he advised her nuns on the course of study they should follow. These nuns of Barking could all read and write and some were able to compose Latin verses. One of their number, Cuthburga, sister of King Ina, founded the abbey of Wimborne, of which she became the first abbess. Her successor, Tetta, proved herself as able an administrator as Hild had been at Whitby, and among her pupils was Eadburga, who became Abbess of Minster, where she developed into an astute business woman, buying new properties to endow her house, importing goods from abroad, buying ships and engaging in the building of various extensions to her house. Like many other English abbesses at this time, she corresponded in Latin with the heads of other monasteries and convents, both in England and on the Continent, exchanging books and other gifts and sometimes paying visits.

The nuns, besides working on the farmlands attached to their abbeys, employed much of their spare time in weaving and embroidery, crafts which they sometimes taught to the women and girls in the district, and a few may have given elementary lessons in reading to small classes of boys and girls.

In the personal relationship of English men and women at this time, monogamy was the rule. The moral code was strict and for women the punishment for unchastity was severe, but socially and economically women were on an equal footing with men and were entitled to hold land in their own right.

During the eighth century, the monks continued to compile their textbooks for the instruction of their pupils and Alcuin, the Yorkshire priest who became tutor to the sons and daughters of Charlemagne, started the fashion for arithmetical problems which were astonishingly like those of our own schooldays—those workmen, A, B and C who were eternally building brick walls, the man who spent his life unproductively filling and emptying a bath, the goat which spent its days cropping grass at an unnaturally steady rate of consumption, never pausing for breath.

Here are two examples which were worrying children more than a thousand years ago, and half a century before King Alfred was born.

'The swallow once invited the snail to dinner; he lived just one league from the post, and the snail travelled at the rate of only one inch a day; how long would it be before he dined?'

And again: 'An old man met a child. "Good day, my son" says he. "May you live as long as you have lived, and as much more, and thrice as much as all this, and if God give you one year in addition to the others, you will be just a century old." What was the lad's age?'

Towards the last quarter of the century the saintly and well-beloved Bede was born, who became abbot of the monastery at Jarrow and the first English historian. The books he wrote for his pupils contained nearly all the knowledge that was then available on the natural sciences, natural history, botany, mathematics and astronomy. A studious nun at this time would have had access to the works of Aldhelm and Bede, the travels of Pliny, Aristotle and Cicero and the writings of Virgil.

Yet most English boys and girls knew nothing of these matters. They grew up in their isolated villages, learning only the lore of the countryside and the folk stories and songs told them by their parents or travelling minstrels, with perhaps a little religious teaching from a visiting priest.

By the end of the eighth century a decline in learning in the nunneries had become apparent, perhaps because there was a lack of abbesses with intellectual aptitude. It was at this time that the custom of fosterage developed, whereby boys and girls of noble families were sent as foster children to other families of similar social standing for training and education, some of the children of the more important families being received by the royal court. It was a Saxon custom, brought to England from the Continent, and may have had its origins in the holding of distinguished young prisoners as hostages.

In A.D. 782 Alcuin was persuaded to cross from England to administrate the school established by Charlemagne at his palace, and here he taught, on English lines, Charlemagne's children and foster children and also a few adults, including Charlemagne's sister, Gisela, abbess of Chelles, but Charlemagne insisted that the girls, in addition to the studies they shared with the boys, should also be taught spinning and weaving, embroidery and similar handicrafts.

A few years later Charlemagne ordered every monastery to establish a reading school, free to all children, whatever their position in life, the curriculum to include reading, writing and arithmetic and a study of the psalter. By A.D. 797 every parish priest was required to keep a school and receive all pupils who came to him. No fee was expected but it was made known that a freewill offering would be acceptable.

Throughout most of the ninth century these opportunities were extended to girls as well as boys, but at the close of the century came the beginning of the end, when the Bishop of Soissons decreed that the girls should be excluded from all the schools under his jurisdiction.

In England the girls fared even worse, for at this time the country was ravaged by the invasions of the pagan Vikings, during which dozens of monasteries and nunneries were destroyed and never restored. When King Alfred succeeded to the throne of Wessex, the only part of the country free from Viking domination, he declared that 'there were few men south of the Humber who could understand their ritual or read a Latin letter. South of the Thames he knew not one such.'

He set aside a sixth of his revenue to establish schools for boys of both gentle and humble birth. It is uncertain whether girls were admitted or whether any provision was made for them, apart from that available in the remaining Wessex nunneries, but at Alfred's court his daughters received the same education as their brothers, all of them taught, by both men and women teachers, to read and write in Latin and English and to study the Bible and Saxon literature.

There was a dearth of teachers in England and King Alfred sent to France for scholars to preside over the abbeys he founded at Winchester and Athelney, while he himself helped to translate many books for them from Latin into English, including the works of Bede: and his annotations and comments formed the basis of the Anglo-Saxon Chronicle.

Throughout Northumbria, Mercia and East Anglia during the tenth century, the conquering Vikings, despite constant wars, began gradually to assimilate the civilization of the English and adopt the Christian faith.

In Wessex the eight daughters of King Alfred's son, Edward, were all carefully educated, and the tradition of training and education for the royal princesses was continued for the next two or three generations of the family, some being taught at the palace school, others at the abbeys of Winchester or Wilton, where, in addition to their scholastic studies, they received a training in needlecraft and the embroidery of Church furnishings—copes, chasubles, stoles and altar hangings —for which England was becoming famed.

Late in the tenth century there was a revival of monastic life throughout the country, and since it was now ordained that only those who had learnt their Creed and Pater Noster could receive a Christian burial in a hallowed grave, it became a matter of grave importance to the Church that every child in the country should receive at least this amount of education. Much of it was given in the churches, but priests were frequently ordered to keep schools for free instruction in every village, which should be accessible to both girls and boys. These were mostly very small gatherings within the church porch, where the children learnt their Latin prayers by heart, though knowing nothing of the language.

At the end of the century and during the early years of the eleventh century, England was again invaded by the Danes, and under the Danish kings there was a decline in learning among the clergy. The monasteries were under the Benedictine rule and when the rule was translated from Latin into English, and a knowledge of Latin was no longer a necessity for the nuns and monks, some no longer studied the language.

At the court of Edward the Confessor, however, the tradition of learning among the Saxon princesses was maintained. Edith, Edward's wife, who was the daughter of Earl Godwin, was carefully educated and also a superb needle-woman, having learnt the art of embroidery at Wilton Abbey: and his great-niece, Queen Margaret of Scotland, wife of Malcom III, was a student all her life and a patroness of scholars. She was sternly devout, and after the Conquest she was greatly influenced by Lanfranc, the Norman archbishop of Canterbury, who continued to be her adviser in spiritual matters after her marriage to Malcolm III.

She spent much of her time in prayer and meditation and gave dutifully to the poor. She founded a school of church embroidery for the ladies of her court and other Scottish noblewomen, but the régime was strict. Only in her presence was any man allowed into the room where they worked, for no 'unseemly intimacy with men, never any impudent levity' was countenanced, and 'none of them would have dared even to use a low word, let alone do anything detestable'.

Not surprisingly, her eight children had a joyless childhood, and the governor of the royal nursery was told to restrain them 'with threats and whippings whenever they erred in infantile naughtiness'.[1]

To the boys, Margaret herself gave religious instruction,

[1] *St. Margaret of Scotland*, Lucy Menzies, 1947, pp. 107–114, 137–138.

but the two girls, Mathilda and Mary, were sent to their Aunt Christina, who had become Abbess of Romsey and was eventually to be Mother Superior of Wilton Abbey. Queen Margaret intended both the girls to enter the Church and after her death they stayed on with Christina. Mathilda was, in some respects, as scholarly and devout as her mother, but, despite all Aunt Christina's furious bludgeonings and arguments, she had no intention of staying in the convent for the rest of her life. Christina sounds a termagant. She insisted on Mathilda wearing the black veil of the votaress. 'I trembled under my aunt's rod,' said Mathilda. 'When I threw off the veil she tormented and insulted me with sharp blows and shameful words, so that in her presence I wore it, groaning and shuddering, but whenever I could get out of her sight I flung it on the ground and trod it under foot.'

Christina had met her match, for Mathilda left the convent to become the queen of Henry I. She was the last of the scholarly Anglo-Saxon royal ladies, a good and devout woman, the patroness of musicians and poets and the benefactress of many religious houses and hospitals.

Chapter Three

MEDIEVAL ENGLAND

WHEN KING WILLIAM of Normandy landed in
England in 1066 this was still a pioneer country, with
only half a million acres of cultivated land. In the
heart of the country and to the west were vast stretches of
forest and woodland, heath and moors, to the east and south-
east miles of unreclaimed marshes and fens. Wolves still
prowled in the forests of the north and men hunted the stag
and wild boar as far south as London, in the forests of Epping
and the woods of Hampstead. The widely scattered population
was something between a million and a half and two million.
They lived by the land and were self-sufficient.

It was a Christian country, but to many of the peasants,
living in remote hamlets or isolated homesteads, far away
from the nearest church and the influence of the priest, Christianity can have been little more than a new mystery, the cross
a symbol to be revered in order to bring good fortune and
avert evil, a rune of great power which it would be wiser not
to ignore.

Though the feudal system which William created in England
was a military one and legally different from the old Saxon
arrangement of master and vassal, the lives of the English
peasants did not change a great deal. Such great landowners
as had not been killed during the Conquest were virtually
dispossessed, for they had to sell much of their land to purchase
the right to remain on what was left. The earldoms of Northumbria, Mercia and Wessex were abolished and sheriffs
appointed for the government of each county, while the

counties were divided into hundreds and the hundreds into manors.

King William allotted large tracts of land to his Norman barons, who paid him feudal dues and agreed to provide him with soldiers when the need should arise. The barons sub-divided their lands among their military followers and sub-tenants, who in their turn, along with such farmers and peasants who happened to be established there, had to swear a similar oath of allegiance to him, pay dues or work for him and serve in time of war.

According to the Norman census in the Domesday Book, there were only 300,000 families in England during the eleventh century, of which 9,300, including the clergy, were large landowners and 12,000 owners of small estates. The rest of the populations were yeomen and villeins, who owned small plots of land, and the landless labourers.

Social distinctions were intensified and more rigidly defined. Everyone had his level in society and anyone who dared question it was sharply reminded that his place in life had been ordained by God and was part of the unalterable scheme of things.

This argument began to be applied to women. Though they worked alongside the men, for the same wages, and had been entitled to hold land in their own name, the feudal system tended to restrict some of their legal rights.

While the Norman barons built their castle strongholds, Lanfranc, the Archbishop of Canterbury, set about reorgani-zing such English monasteries as survived and King William began a great building programme of monasteries and churches. For his magnificent new stone buildings he borrowed heavily from the Jewish moneylenders who had followed him from the Continent, but numbers of very small and simple churches were also built, and by the end of the eleventh century nearly every village had its Christian church, however humble, and appointed priest.

For the majority of English men and women the most important influences in their lives were now their feudal overlords and the Church. These peasants had no education and few had ever travelled more than a few miles from the place of their birth. The Church services were conducted in Latin and were largely incomprehensible to them, but they attended Mass regularly, some because of a true faith, others for fear of the consequences if they stayed away. And they did dutiful obeisance at the wayside crosses which were built throughout the lanes and by-ways of the lonely countryside.

As in Saxon times, the Church was faced with the task of teaching these people the principles of the Christian religion, the meaning of the prayers and psalms they haltingly repeated by rote, and the stories and philosophy of the Bible. This was partly done visually, by the paintings on the church walls which depicted stories from the Old and New Testaments, spiced with horror pictures of the sufferings and torments of the damned in hell and their terrible remorse on the day of Judgment, but parish priests were also ordered to teach their flocks the Creed and the Lord's Prayer, without which knowledge they were not admitted to the sacrament, and by the end of the thirteenth century the ten commandments and the Ave Maria were added to the list.

As in Saxon times, the priests held small schools, usually in the church porches, to which boys and girls came for elementary instruction, but they seldom learnt more than the bare minimum to see them through the Church service, for many of the parish priests were themselves by no means well educated. Some had come from peasant families and had become first associated with the Church by helping the priest as a server. The priest, in return, gave the server a few Latin lessons: and the server could rise to become a 'holy water clerk', for which he would have received a small stipend, enabling him to afford to pay for more Latin lessons from a visiting master.

Though the education of the peasants was so restricted, for children of the upper classes it was a social necessity. With the advent of the Normans, French became the official language of England, spoken by the King and his Court, the barons, the nobility and the clergy, while the peasants and lower orders continued to speak their mother tongue. Latin, too, was a spoken language amongst the learned and the members of the Church, who were able to converse in it as easily as in French.

The Normans introduced to England the literature of Europe, which almost entirely supplanted that of the Saxon period, save in monasteries remote enough to escape direct Norman influence.

Along with many other romances, the Arthurian legends and the Beowulf stories, which had existed in England, as elsewhere in Europe, long before 1066, were re-introduced, imbued now with a new spirit of romance, which had first manifested itself in the languorous warmth of Provence and had been stimulated by the stories told by the Crusaders returning from their adventures in the East.

Early in the twelfth century Geoffrey of Monmouth developed and embellished the King Arthur stories and they were re-written by later writers and also translated from Latin into French. The tales were re-told by the wandering minstrels. The older legends of Merlin, the magician, were added to the cycle, as well as the independent Breton story of Lancelot, who was tempted by the love of a woman from his knightly duty. Thus the rough savagery of the earliest versions of these stories became romanticized into tales of knightly grace and chivalry. Walter de Map, court poet to Henry II, re-wrote them yet again, this time associating them more closely with the Christian Church by adding the story of the quest for the Holy Graal and the adventures of the most courtly of all the knights of the Round Table, Sir Galahad, who was 'sans peur et sans raproche'.

It thus came about that while women were being stripped of their legal rights, they were being romanticized, by way of compensation, for amongst the upper classes of medieval England romantic love became high fashion, and every girl dreamed of the lifelong devotion of some pure-hearted knight.

To this end, young girls were carefully trained in rules

which, though similar to those laid down by the Christian fathers, for the upbringing of Christian maidens, were for a different and more tangible purpose—the enduring love of a personable young husband.

High born girls were taught deportment and table manners, the correct conventions when greeting a stranger or welcoming a guest, the arts of conversation, singing and music and the skills of needlecraft. In the Romances, the heroines were usually the daughters of kings and princes, so it followed that they had been carefully educated in the royal tradition and that some were skilled healers or even wise in necromancy: but in practice, compared with the importance paid to the social graces, intellectual attainments did not play a large part in the new conception of a girl's education.

Monks and nuns were now in separate establishments and the seats of learning were still in the monasteries, on which William had bestowed valuable lands, and to a lesser extent in the nunneries.

The most important monastic order in England was that of the Benedictines, and at these monasteries travellers were always given food and a bed for the night. There was an almoner's office for distributing money to the sick and needy and sometimes a school for the sons of gentry and also an elementary school for poor boys. Nunneries were run on similar lines and occasionally they conducted small schools for a few girls whose parents could afford to have them educated, but nunnery schools for girls who were not intending to take their vows were often frowned on by the bishops, and from time to time, unless they were particularly short of cash, they were forbidden, mainly because it was felt that such close contact with the outside world would be too distracting for the nuns.

In early medieval times, in addition to the women who entered the convents, there were a number of anchoresses throughout the country, who lived in seclusion, either alone, with a maid servant, or in very small communities: and occasionally some of them took a few girl pupils, but the

Church disliked the practice, declaring that an anchoress ought to think only of God.

During the twelfth and thirteenth centuries movements were afoot throughout Europe which were to undermine the prestige of the monasteries and nunneries as places of learning and, at the same time, sorely to affect the education of girls for many years to come.

Returning Crusaders stimulated a renewal of interest in the literature and philosophy of Greece and Rome and also introduced the learning of the East, including the elements of science, particularly physics and mathematics.

Scientific knowledge was not welcomed by the Church, but the spark of scientific enquiry once struck could not be extinguished. Wandering scholars visited the cities of Europe and lectured to the people, and they were received with so much interest that they soon established themselves in small schools, which were the first universities. The earliest in Europe were probably at Bologna and Parma, but by about the middle of the twelfth century the schools at Oxford were established and early in the thirteenth century a group of scholars left Oxford to settle in Cambridge.

With the establishment of the universities, in which girls had no part, the monasteries lost their prestige as centres of learning, and the educational standards of the nunneries fell even lower. In fact, many medieval nuns could probably not write at all, even though they may have been able to read, and they spent their leisure time in sewing and embroidery, spinning and weaving. Eventually they were concentrating almost entirely on moral training and could offer very little real learning to any girl coming to them for an education.

Yet the Church still ordered and controlled the lives of the people and the priests still held their schools, either in the Church porch or perhaps, by now, in small, separate village schools. By the end of the fourteenth century two books had been compiled, with which everyone was expected to be familiar. These were the primer or psalter and the ABC, which contained the Pater Noster and Ave Maria, the Creed and the ten commandments. They were still in Latin, although the study of Latin, which remained the language of international finance, commerce and the professions, had declined both in the religious houses and at Court. At the same time, as the distinction between Normans and English faded, after two or three hundred years of Norman rule, English was more used in general conversation than French, although it was still something of a social distinction to be able to speak it. The convents, by now very class conscious, tried to make a knowledge of French obligatory for their nuns, particularly when so few had Latin, but ultimately, needing the dowries of the novices, they had to admit women who spoke only English.

In 1362 it was ordered that English be used in courts of law and the following year the Chancellor spoke in English during the opening of Parliament. Bishops and clergy gave their sermons in English and John Wycliff, preaching his new and revolutionary doctrine against the established church, wrote his pamphlets in English.

By this time the main purpose of the convents as places where women could dedicate their lives to the praise and worship of God was lost in the more practical idea that they were places where unmarried women of high birth could respectably live out their lives. It would be unfair to say that none had a real vocation, but the fact remains that a large number had been sent by their fathers, to get them out of the way. Medieval society had no place for the spinster who had passed the usual age of marriage, and even if she were still young, marriage dowries were a heavy burden, particularly when there were several girls in the family. Few nuns were accepted in the convents without a substantial payment, but for a parsimonious parent this was usually a more economical proposition. And once the girls had taken their vows, they lost the right to any inheritance which might have been coming their way, for in the eyes of the Church they were dead to the world. The money therefore reverted to the family, and this, in some cases of unscrupulous and mercenary parents, could have been sufficient reason for placing the girls in the convent when they were still young.

The number of nuns in England was never very great and
during the fourteenth and fifteenth centuries, although there
were more than a hundred nunneries throughout the country,
only four had more than thirty inmates, apart from the
servants, and there were probably never more than two thous-
and nuns. Life within the convent walls had become very
different from the placid existence of the old days. Closely
confined and with no real vocation, they grew jealous and
peevish, lax in their religious duties and increasingly inclined
to the pleasures and diversions of the outside world from
which they had been arbitrarily banished.

In vain the bishops, on their regular visitations, after listening
to their complaints against each other, begged them to lead
more seemly lives and passed new rules for them.

'None shall push up against another wilfully, nor spit upon
the stairs going up and down, but if they tread it out forthwith'
ran one new order, after what must have been a particularly
stormy session of airing petty grievances.

Throughout the day and night the nuns had seven monastic
offices to say, although by this time they could barely understand a word of the Latin in which they were written. They
were frequently reproved for arriving late for the services,
falling asleep in the middle of them, leaving early or gabbling
through their prayers with indecent haste.

When they were not at their prayers, they worked at their
embroidery, helped in the convent garden or studied their
psalter and any other holy books which the convent possessed:
and if, against the wishes of the bishops, there were a few small
girls boarding at the convent for their education, they might
help in teaching them to read and sing and acquire such good
manners as Geoffrey Chaucer's Lady Eglentyne possessed.

> At mete wel y-taught was she with-alle;
> She leet no morsel from hir lippes falle;
> Ne wette hir fingres in hir sauce depe.
> Wel coude she carie a morsel and wel kepe,
> That no drope ne fille up-on her brest.

For large parts of the day strict silence had to be observed in the convents, particularly during meals, and this disability they overcame by the use of an ingenious sign language. A sister who wanted fish would 'wag her hands displayed sidelings in manner of a fish tail'. For milk she would 'draw her left little finger in manner of milking'. For mustard she would 'hold her nose in the upper part of her right fist and rub it'. Debarred even from asking someone to pass the salt, she would 'fillip with her right thumb and forefinger over the left thumb': and for wine the sign was to 'move her forefinger up and down the end of her thumb afore her eyes'.

Far from being refuges of the poor, wealthy women would sometimes stay at the nunneries as paying guests, but the bishops disapproved of this custom even more than that of taking in small girls for their education. Another outrage to the bishops was that the nuns were constantly changing the style of their habits, to match the changing fashions of the outside world, but an even greater bone of contention was their habit of keeping pets. Dogs were the favourites, but they also acquired monkeys, squirrels, rabbits, birds and occasionally cats, all of which they brought with them to church, provoking more prohibitions in the visitation reports of the sorely tried bishops, who complained of the cost of feeding them, the inordinate noise they made during the services and the 'foul defilement of the church and cloisters'.

When the Bishop of Lincoln tried to impose a rule forbidding the nuns to leave the convent on private visits, they 'ran after him to the gates when he was riding away and threw the Bull at his head, screaming that they would never observe it'.

During the fifteenth century matters grew worse, with an increasing number of scandalous reports. At Godstow the nuns received regular visits from the choirs at Oxford. At Catesby children were sleeping in the same dormitory as a nun far advanced in pregnancy.

One prioress, driven to desperation, was reported to have dragged her nuns 'round the choir by their veils, in the middle of the service, screaming "Liar!" and "Harlot!" at them', and another kicked her erring nuns 'and hit them on the head with her fists and put them in the stocks'.[1]

All over the country things seem to have come to a pretty pass. In York, for example, where an alehouse had been opened within the gates of the convent, two children were found in the company of a nun who had recently 'brought forth a child of her bodie begotten'.[2]

Yet outside the strange, circumscribed world of the late medieval nunnery opportunities for education were developing both within and outside the Church, though they were mainly for boys.

Politically the history of England during early medieval times was the struggle for supremacy between the King, the Church and the Barons, while the ordinary men and women slowly but doggedly discarded the claims of all of them and throughout the twelfth and thirteenth centuries began to achieve their own emancipation, gradually buying themselves free of their feudal servitude. After the signing of Magna Carta, in 1215, the traditional rights of Englishmen became part of the written law of the land and by the end of the century the first English Parliament had met. English merchants and shopkeepers formed the first trade gilds for their mutual protection. The great woollen industry of England began to develop, which was to form the basis of the country's wealth for many years to come. Sheep farmers grew rich and the King's revenue increased handsomely with the customs dues on its export. Henry III was the great Church and Abbey builder but the French relations and friends whom he appointed to administer them became as worldly as the Court, exacting money payments for penances, after confession, and often delegating the observance of Sunday Mass to the perfunctory offices of a half-literate Mass priest, poorly paid by the officially appointed rector or vicar, who was diverting himself elsewhere.

Yet with the expansion of trade, the founding of the universities, even the disastrous wars with France, begun by

---

[1] *Medieval People*, Eileen Power, Methuen, 1924.
[2] *Medieval English Nunneries*, Eileen Power.

Edward III soon after his accession in 1327, which were to last for the next hundred years, horizons widened. Edward III's army in France consisted of only 8,000 men and did not greatly affect the life of the English countryside. Many villeins who had been able to buy their freedom grew prosperous with sheep farming, built large farmhouses or small manor houses for themselves, so that they ranked socially with the old, independent yeomen and were able to have their sons educated at the new schools which were coming into existence.

The Norfolk-born Paston family was founded in this way, the first member of whom there is any record being Clement Paston, a peasant born in the middle of the fourteenth century, who held and cultivated about a hundred acres of land. He was able to afford a good education for his son William, who became a lawyer, bought more land and married an heiress.

The first grammar schools were established at cathedrals and monasteries, where the boys were given instruction in the Latin language. There were song schools at the cathedrals, where boys were taught to read Latin but did not necessarily understand it, and at the monasteries, where the boy choristers also acted as servants to the monks. There were also song schools attached to the universities and hospitals, as well as numerous chantry schools, run by the chantry priests. These priests were attached to the chantries where the dead rested before their burial, their main task being to say masses for their souls: and a benefactor often stipulated in his will that the chantry priest should also run a choir school.

The standard of education varied with the capacity of the priest. In some cases the boys acquired only a superficial knowledge of Latin, which would enable them to sing a few psalms and lead the responses and prayers, but others were given a sound knowledge of the language.

These schools were exclusively for boys, but as the gilds grew in wealth and importance some, particularly the religious gilds, provided schools for both sons and daughters of their members.

The religious gilds of the twelfth and thirteenth centuries

were similar to the Anglo-Saxon frith gilds, and the merchant and craft gilds which emerged later, though primarily organized for commercial and economic reasons, had a strong religious background.

Women were freely admitted to the craft gilds. A widow was allowed to carry on her husband's trade and a daughter could inherit her father's rights. Women could enter business on their own account, after serving the regulation seven years' apprenticeship. At one time the London silk-weavers' gild consisted almost entirely of women and they also played an important part in the woollen industry, at a time when it was the principal source of England's wealth. There are records of women smiths, forgers, plumbers, bell-founders and surgeons. They made provision for their old age by regular payments to their gilds and were able to draw benefits from them during sickness or unemployment and in old age, so it is not surprising that they were given equal chances of education in the gild schools, the curriculum probably including the teaching of reading, writing, arithmetic, the psalter and the ABC.

Chaucer no doubt echoed the general attitude to women at this time when he said: 'God when he made the first woman made her not of the head of Adam, for she should not climb to great lordship; also certes, God made not woman of the foot of Adam, for she should not be holden too low; for she cannot patiently suffer; but God made woman of the rib of Adam, for woman should be fellow unto man.'

And yet it was during the fourteenth century that the status of women and the few opportunities they had for education began to dwindle. The commercial wealth of the country was developing and the population increasing, after the ravages of the Black Death, which had reduced it to little more than two million, but by the fifteenth century there was little mention of women in agriculture, which had come to be regarded as entirely men's sphere, and they gradually disappeared from the ranks of the skilled craftsmen.

During the fifteenth century there was a growing desire for

the education of boys, particularly amongst the rising middle classes. The Church of Rome was at its lowest moral ebb at this time and wealthy gentry and merchants who in the old days had given large sums to the Church now endowed schools, and many more were founded by the gilds, available by this time to all boys, whether sons of members or not. Rich bishops also endowed schools and men of wealth sometimes sent poor boys to them or left bequests for the education of a number of poor scholars, while a good many schools were left a sufficient endowment to be able to give their education freely to boys who could prove that they would benefit from it.

Very little is known about the public education of girls at this time, yet it seems certain that many of them could at least read, and women were very active in the first phase of John Wycliff's Lollard movement against the increasingly corrupt practices of the Church, until it was temporarily submerged during the Wars of the Roses. They were not only willing students of the new doctrine, which challenged the value of the complicated ritual and mysteries of the Roman church, with its papal pardons and pilgrimages to the shrines of the saints, and the truth of substantiation, but they also joined the ranks of preachers and teachers, defying persecution and even martyrdom.

Women such as these had probably received an elementary education in a petty school, where children who were not taught at home, by parents or a tutor, were sometimes sent, about the age of four or five. Occasionally these petty schools were attached to the grammar schools, as preparatory schools, but more often they were separate establishments run by humble men and women of the lower middle classes, who taught both girls and boys alike, for a few pence a week, as a means of livelihood. The children learnt to read and write and perhaps acquired a little elementary arithmetic, but the two standard textbooks they had to learn were the ABC and the primer.

Amongst the nobility, the custom of training their sons in other noble households still existed in the fifteenth century, for there was a lingering belief in the sanctity of noble birth. Those who showed an inclination for scholarship would be taught to read and write French and Latin by the household priest or a visiting monk, but mostly their education was in the skills which would fit them to become knights—estate management and the use of arms, as well as singing, dancing, music and all the courtly accomplishments—but the need for such skills was fast disappearing. The knight in shining armour was no longer a practical proposition, in an age of increasing commercialism, where yeomen's sons and those of the small gentry were being educated and gaining power and prestige as merchants and members of the professions. The medieval knight became the English gentleman and he needed a very different education.

William of Wykeham had founded the grammar school at Winchester in 1382, for the better education of boys who wished to enter one of the learned professions, and in 1442 Henry VI founded Eton, on similar lines, making the provision that a certain proportion of the scholars were to be 'sons of noble and powerful persons'.

Many noblemen's sons now attended these schools but the custom of boarding out continued well into the seventeenth century.

Girls were also sometimes sent away to another household for training. Until the age of seven they and their brothers would have been given the same teaching in religion, manners, morals and reading, either at home from parent or governess, or in a petty school. After that time, girls concentrated on the manifold duties of household management. In manor houses and similar large establishments, where the mistress had the care of foster children and a large household of retainers and servants to manage, this required a high degree of organizing ability. She had to supervise the spinning and weaving and making of the household clothing, the salting, pickling and preserving of winter supplies and check the large quantities of food which had to be kept in readiness for chance visitors, for these great houses were extremely hospitable. In many ways, like the monasteries, they fulfilled the function of inns. Moreover, they distributed quantities of food each day to the tenants and local peasantry, with particular concern for the old and the sick.

This all required careful training and after a few more years at home, learning sewing and embroidery, with music, dancing and perhaps French from visiting tutors, a girl would be sent away to a household of a similar or even higher status and remain there under the care of the mistress until, in her early teens, she was married.

The Paston letters of the fifteenth century give a picture of the responsibilities and cares of a woman left, often for long periods of time, to manage a large estate on her own, and the competent way in which she dealt with the various problems—the buying and selling of produce and stock, the contesting of legal claims, the assertion of rights. They also show that there was no sentimental attitude to children. From the age of two or three both boys and girls were dressed like adults, and they were expected to grow up quickly, with as little fuss as possible.

And often they were treated with heartless severity. Dame Agnes Paston, for example, in a letter to her son's tutor, urged him 'not to spare the lash'. Her daughter Elizabeth was boarded out with Lady Pole before her marriage, which her mother had arranged for her, and when Elizabeth demurred at the choice of an unattractive, middle-aged widower, she was 'beaten once in the week or twice. Sometimes thrice in one day, and her head broken in two or three places'.

Foreigners were puzzled by the English practice of boarding out children, which they considered harsh, and there was justification for this criticism, for there were many abuses. Children, especially those of poor parents, could be apprenticed for a very small fee or sometimes even given away. Cases appeared in the courts of fathers charging foster-parents with receiving money for their children's upbringing and misusing or appropriating it, withholding an education and treating them like servants, while orphans put out to fosterage sometimes never received a penny of the money their parents had left them: and these abuses were to last well into the seventeenth century amongst all classes, from the peerage downwards.

It is very difficult to assess how many people were literate in late medieval times. During the fourteenth century, when the population was about three million, there were probably between three and four hundred grammar schools in England, though most of them were very small, with only one master and perhaps an usher to help him. By the fifteenth century it has been estimated that there was a grammar school for every 5,626 people in England. The priests still held their little schools in the churches and the number of small cottage schools, run by men or women teachers, was increasing.

Just before the introduction of printing, the output of hand-written books on vellum or parchment, inscribed now almost entirely by the monks, was also increasing. They produced volumes of history and romance, some magnificently illustrated, others utilitarian, to meet the growing demand. Nearly every one of reasonable prosperity now possessed a book of prayers and some began to assemble small libraries. Books of Courtesy became popular and were carefully studied by those who had recently acquired their wealth and wished to improve their manners and become gentry.

It was in 1476 that William Caxton, returning from Bruges to London, set up the first printing press of the country, in the City of Westminster. Here, at the sign of the Red Pale, the first book he printed was Malory's *Le Morte d'Arthur*.

The old laborious days of copying were over. While the kings and princes of England destroyed each other in the futile bloodshed of the Wars of the Roses, to settle the claim to the succession to the throne, medievalism faded away.

Caxton's printing press gave the people of England the gift of accessible literature. Books were still expensive and rare, but Caxton claimed to print the best of English poetry and history, as well as 'joyous and pleasant histories of chivalry', for the delight of the increasing numbers of English people who were learning to read. Amongst these was a translation of *The Boke of the Knight of la Tour-Landry*, published in 1484, which had been made 'at the request of a noble lady which hath brought forth many noble and fair daughters which be virtuously nourished'.

This book on the upbringing of girls had been written in France in 1371, and for the next hundred and fifty years it was widely read throughout Europe, as the standard manual of behaviour desirable in every girl of gentle birth who hoped to achieve perfect womanhood. The advice was pretty conservative, repeating all the admonitions of St. Jerome on manners and morals, but somewhat debased by the implication that this behaviour was not merely an end in itself but the best way to catch a rich husband and the finest insurance for a passport to Heaven.

Unlike many men, the Knight thought it a good thing for a girl to be able to read her psalter and write her own letters, but felt nothing more was necessary.

There was another book of courtesy published about this time for women lower down the social scale—*How the Good Wiff Taught Her Daughter*—giving very similar precepts—the modest demeanour, regular church going, no loud laughter or yawning—but it also warns against the perils of over-drinking in taverns and gives some handy hints on the diplomatic handling of irritable husbands.

> So maist thou slake his mood
> And be his dere darlynge. . . .

Some women were, of course, intellectually far in advance of the ignorance and ineptitude suggested by these works, but many, perhaps the majority, were not, and for many years to come the chief aim of a woman's education was thought sufficient if it enabled her to withstand what the Knight described as 'the perilles of the sowle'.

During most of the fourteenth and fifteenth centuries the throne of England was so much in dispute that the Court had little influence on the upbringing of women. The queens, many of whom came from foreign courts, mostly could read and write some English and French. They had a good knowledge of music and they continued the tradition of beautiful needlework. Anne of Bohemia, Richard II's queen, was highly educated and greatly loved: and to Wycliff's delight, she possessed copies of the gospels in Czech, German and Latin. She and her Bohemian courtiers were sympathetic to Wycliff's work and made it known to John Huss and the leaders of the European movement for the reform of the Church. Edward IV's wife, Elizabeth Woodville, an English noblewoman, had literary tastes and, like Edward's sister, Margaret of York, was a patroness of Caxton. She possessed several valuable books in both English and French, was a skilled embroideress and saw to it that her daughters were carefully educated. Margaret of Anjou had first founded Queen's College, Cambridge, but Elizabeth Woodville added to the foundation and thereafter it was known as Queens' College.

It was Lady Margaret Beaufort, mother of Henry VII, who was the outstanding woman of intellect of the late fifteenth century, though she had had no more formal education than any other English noblewoman of her time. The beauty of her embroidery was outstanding. She could read and write English. She understood French but had very little, if any, Latin. Yet she possessed many books, including volumes of Froissart, Boccacio and Chaucer, and many other histories, romances and poems. And being a book lover, she appreciated more than any other royal lady the significance of Caxton's printing press. She gave him every encouragement and herself compiled for his press the *Ordinances and reformations of apparel for princes and estates, with other ladies and gentlemen, for the time of mourning* and translated from the French the *Mirroure of Golde for the sinfull soule*, neither of which has the feel of a best-seller, admittedly, but they were considerable achievements for a woman of the time.

Inspired by the new spirit of learning of the Renaissance, she founded Jesus College, Cambridge in 1496 and Christ's College, Cambridge in 1505, while at both Oxford and Cambridge she endowed perpetual readerships in theology.

These foundations helped men and not women, but the Lady Margaret had proved to the world that women were capable of academic studies, and that in itself, after the long years of decline in women's education, was a step forward.

The nunneries were entering the last phase of their existence before the Reformation and their dissolution. Many by this time were hard pressed for funds. The old rules forbidding them to take lay pupils were forgotten and many of the houses were now accepting girls, either as boarders or day pupils, and also a few young boys. Some were orphans of the Wars of the Roses. Others were sent there as an alternative to being boarded out. And the nunneries were no longer socially exclusive, for the children of yeomen and merchants were known to have attended them at this time, as well as the children of the gentry.

Very little is known about these nunnery schools and they were very small, seldom having more than thirty pupils. The curriculum was little different from that of a century earlier, comprising reading and writing, music, instruction in good manners, with needlework for the girls. Some of the nuns were probably sufficiently literate to teach the children themselves, provided the bishop had issued the licence which it was necessary for all teachers of the young to hold, and one or two may even have been able to give rudimentary instruction in French, though by this time very few of them knew the language.

The boys, who seldom stayed after the age of seven, often had visiting tutors, and the girls may also have had them for special subjects such as French, and also for music, for the playing of the clavichord, lute, harp, recorder and all the other musical instruments which were being devised during the late fifteenth and early sixteenth centuries, was becoming an increasingly popular and, indeed, socially necessary accomplishment for young women of birth and fashion.

Chapter Four

TUDOR ENGLAND

WITH THE ACCESSION of the Tudors, the old medieval traditions in England gradually passed away. Such families of the old nobility who had survived the Wars of the Roses turned their ancient and uncomfortable castles into dwelling houses, or leaving them to crumble into ruins, moved into simpler and more practical manor houses, similar to those in which the new landed gentry were now living—men who had grown rich on English wool.

Some of the yeomen of the English countryside worked the farms which their families had owned for generations. Others rented them from the hard-pressed nobility or from the monastic houses.

Wycliff's attempts at religious change during the previous century had had little immediate effect, and the Church was as rich and powerful as it had ever been, owning a fifth of England's wealth in land and buildings, and prospering on rents and tithes: and many of the bishops were also counsellors of state, thereby wielding secular as well as ecclesiastical power.

More landowners were turning from arable farming to the more profitable rearing of sheep, which entailed less labour. At the same time, the population was increasing and labourers who, a few generations earlier, had been in a strong enough position to demand higher wages, now sometimes had difficulty in finding work. Some made their way to the towns, where increasing trade and foreign commerce offered more opportunities, but unemployment grew into a serious problem and hundreds became homeless vagrants, who lived as best they could, sleeping in the woods and forests and seeking food and alms from the monasteries, which served them well at this time and became true havens to many a starving and desperate man.

During all the upheavals of the early part of the fifteenth century and the bitter feuds of the Yorkists and Lancastrians, there had been little opportunity for the development of education. The Church had become lax and their interest had flagged. In London the monopoly of establishing schools rested with the bishop, and by 1450 so many old-established grammar schools had ceased to function that there were only three left in the entire city.

Life moved slowly. Four-fifths of the country's three million people were country dwellers, the pace of their lives controlled by the quiet rhythm of the seasons, but events which had taken place in eastern Europe began gradually to affect the west, eventually making themselves felt on this small island on its north-western fringe.

During the Barbarian invasions of the fourth and fifth centuries the capital of the Roman Empire had been moved to Constantinople, and here, throughout the long years, succeeding generations of Greek scholars had kept alive the learning and traditions of the old Empire. The western world had made contact with the Arabs and this eastern Empire during the thirteenth century, but during the succeeding years, as the Greek scholars of Constantinople watched the advance of the Turks through Asia Minor, they took the precaution of moving to the Aegean Islands and the mainland of Italy with their treasures, thereby re-introducing to Europe, with far greater impact, the ancient pre-Christian classical culture.

In Rome and Florence began the Renaissance, a revival of interest in art and literature, philosophy and science, inspired by the writings of ancient Greece and Rome: and eventually the culture of the whole of western Europe was to come under its influence.

With the fall of Constantinople to the Turks in 1453, the ancient trade routes between the Italian city states and the East, by way of Syria, were blocked. The mariners of western Europe began to explore the Atlantic, hoping to find an alternative route to the East by sea. Before the end of the fifteenth century, Bartholemew Diaz had rounded the Cape of Good Hope, Christopher Columbus had landed in the West Indies and John Cabot, financed by Henry VII, had discovered Newfoundland.

In England these discoveries had little immediate material effect and it was to be another generation or more before men's thoughts turned to colonization, but mentally and spiritually the impact was revolutionary. To people who had been brought up to believe that the world ended in a vague cloud, somewhere beyond the Atlantic horizon, it came first as a shock and then as a stimulus. They realized that they had been accepting as fundamental truth much which was patently false. The fallacies of their old geography lessons were now all too obvious, for a start. It set men thinking, questioning, experimenting. Within the next few years Vesalius, the Flemish student of anatomy and physiology, was to disprove the theories of Galen and Aristotle, on which doctors had been trained for more than a thousand years, and Copernicus was to show that, contrary to the teaching of the Church, the earth was not the centre of the universe but a sphere moving round the sun.

Erasmus, the Dutch theologian and scholar, and a leader of the new learning of the Renaissance, paid a visit to Dean Colet at Oxford early in Henry VII's reign, and several years later he returned to meet Sir Thomas More. These three men were deeply concerned at the widening gulf between the conduct of the organized Church in Europe and the concept of Christianity expressed in the New Testament: and Erasmus, steeped in the literature and philosophy of Greece and with a brilliantly clear mind, was saddened to see the obscure ritual of the Church enmesh so many of its members in a tangle of vague superstition. Henry VII was also deeply interested in the new learning of the Renaissance, but he remained a devout Catholic all his life, showing no sign of doubt in the omnipotence of the Church of Rome, despite the growing feeling amongst an increasing number of English intellectuals, influenced by Erasmus, that they could no longer accept some of its doctrines.

With the changing concepts of religion and of life in general, many fine and promising words were written about the education of girls, remarkably few of which were to bear fruit: but Sir Thomas More set an example, not only by the way in which he supervised the education of his own daughters, but by the kindness with which he treated them.

Under his training and that of her tutors, Margaret, the eldest girl, became an accomplished scholar and linguist, amply proving her father's contention that learning may 'equally agree with both sexes. . . .'

When he was away from home, Margaret and the other children wrote him a letter in Latin every day. Margaret also wrote a number of Latin poems and orations and translated into English the Latin work of Erasmus on the Lord's Prayer. Her Greek was as sound as her Latin and she also studied philosophy, astronomy, arithmetic, logic, rhetoric and medicine.

Amongst the visitors to their riverside home at Chelsea was Juan Luis Vives, a Spaniard born in Valencia, who had become a pupil of Erasmus at Louvain University and came to England in 1523 to teach the new learning at Corpus Christi College, Oxford.

Henry VIII asked Vives to draw up a plan of education for the seven-year-old Princess Mary and to supervise her studies. Vives devised a course of reading which included Cicero, Seneca, Plutarch and Plato. She was also to study the works of the Christian Fathers and read her Bible twice a day: and he recommended a study of More's *Utopia* and some of the work of Erasmus, all of which must have been pretty heavy going for a seven-year-old.

Queen Catherine, herself a woman of intellect and scholarship, and greatly drawn to Vives, as a fellow-Spaniard, commissioned him to write *The Instruction of a Christian Woman*, but this was not translated into English until 1540, after Catherine's death. And despite the high standard of education he had set for Princess Mary, he seems to have regarded the intellectual capacity of most women as negligible and saw no place for them outside the home. He granted that education had a stabilizing effect on a woman's character, and made her more amenable to reason, but said that the new learning should be for men only and that women would do better to keep to the old routine of reading and writing, needlework and household duties.

Sour as all this was, he did lay stress on the importance of the mother in the early training and education of her children, particularly in regard to proper speech and good behaviour: and on the broader social problem of the treatment of the poor, Vives was less pompous and more practical. He advocated differing treatments for the various kinds of poverty. Begging should be prohibited and all paupers able to work given some useful employment. Hospitals should be provided for the sick and infirm, asylums for the insane, and the children of the poor should be educated so that they could support themselves in later life, thereby breaking the vicious circle of pauperism. Abandoned children should be cared for in an orphanage until they were six and then sent to a school which provided maintenance as well as education and training. Boys were to be taught to read and write, but 'let them first of all learn Christian piety and the right way of thinking'. The quicker learners should stay on, help with the teaching of the younger children and continue their own education to prepare themselves for entering a seminary to train for the priesthood. The rest should be put to whatever trade or occupation for which they showed an inclination or aptitude. The curriculum for the girls was the usual one of spinning, sewing, weaving, embroidery, cookery and household management, but Vives did concede that 'If any girl show herself inclined for and capable of learning, she should be allowed to go further with it,' though he had no end in view for her and he disapproved of women teachers, on the assumption that few could grasp plain facts and would therefore teach things all wrong.

It was only three years after Vives' arrival in England that

King Henry began his divorce proceedings against Queen Catherine. She turned to Vives for help and advice, but he was no lady's man and as a Spanish Catholic he felt the position too delicate and dangerous to handle. Even so, he was arrested, imprisoned for a time and banished.

There began the long quarrel with the Pope, culminating in the final breech, in 1531, when Henry proclaimed himself the head of the Church of England. And four years later Sir Thomas More, refusing to take the oath of supremacy, was arrested, tried and beheaded.

By this time the King had married Ann Boleyn and the Princess Elizabeth was two years old. Within the next year, Ann was executed and the King had married Jane Seymour. And in 1537 Prince Edward was born, but Jane died in childbirth.

King Henry built a palace at Chelsea, close to Sir Thomas More's old house, for his two small children, who were put under the care of Lady Bryan. From the outset, they were carefully trained and educated. Elizabeth in particular acquired a sound knowledge of Greek and Latin and was an accomplished musician and elegant dancer. She was cleverer than Edward but they loved each other dearly. Like the children of the grammar schools, they spoke to each other in Latin and wrote to each other in Latin when they were separated.

The dissolution of the lesser monasteries had taken place in 1536 and by 1539 the abbeys had been suppressed. Some of the buildings were turned into manor houses but the rest were either deliberately destroyed or left to fall into ruin. Some of the abbots and priests became Protestant clergymen in the newly-established Church of England. Others were pensioned off and cast into the world to live as best they could or seek protection in monasteries abroad. The valuable estates they had been forced to abandon fell into the hands of the King and many he sold to wealthy yeomen and merchants, who established themselves as a new landed gentry. Grammar schools attached to the abbeys and monasteries inevitably disappeared with the Dissolution, but some of the funds from the endowments—

though by no means all—were used in re-establishing some of the old schools or founding new ones. Henry VIII himself re-founded eleven important cathedral schools and by the end of his reign fifty new grammar schools had come into existence.

The closing of the nunneries was no great loss to the cause of girls' education, for the nunnery education had become almost negligible. Nevertheless, an opportunity was missed at this stage, despite the protests of many educationists, to use the money derived from the nunnery estates to establish girls' schools comparable with the new grammar schools for boys.

Many excuses were made but the general attitude was that the money could be put to far better purpose. Good or bad, the nunneries were all swept away and there were no reprieves.

Amongst the casualties of the Dissolution was the convent of the Grey Friars, which since 1225 had been established on the north side of Newgate Street in the City of London. Here in 1327 the Friars had built their beautiful church and a century later Richard Whittington had added a magnificent library for their valuable collection of books: but after the Grey Friars had been disbanded, the convent[1] stood empty and neglected.

For the increasing numbers of unemployed and destitute in England, their problem aggravated by the growing practice of enclosing the common lands, this was the time of even more terrible hardship, for although the closing of the nunneries had had little social effect, the suppression of the monasteries was disastrous for those who had turned to them for shelter and food during their hopeless search for work. In London they lived as best they could, in squalor and near starvation, with nowhere to turn for the succour which the monasteries had been able to give them.

Only a few weeks before he died, King Henry, on the advice of Sir Thomas Gresham, bestowed the convent of the Grey Friars and their church on the City Corporation, for the relief of the poor, provided the citizens contributed to the funds for its maintenance. The church, re-dedicated as Christ's Church,

---

[1] The term 'convent' was used to describe a religious community of men as well as of women.

was to be regarded as a foundation of King Henry VIII and opened for public worship.

A month later Henry was dead and the boy king, Edward VI, was on the throne. The exchequer was low and his regents were occupied with the Chantries Acts, by which more than two thousand chantries and chapels were to be dissolved, and their estates sold to private purchasers, on the grounds that they were improperly administered and had been turned to superstitious uses. This was another serious threat to the cause of education, for so many of the chantries had schools attached to them: and in many cases the purchasers felt no obligation to continue them. In the course of these transactions some three hundred grammar schools disappeared and also the song schools. The government promised to use some of the confiscated money to establish many more grammar schools but all it achieved was a few dozen and in the end Edward VI's government sacrificed far more schools than it ever established. Hugh Latimer appealed to the rich to donate to the furtherance of education the money they would have spent on chantries and pilgrimages, but these pleas yielded little until the reign of Queen Elizabeth a generation later.

Nothing was done about the Grey Friars convent and from time to time it was used as a storehouse. And in the meantime the numbers of paupers and orphans, disabled and sick, most of them totally ignorant and near to starvation, still haunted the narrow lanes and alleys of London, a living reproach to the newly-established Church of England. The church and hospital of St. Bartholemew was doing valiant work, admitting as many of the destitute as they could, but the almoners said that the numbers in need were so great that they were hardly making any impression on the problem and were taking in less than a tenth of those desperate for help.

One Sunday in 1552 Bishop Ridley, the Bishop of London, preached at Westminster before the young King Edward, on the subject of mercy and charity, making an eloquent plea for the plight of London's poor. The message went home and Edward sent for the bishop to make practical plans. The result of that meeting was a letter to the Mayor, Sir Richard Dobbs, which Ridley himself delivered to him that same evening. The following day Sir Richard invited the bishop, two aldermen and six councillors to dine with him and make the first plans. They decided to enlarge this committee to include six aldermen and twenty-four commoners.

They adopted Vives' method of classifying the poor into three categories, firstly the poor by impotency, which included the orphans, sick, aged, blind and lame, secondly the poor by casualty—wounded soldiers, decayed householders and others who had fallen on hard times through no fault of their own—and thirdly the thriftless—the wastrels, idlers and petty criminals.

In all there were 2,100 people to be cared for and the categories into which they fell were further subdivided. For the sick and wounded the religious house founded in honour of Thomas à Becket was to be restored and known as St. Thomas's Hospital, to supplement the work of St. Bartholemew's, and a separate lazar house established for the lepers. For the orphans and children of the poor—both boys and girls—it was decided that the Grey Friars house should be re-established as Christ's Hospital.

There remained the able-bodied, uneducated unemployed, some rascals, some merely helpless and thriftless.

On the right bank of the broad estuary of the Fleet river, where it flowed into the Thames, was the royal palace of Bridewell, standing in the precincts of the holy well of St. Bride and the little church which had been built alongside it. Wolsey had acquired this land but Henry VIII had claimed it and built here a beautiful red-brick palace, similar to that of St. James, with stone facings and out-of-date but impressive turrets. It was here that his last quarrel with Catharine of Aragon took place and after she had left for ever the king also deserted the palace, allowing it to be used as a residence for the French ambassadors.

King Edward inherited the Bridewell Palace and Bishop Ridley now begged him to allow it to be used for the third

main category of the needy as a place of corrective detention—
a house of reform, discipline and employment, where by
technical training, education and correction the men and
women housed there would be transformed into worthy
citizens. It was a wise and merciful policy, far in advance of
most sixteenth-century thinking, and the young king, only a
few weeks before his death, granted his charter to the Bridewell
Hospital.

The ambassadors moved out, albeit somewhat unwillingly,
and the new inmates moved in. However, during Queen
Mary's brief reign, the Bridewell Hospital did not function as
the original governors had intended, the detention being more
apparent than the correction, although they were given plenty
of work to do. There were two treadmills, each using eighteen
men at a time, which were used for grinding corn. In the
smithy nails were made and offered for sale. The women wove
cloth and baked bread. Though far from the original idea of
providing a useful training for the homeless and indigent, the
idea of putting prisoners to work spread through the country,
and when other towns opened gaols as penitentiaries for
vagrants and vagabonds they were called 'bridewells'.

St. Thomas's Hospital and Christ's Hospital fared better. In
the autumn of 1552 St. Thomas's admitted two hundred sick
and aged persons and on November 23 of that year three
hundred and eighty boys and girls arrived at Christ's Hospital,
one hundred of them babies. This may be claimed as the opening day of the first endowed boarding school in England for
girls, and since it flourishes to this day in Hertfordshire, it may
also be claimed as the opening day of the oldest girls' school in
the country.

The governors had agreed that the purpose of Christ's
Hospital would be to supply meat, drink, clothes and lodging
to the needy children of London, as well as learning and officers
to attend upon them. Babies and those too young to learn were
to be cared for in the country.

Appeals for funds were sent to the clergy, church wardens
and sidesmen of every parish in the city and to every house-

holder of substance. Collecting boxes were handed to the land-
lord of every inn and to the wardens of every company. The
response was generous and quick. Within six months the old
monastery building had been renovated and made ready to
receive five hundred children. Mr. Calthorp, a member of the
committee, contributed five hundred feather beds for them,
with straw mattresses, blankets and sheets. And these were
luxuries indeed, which many worthy and prospering country
people did not yet enjoy in England, still making do with
straw pallets and a log of wood for a pillow.

The staff was assembled and included a grammar master,
his assistant, the usher, a writing master, two elementary
teachers for the petties, a music master, a surgeon, various
assistants and also a matron, Agnes Sexton, who had twenty-
five women under her. One of her duties was 'twice or thrice
in every week' to 'arise in the night and go as well into the
sick ward as also into every other ward, and there see that
the children be covered in their beds, whereby they take
no cold', a remarkably gentle and humane touch in a world
where so many children had known nothing but neglect and
cruelty.

The first problems in dealing with the assortment of poor
London children who arrived at the hospital more than four
hundred years ago were discipline and hygiene. Some of the
children were said to have 'died of the hygiene', terrified
perhaps by their first serious encounter with soap and water,
and there were certainly some who, in the early days, were
afraid of so large an institution and tried to run away. They
'would watch duly when the porters were absent that they
might steal out and fall to their old occupations, so that a
number of them were punished before they could be brought
to abide within the bounds of their houses', but it was only a
matter of weeks before they all settled down contentedly,
beguiled by the comfort and kindliness of the place, the regular
food, not to mention the feather beds, which were rare even
in the days of Queen Elizabeth.

The records do not show how many girls there were at the

hospital during the early years, but as there were six masters and only one mistress, they were clearly in a minority. Their ward, with forty beds, was part of the Whittington library over the north cloister, next to the maidens' 'schoole' in the ditch playground. This does not sound particularly salubrious, but in the fullness of time the ditch was filled in.

By Christmas the girls were in a uniform of 'russet cotton with kerchiefs on their heads' but by the following Easter this had been changed to the blue dress, white, green or blue apron and white cap and collar which they were to wear until 1875.

The girls' education was far more limited than that of the boys, comprising for many years only reading and needle-work, with the Bible as their only book. Their school hours were seven till eleven in the morning and one to five in the afternoon, with half holidays on Thursdays and Saturdays: and two or three times a week they were given lengthy and searching catechisms, the purpose of which was to teach them the Christian religion according to the Catechism of the Church of England, so that the children would be ready at all times 'to give an account of the fundamental truths'. The catechizer also had to see that the girls behaved reverently in Church, that they had good manners and behaved respectfully to all persons and deported themselves properly in their wards.

The accounts for the hospital show that in June, 1553, 6s. 8d. was paid as salary to the governess and there were also small payments to Goodwife Smoothing and Goodwife Saepsched—the wives of the steward and the porter, both of whom seem to have combined the duties of schoolmistress and nurse.

This was the year that the young King died. On his accession, six years earlier, at the age of ten, he had been moved to the palace at Greenwich, and the widowed Catherine Parr, herself well educated, and with a court of women who studied Latin and Greek as carefully as the scriptures, retired to the palace at Chelsea, where Princess Elizabeth still lived, with her governess Mrs. Ashley.

The standard of learning remained very high throughout

Tudor times amongst the royal queens and princesses and the women of the nobility. Nicholas Udall, that grim headmaster of Eton, notorious for his flogging, inflicted, as one victim ruefully recalled, 'for fault but small or none at all', remarked in a letter to Catherine Parr on the studiousness of these young women of noble birth, who read and studied as easily in Greek and Latin, French and Italian as in English.

Jane Seymour and Katharine Howard had both been well educated and spoke French fluently, while Ann Boleyn had been carefully trained from the age of seven, when she was taken to France as one of the retinue of the accomplished Mary Tudor, on the occasion of her marriage to Louis XII. But Anne of Cleves, like the rest of her countrywomen, had neither learning nor accomplishments, save her needlework.

Catherine Parr re-married, but her new husband, Tom Seymour, made such unseemly overtures to the fourteen-year-old Princess Elizabeth that she was removed to Cheshunt. Here, from 1548 to 1550, her tutor was the Greek scholar, Roger Ascham. She became a brilliant linguist, equally fluent in French, Italian and Latin, and in later years Ascham declared that there were not four men in the whole of England who understood Greek better than Elizabeth.

Born in 1537, a year or two after Elizabeth and only a few months before Prince Edward, was Lady Jane Grey, granddaughter of King Henry VIII's younger sister, Mary. From the age of nine, Jane was brought up at Catherine Parr's Court and stayed with her until Catherine's death in 1548.

Few doubted that the frail and ailing young King Edward would die very soon, and in order to save the Protestant succession Jane's father had planned to marry her to Lord Guildford, son of the Lord Protector, the Duke of Northumberland, and when the time came, put her on the throne, in place of the rightful heir, the Catholic Princess Mary. To this end, Jane had been carefully brought up and educated by her father's chaplain, John Aylmer, and of all the Tudor children, she was perhaps the most outstandingly quick and intelligent. Before she was six she was reading the Bible to herself and learning

Latin, and then she began to study Greek, Spanish, Italian and French, and ultimately Hebrew and Arabic.

John Aylmer was devoted to her but this was the only affection she was to know, apart from that of her young husband, during their brief marriage, for her childhood was wretched, her upbringing by her ambitious parents made spartan and joyless, in marked contrast to that of Sir Thomas More's children of a few years earlier or even of the little girls who were shortly to be living in Christ's Hospital.

Ascham grieved for Lady Jane, for he hated to see a child ill-treated, and in his most famous book *The Schoolmaster*, which was not published until 1570, two years after his death, he wrote: 'Love is better than fear, gentleness better than beating to bring up a child rightlie in learninge.'

After Edward VI's death in 1553, at the age of sixteen, the erudite little Jane Grey, duly placed on the throne but never crowned, was arrested with her young husband after a few days, committed to the Tower, tried at the Guildhall and executed on Tower Green.

The sick, unhappy Mary Tudor succeeded to the throne and the Papal Legate sailed up the Thames to Westminster to receive England back into the Mother Church of Rome. During the next five years of violent and bitter religious persecution, when Bishop Ridley, to whom Christ's Hospital, St. Thomas's and the Bridewell owed so much, was among the victims to be martyred at the stake, Christ's Hospital was at times in jeopardy, but it weathered the storm and by 1558, when Mary was dead and Queen Elizabeth safely on the throne, it was well launched.

At the same time, the governors of the Bridewell were able to improve conditions. After the Statute of Artificers of 1563, which enacted that every craftsman must serve an apprenticeship of seven years, they introduced a system of apprenticeship at the Bridewell which was available not only to the homeless and destitute, but also to children of poor freemen of the City of London.

The boys' school at Christ's Hospital developed into an important educational establishment comprising several schools

in the same foundation. There were an upper and lower grammar school organized by the grammar master and his usher.
The writing school was endowed in 1577 and a music school
in 1609. The reading school was run by the 'petty' masters and
the girls were taught separately in their 'maidens' school'.
Numerous bequests provided fellowships and scholarships for
the most able boys to pass on to the universities. Boys less
academically inclined, having mastered their ABC and moved
on to the writing school, qualified as apprentices to work in
the counting houses of the city merchants or were sent each
day to the Bridewell, to be apprenticed to such trades as
tailoring, weaving, tapestry, spinning, needle and pin-making.
By providing this technical training as an alternative to an
academic education, Christ's Hospital was unique, and in later
years other schools were to adopt the same plan, but in the
records of this time there is very little reference to the training
of the girls, although the cooperation between Christ's Hospital
and the Bridewell was close. The Bridewell baked all the bread
for Christ's Hospital. Some of the Christ's Hospital boys
received a preliminary training in such crafts as spinning and
needle-making before beginning their apprenticeship at the
Bridewell. And in 1644 there is a record that Mr. Drake, one
of the Christ's Hospital governors, seeing five little girls and
a small boy at the Bridewell, far too young to take part in the
work of the hospital, arranged for them to be taken in at Christ's
Hospital until they were at least twelve years old, in exchange
for the apprenticeship of five of their older boys.

Children stayed at Christ's Hospital until about fourteen or
fifteen years of age, when, if they were not passing on to the
university, suitable work or apprenticeship was found for them.
The girls would have had little difficulty in finding work as
seamstresses in some substantial household, though there are
no precise details of their destinies at this time, and even a
century or more later, when John Evelyn visited the school,
though he was full of praise for their appearance and their
singing, he was vague about their future.

In the early days and up until the eighteenth century, girls took their meals in the same hall as the boys, at their own table, and the food was ample. Beef, mutton, fish, bread, milk, butter, cheese and beer all appear in the accounts of the sixteenth century, but the infants did not always fare so well. On admission they were sent away from London to the country, mainly to Hertfordshire, where they were boarded out in batches of eight or ten, in private households, and stayed until they were about ten years old. The hospital paid for their clothing and board and they were visited as often as possible by the matron or one or other of the governors, but there were sometimes complaints from the children that they were ill-treated or underfed. Occasionally, conditions were so blatantly bad that they had to be moved, and ultimately it was arranged that they should be visited every quarter, for an examination of their diet and clothing and to check that they were receiving proper instruction from a local schoolmistress.

At Christ's Hospital, the girls spent hours of their time in sewing. They sewed their own caps and collars, as well as the nightshirts and neckbands of the boys, and they stitched all the household linen. With the boys, they attended the services at Christ Church, sitting at the end east of the north gallery. In Easter week they marched through the City to attend the sermon at St. Mary's Spittal and then to the Lord Mayor's house to receive his annual gifts: and although in the years to come the scope of their education gradually broadened, until, after many vicissitudes, Christ's Hospital Girls' School was to become the distinguished school that it now is, at the end of Queen Elizabeth's reign we must leave the poor young things at their interminable sewing, their Bible reading and their catechisms.

Yet their condition was infinitely happier than that of the children of the Bridewell. In its early days it had been commended as a good school, where children were brought up in godliness and the idle and unprofitable drones set to useful work. But before the idle could work they had to be corrected and cells were adapted from the old servants' quarters and stables of the palace to accommodate them. Before long

1. King Edward VI, whose brief reign (1547–53) saw the foundation of numerous grammar schools and the schools at Christ's Hospital and the Palace at Bridewell.

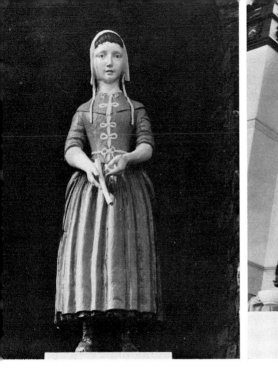

2. Christ's Hospital School. *Top left:* A statue of 1778 showing the girls' uniform at the time. *Top right:* Girls drinking from traditional bowls in the dining hall. *Below:* The main courtyard of the old school buildings in London.

the cells, intended in the first place for brief periods of correction, were increasingly used for prisoners who had no intention of reforming. These included the religious prisoners of the late sixteenth century, among them the Puritans, and in particular the Congregationalists, and also the Roman Catholics who, with the growing threat of Spanish invasion, represented a political danger as well as a threat to the supremacy of the Church of England.

These prisoners were flogged and tortured and died in the Bridewell, and the original purpose of St. Edward's Hospital as a place of rehabilitation and useful occupation was overshadowed and for a time almost lost.

The governors tried to reassert the rights of the young people whose only crime was their poverty. They were still given instruction in their chosen trades, but there are no records of the fate of the girls at this time and it was to be many years before the children of Bridewell were to receive again the training that the founders had planned for them.

Throughout the country as a whole, many more grammar schools for boys were established in the late part of the century, but the Elizabethans had little interest in the provision of any public education for their daughters.

Fifteen grammar schools had been founded or re-established by Edward VI's government, including Bedford School, though some were very small and poorly endowed. The grammar school at Bath, for example, which was part-hospital, part school, could accommodate only ten people and ten poor boys. Repton was founded in 1557 and during Elizabeth's reign many famous schools were endowed by prosperous merchants or noblemen, or, alternatively, buildings were bequeathed, for which the town agreed to pay the master's stipend. Thame School was founded in 1559, Westminster in 1560, Abingdon in 1562, Felsted in 1564, Rugby in 1567, Harrow in 1571 and Uppingham in 1584. In London, St. Paul's, the ancient Cathedral foundation, had been replaced in 1513 by John Colet's new foundation, and other distinguished Elizabethan schools in London were the Mercers', the Merchant

Taylors', Highgate, St. Olave's, Charterhouse and St. Saviour's, though here again some were very small, St. Saviour's taking only thirty boys.

Mostly they were day schools, serving the needs of local boys, and even the schools which were nationally famous and to which boys were sent from all over the country, such as Eton and Winchester, both of which survived the Reformation, were not at first equipped with sleeping accommodation, the boys being boarded out in the town.

The grammar school boys came from all levels of society, except the lowest, who were thought to have no need of education, and mostly they were free to all who were able to qualify intellectually and had reached the required educational standard. Even Eton and Winchester were free in the early days, their exclusiveness lying in the high cost of their board and lodging.

In 1577 William Harrison, in his *Description of England*, was able to say that 'there are not many corporate towns now under the Queen's dominion that have not one grammar school at the least, with a sufficient living for a master and usher appointed to the same', and the number of schools throughout the country had risen to about three hundred and fifty.

These grammar schools were still under ecclesiastical supervision and masters had to be licensed by the Church, for the success of the Reformation depended not only on a learned ministry but an educated laity capable of supporting and defending the new order against the immensely powerful Roman Church.

However, as early as 1513, when Dean Colet re-founded St. Paul's School, he had vested control in the Mercers' Company and stipulated that the headmaster should be a layman: and by Elizabeth's time it was acknowledged that wealthy citizens and the State should accept some of the responsibility for education, which hitherto had been left in the hands of the Church.

For girls, apart from the few at Christ's Hospital, there were no grammar schools. There is some slight evidence that a few may at one time have been admitted to one or two of them, but the practice did not last for long. In the Harrow rules of 1590, for example, it is stated that 'no girls shall be received to be taught in the school' and as the school had been going for nearly twenty years, this could perhaps imply that they had at one time been admitted, but the governors had had a change of heart. At Bunbury Grammar School in Cheshire, founded in 1594, girls were admitted, but their numbers were limited and none was allowed to remain above the age of nine, 'nor longer than they may learn to read English'. At Uffington School there is a note in the records for 1637 that girls be refused admission, for though it was a 'common and usual course' it was 'by many conceived very uncomely and not decent'.

There were still the petty schools which, at about the age of four or five, they could attend with their brothers for two or three years. They learned their alphabet and numbers from a hornbook. This was a wooden tablet with a handle, on which was pasted a paper printed with the alphabet, the numerals and the Lord's Prayer, the paper being protected with a thin sheet of horn. They learnt to read and write and acquired some simple arithmetic, with perhaps, in the last year, a little Latin, for the boys, going on to grammar schools were going to study little else and would be obliged to talk to each other in Latin during school hours, on pain of severe punishment.

When the girls left the petty school some were taught at home by their mothers, or by tutors and governesses. Some were sent to other households, to acquire a training in home management, with perhaps a few accomplishments thrown in for good measure. The rest received no further education at all.

Although there was such a lamentable lack of public provision for the higher education of girls throughout the sixteenth century, at the Elizabethan Court and amongst the nobility there were still many women who had been highly educated in the earlier Tudor tradition.

There were the women of Margaret Roper's generation, a few years older than the Queen, who were skilled in herbal medicine and distillation, admirable housewives and cooks, who spent their leisure time in needlework, embroidery and silk-spinning, reading the Bible, studying history and writing or translating works into English or Latin. There was also the younger generation, who were outstandingly skilled in music and the playing of the lute and virginals: and both young and old, according to William Harrison, had, for the most part, a sound knowledge of Greek and Latin and were no less skilled in Spanish and French.

Gradually the Renaissance enthusiasm for the study of the Classics waned before the easier fashion for Italian poetry, which began with the publication in English, in 1561, of Castiglione's *Courtier*. The romantic accomplishments of poetry, music and dancing were now considered more socially acceptable for a young woman of gentle birth than a knowledge of Greek and Latin, and she was given a new set of rules, in which modesty, temperance, sweetness and gentleness were the attributes to be commended. Intellectually she lost ground.

Amongst high and low, whether educated or illiterate, necromancy died very hard in England, as elsewhere in Europe. It lingered on in the festivals of the countryside and also in people's most private and personal way of thinking. Witches were still hunted and magic and sorcery still practised.

Dr. John Dee was the most famous of the Tudor wizards, a Cambridge graduate who dabbled in astrology and necromancy. During Mary Tudor's reign he had been accused of using enchantments and spells to bring about her death, and had been forced to leave the country in a hurry, but by 1555 he was back again, and when the coronation plans of Queen Elizabeth were being made he was invited by Lord Dudley to consult the stars and the spirit world, so that the most propitious time for the ceremony could be chosen.

He met the Queen and gave her a few lessons in his occult arts, but she must have grown sceptical, for she never kept her promise to take more lessons, though at the end of his life, when he fell on hard times, she was generous to him.

Witch hunting was still rife throughout the whole of

Europe, though in England it was not to reach its climax until the days of Matthew Hopkins in the seventeenth century. The year before Henry VII came to the throne, the Pope had publicly denounced the widespread practice of witchcraft in Germany, and before the end of the fifteenth century nine hundred German men and women, alleged to have been witches, had been put to death. In one city alone, during the course of three months, five hundred had been burnt at the stake. The fear spread throughout Europe and in England and Scotland the laws against witchcraft were renewed and applied vigorously.

During the early part of the sixteenth century there are few records of burning for witchcraft in England but in 1576 three children and a servant girl were placed in the pillory for alleged sorcery and the following year a waxen image of Queen Elizabeth was found. Her advisers at once consulted Dr. Dee on the best way of protecting her and counteracting any possible attempt on her life by witchcraft.

The incident provoked another witch hunt. Simon Pembroke, for example, was noticed to have had a run of amazing good luck at dice and was summoned to appear before the court at Southwark to give an account of himself. He seems to have died of fright, just as he was offering a bribe to the proctor, and on his body were found a talisman in the form of a small tin human effigy, holding three dice, and also 'five devilish books of conjuration and most abominable practices'.

But the most notable conviction for sorcery was in 1590 when three people were put to death for bewitching the five children and other members of the household of Sir Samuel Cromwell of Huntingdon. The property of the sorcerers was confiscated and with the proceeds Sir Samuel created a fund for a sermon on the evils of witchcraft to be preached in Huntingdon every Lady Day.

It is difficult to estimate how widespread the practice of witchcraft was in England, but in the middle of the century one investigator estimated that there were about five hundred practising sorcerers and sorceresses, with concentrations in

Norfolk, Hertfordshire, Worcestershire and Gloucestershire. They used crystal balls for divination and apprehended thieves by the 'sieve and shears' method. Shears were plunged into the wooden sides of a sieve, which was then held upright, balanced by two people on their fingers. The names of likely culprits were called and when it came to the name of the real thief, the sieve was said to give a sharp turn, a method which gave ample scope to an unscrupulous enemy and must have sent many an innocent victim to his fate.

This widespread faith in the occult, often mixed with the baser religious beliefs which were barely distinguishable from magic, shows how superficial and confused was the education of so many people during Tudor times, compared with the outstanding intellectual achievements of the small minority of soundly educated English men and women.

In Germany, early in the sixteenth century, Martin Luther, already excommunicated by the Pope for his protests against the growing corruption of the Roman Catholic Church in the granting of indulgences, had created his own following, with his own brand of Protestantism: and in 1530 he wrote a 'Sermon on the Duty of Sending Children to School', which was sent to all his pastors, to be read to their congregations.

Luther wanted free schools established for children of all classes. He agreed that many children were needed at home—to help in the fields and the household, but pleaded that both boys and girls should be spared them for at least an hour or two's schooling each day.

In his 'Sermon on Married Life' he exhorted parents to give their children a good education as a means of acquiring merit for themselves and reforming Christendom, and in the address 'To the Christian Aristocracy of the German Nation' he said: 'And would to God that every town had a girls' school, in which the little maids might hear the Gospel for an hour daily, whether in German or Latin.' He urged that 'the best of schools should be instituted in all places, both for boys and girls . . . that men may be well able to rule land and people, and that women may know well how to rear children and to order house and servants'.

'To train youth aright is essential not only for their own sake but also for the welfare and stability of all our institutions, temporal and spiritual alike,' he maintained, words which have been echoed time and time again up to the present day.

Thomas Becon was one of the first Englishmen to call for the establishment of girls' schools in England. A professed Protestant, he had been chaplain to Cranmer and rector of St. Stephen Walbrook, and in 1554, during the Marian persecutions, had fled to Strasburg, but on his return to England he had been restored to his old benefice.

Like many returned exiles, he had brought back new ideas from Europe in regard to education, and in a religious manual called *A New Catechism*, which he wrote about the middle of the century, he pleaded the wisdom and reasonableness of providing schools for girls as well as boys. 'Is not the woman the creature of God as well as the man, and as dear unto God as the man?' he asked. 'Have we not all our beginning of her? ... Can the mothers bring up their children virtuously, when they themselves be void of all virtue?'

Becon's advice was not heeded and a few years later the schoolmaster Richard Mulcaster, who in 1561 was appointed the first Master of the Merchant Taylors' school, was again taking up the cause of girls' education, for he wanted to see the same educational opportunities for elementary training, not only for rich and poor boys alike, but for girls as well as boys, although he considered boys 'more worthy and more important in the body politic'. Both boys and girls must be taught to read, 'alike for the training of the mind in the process of acquiring it, and for its usefulness after it is acquired'. They must learn to read English before they start Latin and should be able to read before they are taught to write. He advised lessons in drawing, as a necessary preliminary for those who were later going to study astronomy, geometry and geography, and also singing and music.

He did not think women had any aptitude for mathematics

or the learned professions, but said: 'Is not a young gentle-woman thoroughly well equipped who can read distinctly, write neatly and swiftly, sing sweetly and play and draw well, understand and speak the learned languages, as well as the modern tongue approved by her time and country, and who has some knowledge of logic and rhetoric besides the information acquired in her study of foreign languages? If in addition to all this she be an honest woman and a good housewife would she not be worth wishing for and worth enshrining?'

He also allowed that a girl's education could have practical uses. 'If a young maiden is to be brought up with a view to marriage, obedience to authority and similar qualities must form the best kind of training,' he said, 'but if from necessity she has to learn how to earn her own living some technical training must prepare her for a definite calling. . . .'

The results of all this high thinking are not easy to find during the closing years of the sixteenth century, but about this time a few schools for girls were opened by refugees from the religious persecutions of France and the Low Countries, mainly for their own children, in London, Kent and the eastern counties, and some of these, which English girls were also able to attend, began to concentrate on the teaching of industries.

The greatest hindrance to the establishment of more schools for girls was, of course, the problem of teachers. A few women needing to earn a living established themselves in small schools, but all they had to offer was a knowledge of reading and writing, which they themselves had acquired at a dame's school, and such additional education they may have managed to give themselves by their own reading. There is no evidence of their having been given the necessary licence to teach, and schoolmasters regarded them with suspicion and resentment.

Chapter Five

THE EARLY STUARTS
AND THE COMMONWEALTH

BY THE TIME James I came to the throne, in 1603, there were grammar schools in most towns of England as well as petty schools: and there were petties or dame schools in the majority of small villages, where for a few pence a week, girls and boys could learn to read. How many availed themselves of these opportunities it is impossible to say, but people were probably not so illiterate as is often supposed. There were more books available and they were cheaper. By the end of the century many more girls could read than at any previous time and as people became more literate the general level of culture rose.

Sir Thomas More had suggested that about half the population of four or five million were able to read during the middle years of the sixteenth century, though this does not mean that they could also write, while a knowledge of arithmetic was even rarer. And where a small boy might have been taught reading, writing and arithmetic, it was often considered more suitable for his sister to learn reading, knitting and sewing, but it is unprofitable to generalize. An intelligent little girl could easily enough have taught herself to write after a fashion, once she had learnt her letters.

In 1596 Edmund Coote, a master of the school at Bury St. Edmunds, aiming to overcome the problem of the shortage of men and women with sufficient education to be able to teach, published a book called *The Englische Scolemaister*, which was intended both as a textbook for the pupil and a guide for the teacher, who could work on the principle of keeping a page ahead of the child. In the preface he said he had written it for the unskilful who wished to make use of it for their own private benefit and also for such men and women of trade such as 'Taylors, Weavers, Shoppekeepers, Semsters and such others as have undertaken the charge of teaching others.'

This book was popular all through the seventeenth century and by 1684 was in its forty-second edition, being used by men and women who, though they had but little education themselves, managed to keep school for the children of humble parents and pursue their own trade at the same time.

In Tudor times the fashions and manners of the Court and the scholarship of so many of the royal princesses and women of the nobility had a beneficial effect on the habits and ways of thinking women of the gentry and middle classes. 'You should look to the Court' is the advice to be found in many a book on etiquette. But with the advent of James I they looked in vain for a lead.

King James was a man of considerable learning and not a little wit, but he had very little interest in women and none at all in their education. 'To make women learned and foxes tame,' he said, 'had the same effect—to make them cunning.'

Separated from his mother, Mary Queen of Scots, before he was a year old, he had had a lonely and spartan childhood, brought up by the dour Regents and nobles of the Scottish Court: and although John Knox had died about the time of James's birth the young prince must have read that sour old Scotsman's views on women in his pamphlet *First Blast of the Trumpet Against the Monstrous Regiment of Women*, in which he declared that 'Nature doth paint them further to be weak, frail, impatient, feeble and foolish; and experience hath declared them to be inconstant, variable, cruel and lacking the spirit of counsel.'

James's wife was the Lutheran Princess Anne of Denmark. On her voyage to Scotland, for her marriage, she had been nearly shipwrecked off the coast of Norway and several unfortunate women, both in Scotland and Norway, were afterwards charged with having raised the storm by sorcery and were burned as witches.

Anne found the cold Protestantism of Scotland little to her taste and secretly preferred the colour and pageantry of the Roman Church. The people of Elizabethan England viewed with misgivings the unattractive, slovenly-looking King, with the strange Scottish accent, who came from a country which few of them had ever visited and for which none had any regard. Nor were they reassured when Anne followed him to Windsor, to take possession of her new fortune, which included Elizabeth's vast wardrobe of dresses, and prepare for the coronation in London, where she refused to take the sacrament of the Church of England.

She seems to have had few intellectual gifts. Shortly after her arrival in London she set up a separate court at Somerset House, which for a time was known as Denmark House, and here her principal diversions were to perform in masques and adapt for her own use Elizabeth's large collection of Spanish and French farthingales, a fashion which King James heartily disliked. 'The impertinent garment takes up all the room,' he grumbled.

Many of the masques were written for her by Ben Jonson and most were designed and produced by Inigo Jones, who must have been sorely tried by her at times. In 1610, for example, when a new masque was written to celebrate the investiture of Prince Henry as Prince of Wales, she was cast for the part of Tethy, the mother of all the river gods and goddesses. Inigo Jones designed her dress of silver gossamer, with a sky-blue train festooned with seaweed of gold brocade, but to the consternation of the producers, she insisted on wearing it over her huge farthingale and with her customary enormous ruff.

Her daughter, the Princess Elizabeth, did not receive an education in any way comparable with that of the Tudor princesses. She was boarded out with Lord and Lady Harrington at Combe Abbey, near Coventry, during her childhood, where she was happy enough but learnt no more than the customary reading and writing, music, dancing, French and Italian.

This custom of boarding out girls of noble birth lasted well into the seventeenth century, but now the first boarding schools for girls of the wealthy appeared. The heads of these new schools did not need to have any particular scholastic qualifications themselves, provided they were sufficiently well born to be able to supervise the manners and behaviour of the girls and oversee their material welfare, for a supply of visiting masters and mistresses became available as more refugees from the religious persecutions of Europe arrived in England, needing a means of livelihood. Here again the Church influenced the foundation of these schools, for the Catholic sympathies were still very strong in England, particularly amongst the women, and the Church of England sought to produce a generation of staunch Anglicans.

Only two years after King James's accession, the Gunpowder Plot showed how strong was the Catholic opposition, and it was known that a number of important families were smuggling their daughters over to France and Belgium for a Catholic education. Several English nunneries were established there, with endowments from wealthy English Catholic families, and a number of girls remained in them, taking the veil. King James declared that it was the women who were 'the nourishers of papistry' and preachers reproached them for their 'insolence and impudence', two of the most unlikely words, one would have thought, to describe religious conviction.

These were years of fear and tragedy, with families divided and the recusants in hourly danger. Boys and girls were intercepted as they were being smuggled secretly over to the Continent and brought back to England. Royal proclamations demanded the recall of children who were already abroad, so that they could be educated in the Protestant faith. An Act of 1624 proposed that all such children over nine years of age should be placed in Protestant places of education, or as apprentices or servants with Protestants, 'at the discretion of the parents if they be willing, but if not, then at their expense according to their position and means'.

Boarding schools for girls, being places where girls of different families came together for their board and education, were called 'public' schools. The first of which there is any record is the Ladies Hall at Deptford, which was established for the daughters of the gentry and nobility. We know very little about it, but probably, as with some of the later schools of this kind, the girls brought their own maids with them and lived in considerable style. On May 4, 1617, the Deptford girls took part in a masque called *Cupid's Banishment*, which was played before Queen Anne at Greenwich Palace. Most of the parts were played by boys or young men, but twelve of the schoolgirls, dressed all in white, with wreaths of white flowers in their hair, represented the nymphs of Diana and had been carefully trained by their dancing master, Mr. Onslow. And at the end, two of their number, both god-daughters of the Queen, were presented to her by the boy who played the part of Diana, Master Richard Browne, the future father-in-law of John Evelyn. The girls offered Queen Anne gifts of their own needlework and one can only hope that the scene was more decorous than at the masque performed a few years earlier at Whitehall, to celebrate the visit of the Queen's brother, King Christian IV of Denmark. On that occasion they were all so drunk that the Queen of Sheba fell into the royal visitor's lap, her attendants collapsed and the King of Denmark passed out altogether.

How long the Deptford school lasted is not clear, but John Evelyn, who spent so many of his later years at Sayes Court, Deptford, makes no mention of it in his diary.

However, a number of similar ones were opened during the following years, particularly around London, in the suburbs of Stepney and Hackney, Putney and Chelsea, many of them staffed with refugees who taught the usual subjects of music and dancing, French, sometimes Italian and always plenty of needlework and handicrafts.

In 1619 Queen Anne died of dropsy. King James was already

a sick man and for the remaining six years of his reign he was absorbed with his young men and boys, so that there were few women to be seen at Court, to give a lead to society in fashion, manners and etiquette.

Prince Charles was only twenty-three when his father died and his marriage to the fifteen-year-old Henrietta Maria of France took place. After the first few stormy years, the young King and his Queen fell in love with each other, and their happy family life was reflected in the decorous conduct of the Court and its fastidiously elegant little King.

'The face of the Court was much changed in the change of the King,' wrote Mrs. Hutchinson, 'for King Charles was temperate, chaste and serious, so that the fools, minions and catamites of the former Court grew out of fashion.'

The English Court became once more a centre of taste and culture, where poetry, music and painting all had their place, but these were also the years when Charles arrogantly dispensed with Parliament and the voice of the Puritans gathered strength.

At the beginning of the seventeenth century the Authorized English version of the Bible was to be found in every village in England as well as in many homes: and for thousands of English country folk it was the only book they knew. It was read and re-read to a wondering audience. People heard it in the churches and many gathered in each others homes for Bible readings, those who could read teaching the others. Familiarity had not deadened the impact of its majestic imagery and poetry, and many found it a clearer guide to life than any cleric had been able to give them. Taking much of the Bible literally, they began to re-shape their lives according to its doctrines and to live more soberly. Sunday was kept as a day apart. They frowned upon Sunday sports and pastimes, archery at the butts, bowls or cricket on the village green, and the cooking was done the day before, so that no labour should disturb a day devoted to prayer and worship. They disagreed with even the simplified ritual of the Church of England. The sacrament, they said, should be 'administered purely, only and altogether, according to the institution and good works of the Lord Jesus, without any tradition or invention of men'.

These Puritans began to form communities of their own, outside the Established Church. The first of the dissenters were the Congregationalists, to be followed by the Society of Friends, the Baptists and numerous other smaller groups, each having its own interpretation of the Christian way of life and worship.

Like the Catholics, they were persecuted, fined and imprisoned. Many, as we have seen, ended up in the Bridewell, but their faith and their numbers grew. One group, the Independents, who had sought refuge in Amsterdam, ventured across the Atlantic in the fragile *Mayflower* and settled in Massachusetts, suffering the most terrible hardships for the first few years.

King Charles disliked the Puritans and during his reign the division between the Established Church and the Dissenters deepened. Trading companies were formed to back large-scale Puritan emigration to America and the West Indies, where the colonists could enjoy political and religious freedom: and here, on free grants of land offered by the trading companies, they grew the increasingly valuable crops of cotton, tobacco and sugar cane, with labour from the developing Negro slave trade.

It was against this background that Charles's quarrel with Parliament reached its tragic climax and the Civil War broke out: and after the King's defeat and execution, Oliver Cromwell, to the dismay of a large minority of more moderate Englishmen, became Lord Protector of the Realm.

For the next eleven years England was ruled by a Protestant military dictator. He served England's economy well but the Puritan determination to impose its own views proved disastrous. The use of the prayer book was forbidden. Even the Society of Friends were not allowed to hold their meetings. The mild pastime of dancing round the maypole was banned and everywhere Sunday games came to an end.

At the same time there was a relentless hunt of men and more particularly women believed to be guilty of witchcraft. Between 1645 and 1647 two hundred women were put to death, the majority of whom were, in all probability, harmless enough, but perhaps suspect because of some physical deformity or mental weakness, though a few may have had hypnotic powers which terrorized their more gullible victims and have deliberately practised the black arts of medieval sorcery.

Matthew Hopkins was the most enthusiastic of the witch hunters. He had various methods of apprehending a woman witch and one particularly unsporting way was to tie her thumbs and toes together and toss her into the village pond. If she did not sink and drown she was deemed guilty and so either way she died. But in the end Matthew Hopkins was himself convicted of sorcery and hanged.

As the century progressed and scientific discoveries were slowly accepted, people became less fearful and credulous, but it was a slow process and new ideas, particularly those involving phenomena not readily explicable, invariably raised protest and suspicion, as Mary Astell was later to lament: and the last trial for witchcraft in England was as late at 1712.

However, in his moral crusade, Cromwell relied more on education than restrictive legislation, for it was to lack of the right kind of education that he attributed much of the misconduct of the country's nobility and gentry. He and his government showed a great enthusiasm for education and made many plans for its reformation and extension, for it was now that the idea took shape that it was the duty of the State to supply education to its people. Yet in these plans girls had no part at all.

In 1644 Milton had published his scheme for the better education of a 'select body of our nobles and gentle youths' and by 1660 he was advocating the foundation of schools throughout all parts of the country, in order to spread knowledge, civility and culture to 'all extreme parts which now lie numb and neglected', while James Harrington, in his *Oceana*, claimed that the formation of future citizens by means of a system of free schools was one of the chief duties of a republic.

3. The Red Maids School, Bristol. *Above:* The school as it was until 1911. *Below:* A needlework class in progress in the early 1900s.

*School for Girls founded by Arch Bishop Tenison in 1696.
In High Street, Lambeth.*

4. *Above:* School for Girls founded by Archbishop Tenison in 1696, situated in Lambeth High Street. *Below:* The Black and White House, Bohemia Place, Hackney, was one of the many girls' schools established there.

Milton, who during the Commonwealth had become Latin secretary to the Council of State, was a stern, unyielding Puritan with harsh traits in his character which seem oddly at variance with his passionate love of beauty and freedom and the culture of the Renaissance. He had been carefully educated, first with a private tutor and then at St. Paul's school, from where he went to Christ's College, Cambridge, but he was an impossible husband. In 1643, when he was thirty-five, he had married Mary Powell, the seventeen-year-old daughter of a Cavalier family, but within a month she had left him, probably frightened to death of him and his austere way of life. By the time she returned, two years later, asking for forgiveness, he had published his treatise on divorce, declaring that the law of Moses allowed divorce for 'unfitness or contrariness of mind' as well as for 'scandalous faults', and in later writings he was even to defend polygamy.

We know nothing of Mary Powell's education, but the three daughters of that unhappy marriage received very little indeed. Mary died in 1652, just about the time that Milton became blind. Four years later he married again, but his second wife and their child were both dead by February, 1658, leaving Milton with his three small daughters, the eldest of whom cannot have been more then twelve years old, to bring themselves up as best they could and read to him endlessly in Latin, Greek, Hebrew, French, Italian and Spanish, of which none of them understood a word.

In 1663, complaining bitterly of his undutiful daughters, he asked his friend Dr. Paget to find him a third wife. Dr. Paget produced his own cousin, Elizabeth Marshall, a young woman of twenty-five, whom Milton married forthwith, and his daughters left home to be apprenticed to the trade of embroidery in gold and silver laces and the making of tinsel laces, by means of which they were ultimately able to support themselves.

Cromwell was happier in his marriage, though he seems to have shown no more regard than Milton for the education of his daughters. His government was strict in the licensing of suitable schoolmasters for the boys and the dismissal of those whom it considered incapable. It administered educational endowments, appointed fresh commissioners to visit the universities and established a permanent board of visitors for the great public schools, but Cromwell was more interested in the reorganization of the universities than in primary or secondary education, and defended them against a strong body of Puritan opinion which wanted to see them abolished. In 1651 he was elected Chancellor of Oxford, where he founded a new readership in Divinity, and although he considered the main function of the universities was to furnish ministers for the Church, and regarded piety more important than learning, he had a profound respect for men of letters and the academic standards at Oxford were high during these years.

Cromwell also tried to found a new university in the north of England and another in London, but Parliament did nothing about it and the only result of his plans was the short-lived college at Durham, founded in 1657, which came to an end with the Restoration three years later.

Cromwell's wife was Elizabeth Bourchier, the daughter of a wealthy London city merchant, but again we know little of her education, apart from the fact that she was an exceptionally skilled if over-careful housewife. Cromwell's households at Whitehall and Hampton Court were organized in the manner of small Courts, and inevitably her Highness the Protectress, as Elizabeth Cromwell was styled, came in for a good deal of criticism. Pamphleteers sneered at her 'sordid frugality', which was unfit for the station in which she had been placed, and Lucy Hutchinson was unusually sharp, saying that Elizabeth's new grandeur suited her no better than 'fine clothes do an ape', while her daughters she dismissed as 'insolent fools', except for Bridget, who alone was 'humble and not exalted with those things'.

Lucy Hutchinson had been most carefully educated herself. Born in 1620, in the Tower of London, she was the daughter of its lieutenant, Sir Allan Apsley, and in 1638 she married Colonel John Hutchinson, who later became Governor of Nottingham

Castle and was one of Charles I's judges, though he testified against Cromwell's usurpation.

In her memoirs of her husband, which she wrote for her children, Lucy Hutchinson described the education her parents had given her. She could read when she was four years old and by the time she was seven she had eight tutors, teaching her languages, music, dancing, writing and needlework. Though her mother was concerned for her health, with so much study, her father insisted that his chaplain teach her Latin, and very soon, although the chaplain was a 'pitiful dull fellow', she knew more of the language than her brothers who were at school.

After her marriage, she translated *Lucretius* into English verse and also part of the *Aeneid*, working in the same room as her children, as they learnt their lessons from their tutors. Colonel Hutchinson was equally interested in the education of his children and spared nothing to provide tutors for both his sons and daughters in languages, sciences, music and dancing.

Yet generally speaking, men during the early Stuart and Commonwealth years did not like their women to be learned and did their best to discourage any intellectual leanings they may have shown. Sir Ralph Verney, for example, thought a knowledge of Latin was actually a 'vice in woman'. 'Good sweet heart', he wrote to his granddaughter during the Commonwealth years, 'beleeve me a Bible (with ye Common Prayer) and a good plaine catichisme in your Mother tongue being well read and practised is well worth all the rest and much more suitable to your sex: I know your Father thinks this false doctrine, but bee confident your husband will be of my opinion.'

During the first part of the seventeenth century, therefore, there was very little progress in the cause of girls' education. Daughters of the wealthy still had their private tutors and governesses or went to one of the few expensive boarding schools. The rest picked up an education where they could, in dame schools, from their parents or by their own wits.

The girls at Christ's Hospital were still stitching away and learning to read and a few other hospitals for the relief of orphans and destitute children were opened. By 1631 there were a hundred and six boys and girls at the Bridewell, being taught pin-making, silk weaving and linen weaving. There was a similar institution in Norwich and in 1634 the Red Maids Hospital was opened in Bristol, for the education of forty poor girls, who were to be taught to read English and to sew or do some other laudable work for their maintenance. The founder was Alderman John Whitson of Bristol and in his bequest he provided for a house for 'one grave, painful and modest woman of good life and honest conversation' to look after the orphans, who were to be dressed in red cloth. The girls were to be apprenticed to the mistress for seven years, and this was a serious flaw in the Alderman's arrangements, for the 'grave and painful mistress' was not always, by any means, of 'good life and honest conversation'. She was allowed to sell the girls' work for her own profit and there were times when a particularly avaricious mistress would exploit the girls shamefully, working them far too hard and teaching them nothing but the work which she was selling.

There were various other schemes for helping destitute and very poor children to acquire apprenticeships, but for girls this usually led to the humblest form of domestic service, although those who were apprenticed to laundresses, seamstresses and the like were occasionally taught to read. For small girls under nine years of age there were also handicraft schools, where they learnt to knit, spin and make lace.

About the same time as the Ladies Hall was opened at Deptford, a girls' school was established at Stepney by a Huguenot family called Freind. In 1638 when Susan, daughter of Sir Edward Nicholas, was boarded there, the quarter's school bill amounted to £7 3s. 7d. but as this included many items for embroidery, including 5s. 4d. for an ounce of silver thread, it would seem that the education here was mainly in needlework of various kinds.

It is difficult to visualize the sad grey suburb of Hackney as the place of green fields and orchards, elegant houses and beautiful gardens that it was three hundred years ago, but at this time, so close to the crowded city of London yet far enough removed to enjoy clear, country air, it became a favourite place for boarding schools, for both boys and girls. And at one time there were so many girls' schools at Hackney that it was known as 'The Ladies' University of Female Arts'.

One of the earliest was Mrs. Winch's school, and here a wealthy orphan girl called Sara Cox was placed by her friends. One summer evening, while she was walking on Newington Common, she was suddenly seized by horsemen with drawn swords, bundled into a coach and carried off to Winchester House in Southwark. The abduction had been planned by the brother of a schoolfellow who had become a doting admirer, but whether or not Sara knew what was going to happen beforehand, history does not relate. She was hastily married in the Bishop's private chapel, but then something went wrong with the planning and by one o'clock the next morning they were all—the abducters, the young husband and his new bride —brought up before the Lord Mayor to give an account of themselves, and Sara was duly restored to her friends and, presumably, to Mrs. Winch.

At Mrs. Salmon's School at Hackney there arrived in 1639, during the reign of Charles I, Katharine, the daughter of a London merchant, who was then eight years old. She could already read and her biographer says that by the time she was four years old she had read the whole of the Bible and could recite long passages by heart. She was very quick and bright at school and began to write the poetry for which she was to become famous: and when she left Mrs. Salmon she studied Italian with Sir Charles Cottrell. When she was about sixteen she married James Phillips and continued to write, translating from the French most of Corneille's two tragedies *Pompey* and *Horace*, but it is by her poetry that she is remembered. She was the 'matchless Orinda' and many years after her early death from smallpox her correspondence with Sir Charles Cottrell was published as *Letters from Orinda to Poliarchus*.

Yet poor Orinda, for all her talents, was no beauty. John Aubrey, though admitting her good nature, said she was pretty fat with a red and pimpled face. Evelyn saw her translation of *Horace* acted in 1668, but makes no comment on it, being more concerned with the outrageous display of jewels worn by Barbara Castlemaine on that occasion, but when Pepys saw it he dismissed it as a 'silly tragedy'.

Only four years after Orinda's arrival at Mrs. Salmon's, Mrs. Perwich opened her school at Hackney, in the Black and White house by the churchyard of the church of St. John at Hackney. This half-timbered house is thought to have been the home of James I's daughter, the Princess Elizabeth, after her marriage to Frederick, Elector Palatine of the Rhine, who had been invited to become King of Bohemia, but lost his throne after only twelve months. Elizabeth, as the exiled Winter Queen, may have spent some years of her long widowhood here and the site is today known as Bohemia Place.

Mrs. Perwich's elegant school was famous and she ran it for seventeen years, during which eight hundred girls passed through her hands.

These were the years of the Civil War and the Commonwealth, and the girls, all from wealthy families, came from every part of the country, bringing their own maids with them. Though the curriculum was circumscribed to the usual music, dancing and needlework, with probably French and Italian, the school was exceptionally well staffed, with no less than sixteen visiting masters to teach singing and a number of musical instruments, which included the lyre, viol, lute and harpsichord. As there were never more than a hundred girls in the school at one time this was generous. The masters included a singing master, Simon Ives, who was also a lay vicar at St. Paul's, and some of whose songs were published in John Playford's Collections, Albert Byrne, who taught the harpsichord and was at one time organist at St. Paul's, Edward Coleman, a gentleman of the Chapel Royal, and the famous

Mr. Hazard for dancing. The school had its own choir and orchestra, which was led for a time by Mrs. Perwich's own daughter, Susanna.

This love of music was as characteristic of Stuart England as it had been in the time of the Elizabethans. Nearly everyone knew the songs and dances of the countryside and every village had its choir, its orchestra of stringed instruments and its bell ringers, every town its band which was ready to perform on important civic occasions. Though the Puritans disapproved of dancing and although there were occasions when they had deliberately destroyed church organs, Cromwell himself was very fond of music and a great deal was published during the Commonwealth years. Even John Milton, though he considered it unsuitable to be introduced in Divine worship, enjoyed it in his leisure hours.

Most people of education could read music and play at least one instrument, so it is not surprising to find music so important a part of the curriculum of a fashionable girls' school. Madrigals were still popular too, especially during the first half of the century, and people often met in each others houses for an evening of madrigals, rounds and glees. Thomas Morley was one of the favourite composers, his *Ballet for Five Voices* and *Canzonets* or *Little Short Songs for Three Voices* having been published at this time: but later in the century the fashion for madrigals declined in favour of the more elaborate solo song, for which an accompaniment on a stringed or keyboard instrument was written.

The craft of needlework must not be dismissed lightly either. The tradition of fine needlework and beautiful embroidery continued all through the seventeenth century. Practically all women's and children's clothing and some men's clothing were made at home, and the stitching on the few garments which have survived is often exquisitely fine and delicate, though some, it must be admitted, is fairly crude.

Clothes were often beautifully embroidered and the Puritans sometimes embellished theirs with texts and holy thoughts, if Jasper Mayne, that amusing if bawdy clergyman-playwright is to be believed. In his play *The City Match*, written in 1639, he pokes fun at a Puritan waiting-maid and makes her mistress complain:

> She works religious petticoats; for flowers
> She'll make Church histories. Her needle doth
> So sanctify my cushionets! Besides,
> My smock-sleeves have such holy embroideries,
> And are so learned that I fear, in time,
> All my apparel will be quoted by
> Some pure instructor.

With the establishment of the East India company at the end of Queen Elizabeth's reign and the arrival of eastern carpets and rugs, the embroideresses became fascinated by Oriental patterns and the skilful blending of colours. In early Stuart times, the Tudor rose was still used a great deal in designs, but within a few years the Oriental influence became very apparent. Patterns, beautifully filling the space they were intended to cover, were composed of stylized birds and animals, trees, flowers, leaves and trailing vines, and were often bordered with a band of pattern based on carnations, pansies and other English garden flowers.

These early Stuart embroideries are easily recognizable and very characteristic of the period, and many have become part of our national heritage, to be found in museums and historic houses. They appeared on cushions and stools, bed covers and curtains for the massive four-posters, window curtains and other hangings, all worked in crewel wool and silk. Night caps, garters and underclothes were all embroidered as well as bed linen, and handkerchiefs were either hem-stitched and embroidered with an elaborate pattern of drawn thread work or bordered with needlepoint lace.

In time the animals and flowers became more naturalistic and human figures were introduced. Pattern became subordinate to the pictorial interest and realism was introduced in the smallest details. Human figures were given wigs of human hair or the hair was embroidered in a knotted stitch to represent curls. Tiny beads were sewn into the work to represent pearl necklaces. The faces were sometimes painted on smooth silk and appliqued to the fabric, though usually they were embroidered in the finest silk, using a small, satin stitch. Figures and animals were stuffed with fragments of frayed silk to raise them and make them look realistic.

These picture embroideries were sometimes worked on cushions and screens, and miniature needlework pictures were used to decorate caskets and book covers. Favourite subjects were royal pageants in which the figure of Charles I often appeared, and scenes from the Old Testament, particularly ones illustrating the stories of Hagar and Ishmael, the finding of the infant Moses, and Susannah and the Elders.

Stump work was popular for a time. It was a form of collage and the human figures in the pictures were raised and often embellished with gold and silver thread. At least one mirror with a wide frame of stump work has survived from the reign of James I. It was very ugly, but even worse was the short-lived craze, later in the century, for pictures worked entirely in coloured beads, but these digressions did not affect the charm of the general run of embroidery, most of which involved a high degree of skill. The pictorial embroideries became so realistic that they gradually grew to be more like toys than pieces of embroidery and the fashion soon died.

As in Elizabethan times, little girls were taught their stitches on samplers of fine linen, using white linen thread and coloured silks. The simplest of these stitches were the cross-stitch, tent-stitch, long and short stitch, crewel stitch and feather stitch, but a great many others, far more complicated, were taught them as their skill developed. Broderie Anglaise or 'eyelet' embroidery was fashionable and the button holes were wonderfully fine.

Very few of the Jacobean samplers have survived and many were lost during the Civil War. At the top there were usually rows of different kinds of stitches. There was often an example of drawn-thread work next and specimens of formal roses, carnations, honeysuckle, love-in-the-mist and strawberries. Then came specimens of birds and animals, particularly the two favourites, the lion and the stag. These were followed by ornamental designs copied from the newly-imported works of art from the East and cross-stitch patterns: and the sampler ended with the letters of the alphabet, verses from the Bible, mottoes or scraps of secular verse.

Like Shakespeare's Helena and Hermia, the girls of Mrs. Perwich's School may well have sat together and 'created both one flower, both one sampler, sitting on one cushion', for Shakespeare had been dead for less than thirty years when the school opened.

These Stuart embroideresses had thimbles and scissors, stilettoes for their eyelet embroidery and spools for their wools and silks. Special tambour needles for working on a tambour or frame have come to light in old workboxes and also small wooden moulds, like short thimbles, on which they made their knotted work.

There were very few pattern books in circulation. Girls drew flowers and plants from nature, under the guidance of their drawing master, and adapted them. They copied pictures and used each others samplers, probably designing their pattern first on paper and then transferring it to the material they were embroidering.

For a girl like Lucy Hutchinson, who was an intellectual, and confessed that 'for my needle I absolutely hated it', all this needlework must have been purgatory, but for many others, who achieved consummate skill, it was a creative outlet which must have given them great pleasure.

Susanna Perwich, who came to her mother's school when she was seven years old, having already taught herself to read, was exceptionally accomplished in all these arts, and she stayed on after her schooldays to teach. Her embroidery included black work, which had been so popular in Tudor times, white work, and work in colour. She also worked in silver, straw, glass, wax and gum and had 'all other parts of excellent well-breeding', which included calligraphy, accountancy, house-wifery and cookery.

But Susanna was destined to die young. She was engaged to be married and when her lover died her heart 'began to be much broken'. As she sank into a decline she turned from her needlework and music to religion, gently 'melting towards God', and in 1661, before she was twenty-five years old, she died, and the whole school attended her funeral in the church of St. John close by.

During her short lifetime, the young Samuel Pepys was living close by, in Kingsland, for in his diary for April 23, 1664, he wrote that he took his wife out to White Chapel, and to Bethnal Green; so to Hackney, where I have not been many a year since a little child I boarded there. Thence to Kingsland, by my nurse's house, Goody Lawrence, where my brother Tom and I was kept when young.'

In Mrs. Perwich's time there were also several girls' schools at Putney, for in his diary for May 17, 1649, John Evelyn records that he 'went to Putney by water, in the barge with divers ladies, to see the Schools, or colleges, of the young gentlewomen'.

No details of these schools have survived. John Evelyn's editor suggests that one of them may have belonged to Bathsua Makin,[1] but there is no direct evidence for this. Yet Putney was already a fashionable place for young women's boarding schools and was to remain so for many years to come.

Thomas Knyvett's younger daughter Muriel, his much-loved Muss, had been at a school at Fulham, run by a Mrs. Randolph, but a friend, Stephen Southalls, writing to her mother, Katherine, in 1641, reported that Muss, then about thirteen or fourteen, was very unhappy there, for the school was hopelessly inefficient and the girls were taught very little. Mrs. Randolph spoilt her own children but treated both her pupils and servants heartlessly. 'She growes moore twitty now adayes then heretofore she haue bin', he said. There were constant quarrels, during which the servants usually walked out, but the unfortunate girls were trapped until their parents removed them.[2]

The climax came when Muss developed smallpox, which it

[1] See p. 99.   [2] Brit. Mus. Egerton MS. 2716, f.377. Quoted in *The Knyvett Letters* (1620–1644), Norfolk Record Society, 1949.

was said could have been avoided if Mrs. Randolph had sent her home sooner, before the infection spread through the school.[1]

In 1643, during the Civil War, when Knyvett was a prisoner of Cromwell for a time, he wrote to his wife suggesting several places where Muss might be sent for safety, in the end saying: 'I think you may doe very well to place Muss at Putny for a while. I beleeve she cost as much wher she is.'

Yet she does not seem to have arrived there, for the following year, in a letter arranging for his wife to join him, he says: 'You must needs disspose of Muss, for I knowe not what you can doe with her heer. She is to big for Putny now.'

Twenty-three years later, Pepys recorded that he had met Theophila Turner, who had come to London 'to put out her sister and brothers to school at Putney' and two years afterwards, on April 19, 1669, he was taking leave of Betty Turner 'who goes to Putney to school tomorrow'.

And by the end of the eighteenth century, according to J. Edwards' *Companion from London to Brighton in Sussex*, 1801, there were five boarding schools for young ladies in Putney, three in the High Street, one in Lower Richmond Road and one in Putney Bridge Road.

It was during the years of the Commonwealth that Dorothy Osborne was writing her delightful letters to William Temple, the man she was ultimately to marry in defiance of her family's wishes. She told him about the wealthy suitors they would have had her choose and shows that a woman of character was quite capable of refusing to submit to the barbarous custom of being married off to the highest bidder agreed to by her family, however disagreeable he may have been, although the custom was to last for many more years.

During the long years of waiting for William, while she was tied to her home in Bedfordshire and her cross-grained, ailing, Royalist father, Dorothy spent her time, after supervising the large household of servants, in gardening, needlework and reading, for she read widely, in English, French Italian and Latin, books of travel, biographies, novels and plays.

[1] *The Knyvett Letters*—Introduction.

Chapter Six

THE RESTORATION

W ITH THE DEATH of Cromwell and the restoration of the monarchy, there was a sharp reaction to the high moral standards which the Commonwealth government had tried to impose, and there were signs that it had begun even before 1660. In 1657, when two of Cromwell's daughters were married, both weddings were accompanied by festivities which scandalized many Puritans. Frances was married to Robert Rich at the Whitehall Palace, where 'they had forty-eight violins and much mirth with frolics, besides mixt dancing (a thing heretofore accounted profane), till five of the clock in the morning' and at Mary's wedding to Lord Fauconberg at Hampton Court there were similar junketings, with a masque composed by Andrew Marvell, in which the Protector himself appeared as Jove.

Writing of his son Henry and his son-in-law Claypole, Lucy Hutchinson said that they were 'two debauched, ungodly cavaliers', while Richard, though gentle and virtuous, was yet 'a peasant in his nature' and 'became not greatness'.

As early as May, 1654, Evelyn recorded: 'I now observed how the women began to paint themselves, formerly a most ignominious thing, and used only by prostitutes.'

England was obviously ready for a change of mood, and Charles II did not disappoint them. On the contrary, he and his Court far exceeded anything that the most rebellious of Puritan youth could ever have dreamed possible. Even by the moral standards of the 1970s it would be surprising for a public figure to appear with his three illegitimate sons by three

93

different women, but on Easter day of 1684 Evelyn wrote that 'the Bishop of Rochester preached before the King; after which his Majesty, accompanied with three of his natural sons, the Dukes of Northumberland, Richmond and St. Albans (sons of Portsmouth, Cleveland and Nelly) went up to the altar; the three boys entering before the King. . . .' And a year later, a few days after the King's death, Evelyn said: 'I can never forget the inexpressible luxury and profaneness, gaming and all dissoluteness, and as it were total forgetfulness of God (it being Sunday evening), which this day se'ennight I was witness of, the King sitting and toying with his concubines, Portsmouth, Cleveland, and Mazarine, etc., a French boy singing lovesongs, in that glorious gallery, whilst about twenty of the great courtiers and other dissolute persons were at Basset round a large table, a bank of at least 2,000 in gold before them; upon which two gentlemen who were with me made reflections with astonishment. Six days after, was all in the dust.'

Even Pepys, who had no great cause for complacency, complained of the King's dalliance in public with Lady Castlemaine.

This standard of behaviour in the Court influenced many aspects of English social life—the theatre, dress and education—and particularly girls' education, for in an atmosphere of this kind, there was little place for women of intellect.

Queen Catharine of Braganza, young, plain, inexperienced and desperately affronted at Charles's neglect, behaved with great dignity in an impossible situation but had little effect on the conduct of the Court.

With the re-establishment of the Anglican Church there was a renewed persecution of the Dissenters, mainly because of a fear, not entirely unjustified, that dissent meant sedition and that the meetings of Dissenters might well be the breeding grounds for political plans to overthrow the new government.

Charles II had no part in this new persecution and pleaded for tolerance: and in the end the problem solved itself, for the number of Nonconformists, including many wealthy merchants and skilled artisans, was so large and their work so important to the economy of the country, that their persecution became impractical. There was a compromise. Some worshipped at their parish church and, like the Catholics, held their own religious services in private. Others refused to conform and in time gained freedom to conduct their own services in public, though this was a matter of economic expediency rather than religious toleration, and it was to be many years before Catholics or Nonconformists were entirely free from certain social prejudices, particularly in regard to education, for they were not admitted to the universities, nor were they allowed licences to teach in the grammar schools.

During the last two or three decades of the seventeenth century the first few, small Quaker schools were founded, but there was no provision for girls, and it was not until the eighteenth century that the Charity schools, which catered for both boys and girls, were in sufficient numbers to be effective.

James II's troubled reign was too short and his love affairs too complicated for the conduct of his Court to have any effect on the social position of the women of England. The education of James's two daughters, Mary and Anne, was controlled by King Charles, who had been determined that they should be brought up in the faith of the Church of England, for the sake of peace, if for no better reason. Their mother, Anne Hyde, had died when Mary was nine and Anne six, and they were sent to live with the Villiers family of six girls and a boy at Richmond Palace. Their Preceptor was Bishop Compton and they were soundly instructed in the teaching of the Church of England, but in other respects their education was in no way different from that of other well-born girls of the time. They had lessons in music and dancing, French and divinity, and there it ended. They were taught no history and nothing of the Classics. At this stage they were a long way from the succession and were given no special training in the duties of royalty, but Anne had an exceptionally beautiful speaking voice and her uncle Charles engaged Mrs. Barry, the actress from the Drury Lane theatre, to give her special training in voice production.

Princess Mary was married at the age of fifteen to Prince William of Orange and departed for Holland: and when in 1689 they returned to England as King and Queen, Princess Anne was already married to Prince George of Denmark and had begun the long series of pregnancies and miscarriages which so seriously undermined her health.

William had little interest in women and treated the garrulous Mary so badly that his chaplain, Bishop Burnett, had on occasion to remonstrate with him: and although at her early death, in 1694, at the age of thirty-two, he is said to have collapsed with grief, for the rest of his reign there were very few women at Court, for he preferred the company of men—particularly his Dutch friends, the Earls of Albemarle and Portland.

He died in 1702, after a fall from his horse, and when Anne succeeded to the throne, although she was only thirty-seven, she was already a sick woman. Not only was her health sapped by her seventeen pregnancies, but she was so crippled with gout that she had to be carried to her coronation in a specially constructed chair, while Prince George, enfeebled by gout and hard drinking, had only another six years to go.

With the Restoration, though there was little or no advance in the provision of public education for the vast majority of girls, many more fashionable boarding schools for young gentlewomen were founded in and around London. Yet few of them showed any inclination for serious intellectual exercise and many were condemned for their snobbery and inefficiency.

In Hackney, Mrs. Perwich was dead and the Black and White house had come into the possession of the Vyner family, though by the beginning of the next century it was to become a school again. Several other fashionable schools had been established close by, however, some of which were lampooned in the Restoration comedies, for the standard of behaviour at the Hackney schools seems to have deteriorated sadly since the days of Mrs. Perwich. The Puritan Joseph Lister refused employment as serving man in one of them, for he found it was a place 'for young gentlewomen to learn to play and dance and sing', which 'did not at all suit him', while Aubrey went even further, condemning them as places where 'young maids learnt pride and wantonness'.

However, they may have been unduly prejudiced. On Sunday, April 21, 1667, Samuel Pepys and his wife 'took coach and to Hackney Church, where very full. . . . That which we went chiefly to see was the young ladies of the schools, wherof there is great store, very pretty; and also the organ, which is handsome. . . .'

In 1675 Ralph Josselin's wife took her two daughters, Mary and Elizabeth, to finish their education at one of the Hackney schools. Mrs. Crittenden was running a school for girls in Hackney at this time and Mrs. Slater's School was in Hackney Lane, just beyond where Laura Place now runs. This was a red brick house approached by an open courtyard, paved with black and white marble, and enclosed by an iron railing, but the first and second storeys of the house were built over the courtyard, so that it was perfectly secluded, and there was a large garden behind. Mrs. Slater's School was particularly fashionable during the early eighteenth century, when it was considered to be one of the most exclusive in London.

Another famous Restoration school in this part of the world was kept by John Playford's wife, in a house opposite Islington Church, where 'young gentlewomen may be instructed in all manner of Curious works, as also Reading, Writing, Music, Dancing and the French language'.

To the west of Sir Thomas More's house at Chelsea, Sir Arthur Gorges had built another large mansion, which remained in the Gorges family until it was sold, in 1664, and became a girls' school for a few years. It was very fashionable and the curriculum conservative, still limited mainly to music, dancing and needlecraft. The first proprietors were Mr. Bannister and Mr. Hart but four years later the school was taken over by Mr. Josias Priest, who had been running a school in Leicester Fields. He was a well-known teacher of dancing who sometimes acted as ballet master at Drury Lane. A few years after moving into Gorges House, he persuaded the young Henry Purcell to write an opera for his girls to perform, and it was for them that Purcell produced his delightful *Dido and Aeneas.*

Among the pupils at Gorges House was little Mary Verney, daughter of Sir Edmund Verney, who, when she was only eight years old, was brought up from her beautiful home at Claydon by her father, her brother and her aunt, being treated on the way through London to a sight of Westminster Abbey and St. Bartholemew's fair at Smithfield. She seems to have enjoyed herself at school, making good progress with her music and other accomplishments, and when she wrote to her father asking if she could learn to 'Japan' on enamel boxes, which was presumably an extra, he wrote back at great length, and in giving his approval said: 'for I admire all accomplishments that will render you considerable and Lovely in the sight of God and man. . . .' all of which seems to have been making very heavy weather of a simple request.

There were several other girls' schools in Chelsea during the seventeenth century and after the death of Mrs. Perwich at Hackney Mr. Hazard, the dancing master, and his wife ran a school in Kensington. After Mrs. Hazard died, in 1682, her husband advertised the fact that he had engaged in her place a lady who would undertake the care of the girls, but the venture cannot have been a great success, for within a year Mr. William Dyer had moved from his school in Chelsea to take over Mr. Hazard's establishment.

It was not unusual for country girls like little Mary Verney to be sent to London to be 'finished' in the arts of music, dancing, needlework and general deportment, as well as perhaps a little French, for appearance and manners were considered of vital importance, both for girls and boys of the upper classes. It was a very worldly age, for these accomplishments were taught mainly in order that the young people should gain an entrance into the right circles and make advantageous matches. Occasionally, of course, there were genuine love matches, like Dorothy Osborne's, but in the main marriages were still business arrangements, not only among the aristocracy and gentry but in the middle classes as well, and although the legal status of women was so low, the wife was expected to bring her marriage portion, and a very substantial one at that.

Schools similar to the fashionable ones in London were to be found throughout the country, but there were not many of them and they were mainly very small. There was one at Westerham, where Frances Courtney and her sister were sent in 1620, and another in Manchester. There were several in and around Oxford, the Virgins' Hall being established soon after the Restoration. In Exeter, Mrs. Crosse, a widow, was keeping school during the 1640s, but when she was suspected of being a witch she lost custom and had to close down.

The first move to try to give girls a solid education based on sound scholarship came from Mrs. Bathsua Makin. She was a highly educated woman and had taught Charles I's second daughter, the Princess Elizabeth, who had died a year after her father's execution. Bathsua was a rather grim looking woman —the kind of intellectual who scared men and whom they deplored—but she was very sound in her ideas and her teaching, and had given the Princess a good grounding not only in French and Italian, but in the Classics and in Hebrew. In 1673 she opened a school for girls at Tottenham High Cross and in the same year she published her *Essay to Revive the Ancient Education of Gentlewomen*, which she dedicated to the young Princess Mary, who in 1689 was to become Queen with William.

She reminded her readers of the education which young gentlewomen received in earlier times and argued that if they were to be given it again they would gain much pleasure and the country would benefit. She deplored the current licentiousness and admitted that the times were not propitious for her suggestion, adding, perhaps unwisely, that if schools were established that gave girls a sound education in the Classics 'how asham'd Men would be of their ignorance, and how industrious the next Generation would be to wipe off their Reproach'.

She offered a compromise with the craze for acquiring mere accomplishments by suggesting a girl spend half her time on these and the rest on ancient and modern languages as well as geography, history, arithmetic, astronomy, cookery and a knowledge of herbal remedies.

It was a brave effort on the part of Mrs. Makin but she was right in her prediction that neither men nor women were yet ready to consider such a radical change in the education of girls. How her school prospered we do not know. Mrs. Elizabeth Montagu's mother was a pupil there and was an important influence on Elizabeth's future as one of the eighteenth-century Blue Stockings, but no other school like Mrs. Makin's seems to have been established for many years to come.

Although in many ways the seventeenth century was a time of great intellectual progress and 'sustained curiosity', during which an astonishing number of scientific discoveries were made, including William Harvey's discovery of the circulation of the blood, Hooke's microscope and Boyle's discoveries concerning the properties of air, their work was little understood outside the select and immediate circle of the Royal Society, of which all three were founder members, and even King Charles, who was seriously interested in their work, sometimes made fun of them. 'Gresham College he mightily laughed at for spending time only in weighing of ayre' recorded Pepys on February 1, 1664.

These new sciences were studied neither in the grammar schools nor the universities, all of which were losing their early vigour, and with boys' education grown so lax there was little hope of girls' education being taken more seriously.

During the latter part of the seventeenth century there were 2,300 scholars in residence at Cambridge and 3,000 at Oxford, most boys going up when they were about sixteen, but the teaching was not outstanding and Anthony à Wood said the decline was owing to the increase of coffee houses and taverns, 'where seniours and juniours passed a great deal of the day'.

The grammar schools which had played so important a part in the education of boys for so many years also fell into disrepute after the Restoration, suspected of having been breeding grounds of dissent and rebellion. They were subjected to more control and expected to conform to the politics of the government.

There were few benefactors willing to replenish old endowments and a growing body of critics, including many statesmen, who thought that boys should not be taken from the useful work of the plough to pore over books, while the controversial Thomas Hobbes declared that the devotion of the grammar schools to ancient history and classical studies tended to promote republicanism.

Many educationists urged that the preoccupation with Latin grammar should be relaxed, so that boys had an opportunity to learn history, geography, mathematics and English composition, all of which were becoming increasingly necessary in a widening world, but for many years little was done, mainly because so many schools were bound by medieval statutes with carefully circumscribed curricula, from which it would have been illegal to diverge.

Another problem was that the grammar schools suffered from a shortage of masters, for Dissenters were debarred by Statute from teaching in them and began to found their own excellent academies, offering a more realistic and useful education, in tune with the changing times and broadening horizons, which included science, mathematics and geography as well as the classics and living languages. By the eighteenth century the reputation of the Dissenting Academies was so high that many sons of Anglicans were sent to them as well as the Dissenting families.

One of the eccentric literary figures of Restoration England was Margaret, Duchess of Newcastle. She was born about 1624 and in 1643 she became a maid of honour to Henrietta Maria. During the Civil War she went into exile with the Queen to France and there met and married another English exile, William Cavendish, who was to become the Duke of

Newcastle. Margaret had none of the traditional housewifely skills and said, reasonably enough, that needlework and embroidery were a waste of time when you could pay someone to do the work for you: and such arts as the making of elaborate confectionery and sweetmeats 'that are good for nothing but to breed obstructions and rot the teeth' were profitless.

With her husband's help she began to write plays, poems and essays. She was an individualist and adopted her own style of dress, so that in her day she was as well known for her eccentric appearance as for her writing. In 1667, after she and her husband had returned to England, she wrote her famous biography of the Duke, to whom she was devoted, and on April 18 of that year John Evelyn visited them at their house in Clerkenwell, being 'much pleased with the extraordinary fanciful habit, garb, and discourse of the Duchess'.

Pepys was not nearly so impressed by her. He went to see 'the silly play of my Lady Newcastle's, called *The Humorous Lovers*, the most silly thing that ever come upon the stage. I was sick to see it. . . .'

When she asked to be invited to a meeting of the Royal Society there was much doubt and debate amongst the members before the visit was allowed, and when she eventually arrived she came in great pomp, being received by the Lord President, preceded by the mace-bearer, at the door of their meeting chamber. She was shown several scientific experiments and as she left John Evelyn escorted her to her coach. Samuel Pepys was also present on that occasion. 'The Duchesse hath been a good, comely woman,' he conceded, 'but her dress is so antick, and her deportment so ordinary, that I do not like her at all, nor did I hear her say any thing that it was worth hearing, but that she was full of admiration—all admiration.'

So he was happy to go home to his Elizabeth that afternoon and spend the evening with her singing in the garden. But Elizabeth had had very little education at all and this was a constant source of vexation to Samuel. They had married in 1655, when Elizabeth was fifteen, and as she had spent most of her life in France with her raffish French father, she spoke and read French more easily than English, but her spelling and writing were atrocious and she knew no arithmetic, nor had she any knowledge of housekeeping. 'Sluttish and dirty', commented Samuel on the state of his house during the early years.

Over and over again the bad cooking—the half-cooked rabbit, the sweet sauce served with the leg of mutton, the blackened roast—was a bone of contention.

Husbands of young wives often undertook the completion of their education and Pepys, who was fundamentally very kind-hearted and indulgent, began to teach his wife music, at which she proved so apt that he engaged a singing master for her as well, and soon she was asking for a dancing master: and all went well until Pepys found that the master was coming twice a day.

He tried to turn her thoughts to more serious matters. He bought a pair of globes and set about teaching her both geography and arithmetic. Soon Elizabeth was coping satisfactorily with addition, subtraction and multiplication and so, wrote Pepys, 'I purpose not to trouble her with division'.

He next found a painting master for her and was pleased with her work until he decided that she was taking too much interest in the master and neglecting her household duties.

And so Elizabeth and Samuel battled on, quarrelling one day and loving each other the next, but Samuel always kept a pretty tight rein. His wife's duty, first and foremost, was to look after his house—had they had any children she would have been even more fully occupied—and her education, scanty as it was, and although it was intended primarily to make her more companionable to her husband, must always be of secondary importance.

John Evelyn, a very different character, and from a higher social sphere, paid great attention to the education of his children, particularly his greatly-loved daughter Mary, who was brought up in the Pre-Restoration, old-fashioned and soberer tradition. In 1682 he took a house in London so that she could receive music and dancing lessons from the best masters, but she had had tutors in many other subjects and when, three years later, she died, Evelyn, broken-hearted, wrote a long account of her graces and accomplishments, describing her knowledge of literature and history and of the Classics and her fluency in French and Italian.

She was eighteen when she died and still unmarried, for her parents had shown uncommon kindness and good sense over the matter. 'There were four gentlemen of quality offering to treat with me about marriage,' wrote Evelyn, 'and I freely gave her her own choice, knowing her discretion. She showed great indifference to marrying at all,' and she told her father that unless he judged it expedient for her, she would prefer to stay at home with her parents and let her dowry be added to those of her sisters.

Chapter Seven

MORE ADVICE TO THE GIRLS

ONE FORTHRIGHT AND endearingly outspoken woman of the seventeenth century, who championed the cause of girls' education and deplored the way it was being neglected, was Hannah Woolley. Hannah was born in 1623 and at fourteen she found herself orphaned and entirely alone in the world, with nothing but her wits and quick intelligence to support her. We know nothing of her parents, but she was a gentlewoman, and had received the usual gentlewoman's education, reading and writing, music, household crafts and needlework of all kinds.

In a rare mention of her family, she bids the reader take notice that 'my Mother and Elder Sisters were very well skilled in Physick and Chirurgery, from whom I learnt a little'.

In order to support herself, she set about running a small school, and in her prospectus she offered to teach:

Works wrought with a Needle, all Transparent Works
Shell-work, Moss-work, also Cutting of Prints, and adorning Rooms or Cabinets or stands with them
All kinds of Beugle-work upon Wyres, or otherwise
Rocks made with Shell or in Sweets
Frames for Looking-glasses, Pictures or the Like
Feathers of Crewel for the corners of Beds
Preserving all kind of Sweet-meats wet and dry
Setting out of Banquets
Making Salves, Oyntments, Waters, Cordials, healing any wounds not desperately dangerous

Knowledge in discerning the Symptoms of most Diseases and
  giving such Remedies as are fit in such Cases
All manner of Cookery
Writing and Arithmetic
Washing black or white Sarsnets
Making Sweet Powders for the Hair, or to lay among Linnen
All these and several things beside too tedious here to relate, I
  shall be ready to impart to those who are desirous to learn.

This seems a formidable list for a fourteen-year-old but,
with becoming modesty, she tells us that, after two or three
years 'my extraordinary parts appear'd more splendid in the
eyes of a Noble Lady in this Kingdom, than really they
deserv'd', and the Noble Lady asked her to become a resident
governess to her only daughter. In less than a year the lady was
dead and Hannah moved on, but during that short time she
had learnt a great deal about the management of a noble
household and also, she implied, of Court etiquette.

In the second household, Hannah stayed for seven years,
first as governess to the children and then as stewardess and
secretary to her mistress. Hannah was happy and took good
advantage of the opportunities offered her. She took great
pains with her letter writing, read widely, improved her French
and Italian and learned 'courtly Phrases and Graces, so how to
express myself with the attendancy of a becoming air. And as
I gather'd how to manage my Tongue gracefully and discreetly;
so I thought it irrequisite to let my hands to lye idle, I exercised
them daily in Carving at Table. And when any sad accident
required their help in Physick and Chyrurgy, I was ready to be
assisting; in those two excellent Arts in this place I acquired a
competent knowledge.'

When she was twenty-four, Hannah yielded 'to the im-
portunity of one I dearly loved' and married Mr. Woolley,
the master of a Free School in Essex, and there they lived and
worked happily for the next five years, until they moved to
Hackney, to establish their own school with more than sixty
boys, all boarders. Hannah confessed that she now had 'many
more Trials for my Skill' for by this time she not only had

four sons of her own, but was in charge of the large household and also undertook the duties of school doctor, treating 'Agues, Feavors, Measzles, Small-pox, Consumption and many other Diseases'. About her treatment of really difficult cases she writes cautiously, 'because there is in those cases a good Judgment required, and I use those things, in those cases which are not Common Receipts, which may as well Kill, as Cure; . . . Experience, with much Reading, must give that understanding.'

About the time of the Restoration, Mr. Woolley died. The school was presumably sold or closed, and Hannah set about the hazardous business of earning her living by writing, in order to bring up her family. Her first three books were collections of recipes, and despite a good deal of trouble with an unscrupulous publisher, they seem to have sold fairly well. In 1666 she married a Mr. Challinor, but two or three years later he died, and by 1674 she was living in the house of Mr. Richard Woolley, in all probability one of her sons, in the Old Bailey in Golden Cup Court, still writing and also running a servants' employment agency.

It was now that she wrote her two important books *The Gentlewoman's Companion*, which appeared in 1675, and a revised and amended edition of *The Queen-like Closet*, which had first been published in 1670.

The Gentlewoman's Companion she describes as a 'Universal Companion and Guide to the Female Sex in all Relations, Companies, Conditions, and states of Life, even from Childhood down to Old Age; from the Lady at the Court, to the Cook-maid in the Country', and in addition to her recipes there is advice on almost every contingency a young woman might have to face in life. Even one troubled with 'a wandering eye' can find a solution in the section on 'the Government of the Eye', and in regard to the ultimate problem of marriage she says: 'Whatever you do, be not induced to marry one you have either abhorrence of loathing to,' which is refreshing to read after Lord Halifax's *Advice To A Daughter*, written several years later, in 1689, when he said: 'It is one of the Disadvantages belonging to your Sex, that young Women are seldom permitted to make their own Choice; their Friends' Care and Experience are thought safer Guides to them than their own Fancies; and their Modesty often forbiddeth them to refuse when their Parents recommend, though their inward Consent may not exactly go along with it.'

Nevertheless, Hannah lays stress on the need for children to obey their parents. 'And think not,' she says, 'though grown up to Woman's estate, that you are freed from Obedience.'

'But of all the acts of disobedience, that of marrying against the consent of Parents is the highest,' she continues. 'Children are so much the Goods and Chattles of a Parent, that they cannot without a kind of theft give themselves away without the allowance of those that have the right to them,' all of which hardly matches her previous advice not to be persuaded to marry anyone they disliked. Moreover, her assumption that women should live in a state of complete subjugation to their husbands and be indulgent to their infidelities, and the soothing advice that 'discretion will bring him home at last', seems out of tune with her independent spirit.

On the question of the education of girls she is sounder. 'The right Education of the Female Sex,' she says, 'as it is in a manner every where neglected, so it ought to be generally lamented. Most of this depraved later Age think a Woman learned and wise enough if she can distinguish her Husbands bed from another's . . . vain man is apt to think we were merely intended for the world's propagation, and to keep its inhabitants sweet and clean; but by their leaves, had we the same Literature, he would find our brains as fruitful as our bodies. . . . Hence I am induced to believe we are debarred from the knowledge of Humane learning, lest our pregnant Wits should rival the touring conceits of our insulting Lords and Masters. . . . I cannot but complain of, and must condemn the great negligence of Parents, in letting the fertile ground of their Daughters lie fallow, yet send the barren Noodles of their sons to the University, where they stay for no other purpose than to fill their empty Sconces with idle Notions to make a noise in the Country.'

She is writing here for girls who are being taught at home by their mothers or governesses and deplores 'the careless neglect of Parents, who think neither God or Nature doth tie them to further regard of their Children than to afford them food, and make them strut in the fashion, learn them to dance and sing, and lastly lay up a considerable sum, for some person whom they value by his greatness not his goodness'.

Education, she says, 'not only fortifies the best inclinations, but enlargeth a mean capacity to a great perfection'. And in an age when appearances, manners and deportment were of great social significance, she laments the state of uneducated ladies who have 'no agreeable discourse' and stand 'like so many Mutes or Statues when they have happened into the company of the ingenious', because they understand nothing of the conversation.

Hannah was a woman of great humanity. She makes a plea for greater kindness to little children and begs parents to take care in choosing governesses, many of whom she has known to be unduly severe. She advocates firmness with gentleness, maintaining that 'blows are fitter for beasts than rational creatures'. 'Let them be lovingly and quietly Governed: not with perpetual Chiding and Brawling, but treat with them mildly and gently; unless you find them Refractory to your Commands; if so, then some Austere language must be used' and 'if by ill-Fate (after all this care) you should have a rebellious and refractory Child, your frequent prayers to Almighty God will be the only way to reclaim them.'

She also has advice for nurse-maids in the handling of their charges, urging them to be 'not churlish or dogged to them, but merry and pleasant and contrive and invent pretty pastimes agreeable for their age'. And in accordance with sound modern precept, she wisely adds: 'Let them be fully employed, but with diversity of things; that will be a delight to them.'

Hannah has a special word for girls who, like herself, had been left, unexpectedly, to their own resources, many after a childhood of affluence. There had been several causes for such problems in England at this time, for although the children of the Civil War were now grown up, the Dutch wars of the seventeenth century and the terrible plague of 1665 had taken a heavy toll. Few of these girls, she knows, will have had the education to teach, as she did, but she advises them to forget the past and enter the service of some noble household and try to acquire the accomplishments of a 'Waiting-woman or House-keeper'. Above all, she begs them to resist any tempting offer to appear on the stage or to take the even easier way by joining a bawdy-house and sinking to a life of degradation and probable crime.

She has an infinite pity for girls who have been left, as she was, entirely alone, and begs parents to make provision for their daughters whenever possible, if not financially, then by giving them a sound education, so that, in the event of their having to earn their own living they can do so honourably, in 'some honest and creditable employment'. 'Such girls as these,' says Hannah, 'shall never lack my assistance. . . . I do love such with my heart.'

We do not know when Hannah died, but it was probably in the 1680s, several years before two more protagonists of girls' education were to have their say. These were Mary Astell and an anonymous writer whom some thought was Mary Astell but seems to have been a Mrs. Drake. Mary Astell was practical and Mrs. Drake all theory. Her little book, *An Essay in Defence of the Female Sex*, was published in 1697 and addressed to the Princess Anne of Denmark, by now in direct succession to the throne. It could well have been a retort to Lord Halifax's *Advice to a Daughter*, which had become widely read and approved, for in it, after warning his cherished Elizabeth on the disenchantments of marriage, and despite the tender warmth and kindly wisdom of much of the essay, he says: 'You must first lay it down for a Foundation in general, that there is Inequality in the Sexes, and that for the better Œconomy of the World, the Men, who were to be the Lawgivers, had the larger share of Reason bestowed upon them. . . . It is true that the Laws of Marriage run in a harsher Style towards your Sex: Obey is an ungenteel word . . . but the supposition of your being the weaker Sex having without doubt a good Foundation, maketh it reasonable to subject it to the Masculine Dominion.'

And as for any who would question the supposition of inferiority or attempt to improve the social status of women, he blandly dismisses the subject by saying that 'it is unwise to break into an Establishment upon which the Order of Human Society doth so much depend'.

Mrs. Drake would have none of this. In her opening paragraphs, she seems to take an unconscionable time to say nothing at inordinate length, but when she does come to the point she shows a sharp observation and an astringent wit.

She begins with the observation Chaucer made three centuries earlier that the 'reason for which woman was created was to be a companion and help meet to Man' adding brightly that 'consequently those that deny 'em to be so must argue a mistake in Providence, and think themselves wiser than their Creator': and she also makes the interesting point that 'amongst country folk the Condition of the two Sexes is more level than amongst Gentlemen, City Traders or rich Yeomen'.

Dutch women, she says, 'manage their Domestic affairs but also keep Books, balance Accounts, and do all the business with as much Dexterity and Exactness as their, or our Men can do', and she has often heard 'some of our considerable Merchants blame the conduct of our Countrymen in this point, that they breed our Women so ignorant of business; whereas were they taught Arithmetick, and other Arts which require not much bodily strength, they might supply the places of abundance of lusty Men now employ'd in sedentary Business. . . . Beside that it might prevent the ruin of many Families, which is often occasion'd by the Death of Merchants in full business, and leaving their Accounts perplex'd and embroil'd to a Widow and Orphans, who understanding nothing of the Husband or Father's business, occasions the Rending, and oftentimes the utter confounding a fair Estate; which might be prevented, did the wife but understand Merchants Accounts. . . .'

This is sound common sense and to the suggestion that a woman has no head for business, she retorts that 'a man ought no more to value himself upon being wiser than a woman if he owe his Advantage to a better education, and greater means of Information, than he ought to boast of his Courage, for beating a Man, when his Hands were bound.'

She suggests, as waspishly as Hannah Woolley, that this assumption on the part of the male of mental superiority is because he fears that if she were given an equal opportunity of education she might easily surpass him, and she is particularly angry and on the defensive at the accusation, which crops up often at this time, and which Hannah Woolley mentions, that 'women's conversation is tedious to men to endure.'

'Let us now look into the manner of our Education, and see wherein it falls short of the Mens, and how the defectes of it may be, and are generally supply'd,' says Mrs. Drake. 'In our tender years they are the same, for after Children can Talk, they are promiscuously taught to Read and Write by the same Persons, and at the same time both Boys and Girls. When these are acquir'd, which is generally about the Age of Six or Seven Years, they begin to be separated, and the Boys are sent to the *Grammar School*, and the girls to Boarding Schools, or other places, to learn Needle Work, Dancing, Painting and other accomplishments according to the Humour and Ability of the Parents, or inclination of the Children. Of all these, Reading, and Writing are the main Instruments of Conversation; though Musick and Painting may be allow'd to contribute something towards it, as they give us an insight into the Arts, that makes up a great part of the Pleasure and Diversions of Mankind. Here then lies the main Defect, that we are taught only our Mother Tongue, or perhaps *French*, which is now very fashionable, and almost as Familiar amongst women of quality as Men; whereas the other Sex by means of a more extensive Education to the knowledge of the *Roman* and *Greek* Languages, have a vaster Field for their imaginations to rove in, and their Capacities thereby enlarg'd.'

But she destroys her point when she argues that women can read the Classics in translation, that Shakespeare, Dryden and all the Restoration dramatists are available to be read in English, and that for many boys a Classical education is a waste of time.

She is at her best when refuting the imputations that women are guilty of vanity, impertinence, enviousness, dissimulation and inconstancy, arguing that on all counts men are as bad or even worse. She scorns the Beau who claims to be widely travelled and after a brief sojourn abroad retains of the language only 'a few modish words to lard his discourse with. . . .' We have all met him and he sounds disconcertingly like someone who has just returned from his first package holiday in Europe. As an example of male impertinence she gives a scurrilous description of the Fop Poet—the literary failure who pretends to be on familiar terms with the stars of the profession which has rejected him. It seems she must have suffered badly from this one: 'He is the Oracle of those that want wit, and the Plague of those that have it; for he haunts their Lodgings, and is more terrible to 'em than their Duns,' she laments. As for vanity, she suggests that 'it is nothing but foolish vanity—what else—makes men involve themselves in the Fatigue and Hazards of War, and intricate intrigues of State, when they have already more than they can enjoy. . . . And it is vanity which makes them wish to leave a Reputation behind 'em in the world, though they know they can't be affected with it after Death.'

The father of today's pub politician she found in the coffee house, where he is 'always settling the Nation, yet could never manage his own Family'. 'He is,' she says, 'a mighty stickler at all *Elections* and tho' he has no vote, thinks it impossible any thing shou'ld go right unless he be there to BAWL for it.' After three centuries of bawling, and picking up the vote on the way, he has not changed very much, but, as our Lady says, in her stylish way, 'after this digression, Madam, let us return to our subject'.

As for accusing women of dissimulation, 'they are the common object on which it is daily practis'd', she retorts. 'A man thinks her ruin a step to Reputation and founds his own Honour upon her infamy. . . . Men insult over the weakness of a too fond WOMAN and *Triumph* in her dishonour. They pursue with so much Eagerness and Impatience what they so soon slight if obtain'd.'

And for the allegation of inconstancy, she declares that women have neither the means nor the temptation 'to be fickle and inconstant so ready as Men have; for Modesty, and the Rules of Decency observ'd among Us, not permitting to us the Liberty of declaring our sentiments to those we Love, as Men may, we dare not indulge a wanton Fancy, or rambling Inclination, which must be stifled in our own Breasts. . . .'

What Princess Anne thought of all this, we don't know, but she was very sympathetic to Mary Astell's proposals.

Mary Astell was born in 1666, the only daughter of a rich merchant of Newcastle-upon-Tyne. She had been carefully educated by a clerical uncle and when she was only twenty-two, she came to London and settled in Paradise Row, close to the Chelsea river side, and here she lived alone, in her charming little house, until her death in 1731. She is said to have been suffering from a broken heart when she first came to Chelsea, but whether her lover had died or jilted her we shall never know.

She was deeply concerned that women should be better educated and was bitterly opposed to the custom of arranged marriages, which was to be found at nearly every level of society. In 1694 she published the first part of *A Serious Proposal to the Ladies for Their True and Great Interest* and three years later the second part, which was dedicated to Princess Anne.

Her proposal was to found a college for the higher education of 'the most neglected part of the World as to all Real improvement, the Ladies'.

Like Mrs. Drake, she pointed out that the reason why women were so often regarded as inferior was not because of anything inherent in their nature, but because of their lack of education. By this time many other writers, both men and women, were realizing how disastrous the situation was becoming. Daniel Defoe wrote: 'I have often thought of it as one of the most barbarous customs in the world, considering we are a civilized and Christian country, that we deny the advantages of learning to women. We reproach the sex every day with folly and impertinence, while I am confident, had they the advantages of education equal to us, they would be guilty of less than ourselves.'

Jonathan Swift, less charitable, merely grumbled: 'Not one gentleman's daughter in a thousand should be brought to read her own natural tongue, or be judge of the easiest books that are written in it,' and Steele spoke of 'the unaccountable wild method in the education of the better half of the world, the women'.

Mary Astell's plan was to provide 'a Seminary to stock the Kingdom with pious and prudent Ladies' and 'to expel that cloud of Ignorance which Custom has involv'd us in ... and to furnish our minds with a stock of solid and useful Knowledge, that the Souls of Women may no longer be the only unadorn'd and neglected things.'

The seminary was to have a double purpose, serving as a place of education for girls who in due course left and were married, but also as a permanent home for women who did not marry, either because they disliked the husbands which had been chosen for them or because their families had become impoverished and had not the necessary bride-price to offer.

William Harvey shared Mary Astell's abhorrence of arranged marriages, but for medical as well as humanitarian reasons. 'We ought to consult more with our sense and instinct, than our reason,' he said, '... A blessing goes with a marriage for love upon a strong impulse.'[1]

As for Lord Halifax's daughter Elizabeth, despite all the loving care lavished on her by her father, she was married at nineteen to the third Earl of Chesterfield, 'a man of morose disposition and violent passions', and after having six children she died, still in her twenties.

Life for a spinster in English society at this time was bleak, particularly if she did not have sufficient education to stimulate her intellectual resources. Most stayed in the home of their

[1] Aubrey, *Brief Lives*.

parents or relatives and very few had the opportunity, like Mary Astell, of living independent lives.

For a sum of £500 to £600 Mary Astell offered women at her seminary a home of 'seraphic celibacy', where they could spend the rest of their lives in study and contemplation. Some might in time join the staff and become teachers, the subjects she recommended for study being logic, mathematics, philosophy and the sciences, which were usually considered beyond a woman's comprehension, and also the writing of the English language.

Here they would be protected from suitors looking for nothing in a wife but her money. They would not be persuaded, imposed on, bought or set up to auction. A woman who had more money than discretion 'need not curse her Stars, for being expos'd a prey to bold, importunate and rapacious Vultures'.

Mary would allow no Dissenters in her seminary and at this stage she was considering only the women of her own upper class, for she firmly believed that social distinctions were part of the divine order, and although she admitted that all good Christians, from the highest in the land to the most humble, would ultimately be admitted to the Kingdom of Heaven, she could not help feeling that the high born in this world could hardly fail to have more privileges in the next.

For girls who would like to marry but had little chance because of the impoverishment of their families, she suggested that 'virtuous and prudent gentlemen' might choose wives from her seminary. 'Such a lady, if she bring less will not waste so much,' and since they were all to be ladies of quality, the suitors would run no risk of tainting the 'purity of their blood'.

For girls who used the place only during their teens, for an education, she recommended that her training would make them better wives and mothers, and, most important of all, capable of teaching their children, for, she said: 'The Foundation of Education on which in a great measure the success of all depends, shou'd be laid by the Mother, for Fathers find other business. . . .'

Yet it was with the fate of the unmarried woman that Mary Astell was so deeply concerned. Seeing her beauty fade and 'quite terrified with the dreadful name of OLD MAID, which yet none but fools will reproach her with, nor any wise woman be afraid of . . . she flies to some dishonourable Match, as her last tho' mistaken refuge'.

The surest cure for the unhappiness of women such as these was the training of the mind, which is true education, said Mary, and this she offered them in the sanctuary of her academy. She made no suggestion of any useful employment for them or consider the possibility of an entry into any of the professions, but said: 'Fain would I rescue my Sex or at least as many of them as come within my little sphere from that Meanness of Spirit into which the generality of them are sunk.'

Many women were very sympathetic to Mary Astell's plan. An anonymous 'great Lady' promised her £10,000 towards the foundation. Who she was is not certain. Many believed it was the Princess Anne, but it may well have been Lady Elizabeth Hastings. However, the college never materialized. The idea was ridiculed by Addison and Steele and many condemned the whole principle of such an establishment as savouring of a Popish nunnery, although Mary had insisted that 'there shall be no vows or irrevocable Obligations, not so much as the fear of Reproach, to keep our Ladies here any longer than they desire'.

Yet Bishop Burnet, one of the objectors to her scheme, held strong views in favour of educating girls. He blamed 'the irregularities of the gentry' on 'the ill methods of schools and colleges' and said: 'The breeding young women to vanity, dressing and false appearance of wit and behaviour, without proper work or a due measure of knowledge and a serious sense of religion is the cause of the corruption of that sex. Something like monasteries without vows would be a glorious design and might be so set on foot as to be the honour of a Queen on the throne; but I will pursue this no further.'[1]

Dean Atterbury, who lived not far from Paradise Row, in

[1] Burnet, *History of His Own Times*, VI, 204.

Church Lane, Chelsea, was a good friend of Mary Astell's, though he did once complain that 'she had not the decent manner of insinuating what she means, but is now and then a little shocking in her expressions'. Quite clearly, she struck home too suddenly and sharply, disturbed too many consciences and caused too many red faces. To her bitter disappointment, the offer by the 'great lady' was withdrawn, but with 'a sort of bravery of the Mind and Soul', Mary went on writing and pleading the cause of women's education and the evils of selling brides.

Defoe was sympathetic to her cause in general but criticized the plan for her seminary as being too restrictive for young girls and, again, too much like the régime of a nunnery. He had his own proposal to make, of an academy where the curriculum was little different from that of other existing schools, but which was built in such a way that it would be difficult for young men to creep in and divert the girls from their studies, and where discipline, without actual spying, would protect them. He would, in fact, have had an act of Parliament to make it a 'felony without clergy for any man to enter by Force or Fraud . . . or to solicit any Woman, though it were to Marry, while she was in the House', a tacit admission that there were some rare goings-on in some of the girls' schools at this time.

'I would have Men take Women for Companions and Educate them to be fit for it,' he said. 'One would wonder, indeed, how it should happen that women are conversible at all, since they are only beholden to natural parts for their knowledge. Their youth is spent to teach them to sew and make baubles. They are taught to read, indeed, and perhaps to write their names or so, and that is the height of a woman's education.'

He suggested a curriculum which would include music and dancing, 'which it would be cruel to bar the Sex of, because they are their Darlings', but also French and Italian and 'all the graces of Speech and all the necessary air of Conversation which our common Education is so defective in that I need not expose it.'

Here is yet another charge that English women lacked skill in the art of conversation, and an anonymous French nobleman, writing a few years earlier, after a visit to England, described them as 'sitting as silent and fixt as statues', entirely lacking in 'assurance, address, and the charming discourse of our demoiselles' and stirring into life only when they can be 'censorious of their neighbours'.

'They should be taught to read books and especially history,' continued Defoe, 'so as to make them understand the world, and be able to know and judge of things when they hear of them.'

Lady Mary Wortley Montagu, the daughter of Lord Kingston, was only a child when Mary Astell wrote her *Proposal*, for she was not born until 1689, but as she grew up the two women became close friends. Her mother died when Lady Mary was very young and she was brought up at her father's country home. From the time she had learnt to read, she became a student, and she taught herself Latin, 'by the help of an uncommon memory and indefatigable labour', having been left 'to the care of an old governess who, though perfectly good and pious, wanted capacity'.

Later she was guided in her reading by the great Bishop Burnet and also by a favourite uncle, William Fielding. When she was still in her teens she began to write poems, made an attempt at one or two romances and, with Dr. Burnet's help, wrote a translation of the Latin version of the Enchiridion of Epictetus. In July, 1710, when she sent him the finished translation for his opinion, she wrote: 'My sex is usually forbid studies of this nature, and folly reckoned so much our proper sphere, we are sooner pardoned an excess of that, than the least pretensions to reading or good sense. . . . There is hardly a character in the world more despicable or more liable to universal ridicule, than that of a learned woman: those words imply, according to the received sense, a tattling, impertinent, vain and conceited creature. I believe nobody will deny that learning may have this effect, but it must be a very superficial degree of it. . . .'

She was having almost to apologize for her learning, for the men who complained continually of the follies of most women were for ever poking fun at those who were highly educated: and in the *Tatler*, the first number of which had appeared the year before, Addison and Steele were merciless.

In a later letter to Burnet, Lady Mary, still very young and inexperienced, was succumbing with unhappy and abject humility to the accepted attitude to women. 'I am not now arguing for an equality of the two sexes. I do not doubt God and nature have thrown us into an inferior rank; we are a lower part of the creation, we owe obedience and submission to the superior sex, and any woman who suffers her vanity and folly to deny this, rebels against the law of the Creator and indisputable order of nature,' she confessed.

Negotiations had been going on for months between her father and Edward Wortley Montagu in regard to her marriage, but the two men could not agree on the financial arrangements. Edward was a difficult character, and as a lover seems to have blown hot and cold according to his mood and his temper, but when the negotiations with Lord Kingston finally broke down and another likely husband was found for Lady Mary whom she loathed, she and Edward, in the face of incredible difficulties, and an enthusiasm on Edward's part which at times can be described only as lukewarm, flouted all the conventions and, in 1712, made a runaway marriage.

It did not turn out particularly well and in the early years he neglected her shamefully, but when he was appointed ambassador to Constantinople, she accompanied him, and it was from here that she began the letters to her family and friends which were to bring her fame.

From Turkey she introduced to England the practice of inoculation against smallpox, at a time when the disease was carrying off nearly a tenth of the country's population each year. When the critics raised their objections, it was Mary Astell who rallied to her cause, in an article in *The Plain Dealer* for July, 1724. She decried the English resistance to anything new and pointed out the sharp decline in the death rate by smallpox of those who had been inoculated. A few years before her death, Lady Mary showed her a manuscript volume of her letters and journals, written during her considerable travels, and although they were not published until many years later, Mary Astell wrote the preface.

Towards the end of her life, Mary Astell, who died in 1731, helped her friends Lady Elizabeth Hastings and Lady Jones, daughter of the profligate Earl of Ranelagh, to found a school for the daughters of the pensioners of Chelsea Hospital, which existed until 1862.

Lady Mary Wortley Montagu and her husband were back in England by 1718 and for a time lived amongst the literary circle at Twickenham, where Pope was her ardent admirer until their ruinous quarrel, when she had the temerity to laugh at him for his infatuation for her. Then they moved to Cavendish Square and followed the fashionable social round for a few years, but when Lady Mary was nearly fifty she left her husband and spent the next twenty years in Italy and France, from where she wrote more brilliant letters, many of them to her daughter, who had become the Countess of Bute.

'To say truth, there is no part of the world where our sex is treated with so much contempt as in England,' she wrote on one occasion. 'We are educated in the grossest ignorance, and no art omitted to stifle our natural reason. If some few get above their nurses' instructions, our knowledge must rest concealed and be as useless to the world as gold in the mine. I am now speaking according to our English notions, which may wear out, some ages hence, along with others equally absurd.'

The notions did wear out eventually, or at least wear very thin, but not for many years to come.

Writing of her first grandchild, Lady Mary said in a letter to Lady Bute: 'You have given me a great deal of satisfaction by your account of your eldest daughter. I am particularly pleased to hear she is a good arithmetician: it is the best proof of understanding: the knowledge of numbers is one of the chief distinctions between us and the brutes.'

'Learning, if she has a real taste for it,' continued Lady Mary, 'will not only make her contented but happy with it. No entertainment is so cheap as reading, nor any pleasure so lasting. She will not want new fashions, nor regret the loss of expensive diversions, or variety of company, if she can be amused by an author in her closet. To render this amusement extensive she should be permitted to learn the languages. I have heard it lamented that boys lose so many years in mere learning of words: this is no objection for a girl, whose time is not so precious: she cannot advance herself in any profession, and has therefore more hours to spare; and as you say her memory is good, she will be very agreeably employed this way.'

Here again she is tacitly accepting that men's place in society is more important than that of women and her further advice stresses this.

'There are two cautions to be given on this subject: first, not to think herself learned when she can read Latin, or even Greek. Languages are more properly to be called vehicles of learning than learning itself, as may be observed in many schoolmasters, who, though perhaps critics in grammar, are the most ignorant fellows upon earth. True knowledge consists in knowing things not words. . . .

'The second caution to be given her (and which is most absolutely necessary) is to conceal whatever learning she attains, with as much solicitude as she would hide crookedness or lameness: the parade of it can only serve to draw on her the envy, and consequently the most inveterate hatred, of all he and she fools, which will certainly be at least three parts in four of her acquaintance. . . .

'At the same time as I recommend books, I neither exclude work nor drawing. I think it is as scandalous for a woman not to know how to use a needle as for a man not to know how to use a sword.'

Horace Walpole was one of the men who scurrilously criticized Lady Mary herself for her learning. His malice knew no bounds when he wrote about her, but this was not entirely scorn for her erudition. He hated her because of her friendship with Miss Kerrey, his father's mistress, who had supplanted his adored mother, and also, quite illogically, but perhaps understandably, because Edward Wortley Montagu had often opposed his father, Sir Robert, in the House.

After writing her views on education to Lady Bute, Lady Mary followed it with another letter, half explanatory, half apologetic, lest Lord Bute should take alarm at the prospect of having learned daughters on his hands.

'Almost all girls of quality are educated as if they were to be great ladies, which is often as little to be expected as an immoderate heat of the sun in the north of Scotland,' she wrote. 'You should teach yours to confine their desires to probabilities, to be as useful as possible to themselves, and to think privacy (as it is) the happiest state of life': and later she points out that study makes solitude agreeable, and that during the seven years in which she has lived in retirement she never had half an hour heavy on her hands.

'My own education was one of the worst in the world,' she said later, 'being exactly the same as Clarissa Harlowe's; her pious Mrs. Norton so perfectly resembled my governess, who had been nurse to my mother, I could almost fancy the author was acquainted with her. She took so much pains, from my infancy, to fill my head with superstitious tales and false notions, it was none of her fault I am not at this day afraid of witches and hobgoblins, or turned methodist. Almost all girls are bred after this manner. . . .'

Sadly for Lady Mary, Lady Bute did not share her mother's views about the education of girls and her youngest daughter, Lady Louisa Stuart, who inherited her grandmother's passion for reading and study, and something of her literary abilities, was harshly discouraged, both by her elders and her brothers and sisters.

In later years she said that they constantly accused her of affectation and conceit, and of trying to be as clever as her grandmother, although this was the first she had ever heard of her existence, for during these years, Lady Mary, having left her husband, was something of a family disgrace.

After Edward Montagu's death, in 1761, Lady Mary returned to London, but within a few weeks she had developed cancer, and before the end of the year she was dead.

Chapter Eight

THE CHARITY SCHOOLS

THROUGHOUT THE EIGHTEENTH century, and well into the nineteenth, the belief that women were mentally inferior to men was constantly aired and, it would seem, sincerely believed by nearly all men and the majority of women: and people like Lady Mary Wortley Montagu were regarded as freakish exceptions.

In the previous century, La Bruyère, in his *Caractères*, had said that women's lack of knowledge was largely their own fault, since there was no reason why they could not read and study for themselves, as Lady Mary and many other women were to do. For the most part, however, he thought they were 'firm set in their ignorance, whether owing to constitutional feebleness, indolence of mind, carefulness for their personal appearance, or a certain instability which deprived them of the power to concentrate'.

Other writers had suggested that there was a physical difference in the structure of a woman's brain which made her unalterably and permanently inferior to a man mentally.

In English society there were women who read the same books as men and talked politics on an equal footing. Some had a great influence on political events and took an active part in electioneering, particularly Georgiana, Duchess of Devonshire, during the election of 1784, when she scandalized the prudes by offering a kiss and a ride in her coach to the hustings in Covent Garden to any Whig voters. Such women lived in freedom, aired their views in public, talked farming and business, wrote and published what they liked, hunted and shot with their menfolk.

Yet they had little effect on the mainstream of opinion which accorded with the defeatist advice of George Lyttelton:

> Seek to be good, but aim not to be great;
> A woman's noblest station is retreat.

This was echoed a century later by Charles Kingsley's irritating admonition:

> Be good, sweet maid,
> And let who will be clever.

Even more strongly held was the belief that the poor should be kept firmly in their place. Those who had learnt to read and perhaps to write a little should count themselves privileged, but this must be the utmost limit of their education, lest they should get above themselves and in time refuse to do the necessary laborious and unattractive services to their betters for which a Divine providence had placed them in the world.

The population of England and Wales at the time of Queen Anne's accession in 1702 was about five and a half million. More than half a million lived in London, but the other cities of England were as yet comparatively small and the majority of the population were country dwellers: and even at the end of the eighteenth century more than three-quarters of the population were still living in the scattered hamlets and villages of the English countryside.

In the opening years of the century, the death rate exceeded the birth rate, partly due to a lack of medical knowledge and hygiene, to epidemic diseases such as smallpox and typhus, to malnutrition and tuberculosis, but also because of the excessive amount of gin that was drunk by the poor, in place of the traditional beer. The habit of gin drinking had been introduced by Dutch King William and his Court, and it was now distilled from English corn in such large quantities that it was cheaper than beer. During the 1730s and 1740s there were said to be between three and four thousand gin shops in London alone and the poor, particularly in London, and to a less extent throughout the country, drank so much of it, to escape from the squalor and misery of their surroundings, that they died in their thousands. At one time excessive gin drinking was the cause of twelve per cent of deaths, and by the middle of the century the government had to take action by imposing a heavy tax on gin and allowing it to be sold only by licence. This checked the death rate and thereafter, with advancing medical knowledge and the establishment of efficient hospitals, the population figures rose sharply, and by the end of the century the figure had reached nine million.

Queen Anne was conscientious and kind, sincerely anxious to do her best for her people, but in an assertion of her hereditary divine right to the Crown she revived the ancient practice of touching for the King's Evil, a business which William III had dismissed as Popish nonsense, and all unwittingly she helped to perpetuate the superstitious mists which Lady Mary Wortley Montagu had described and which lingered on into the Age of Reason.

In 1716 Dudley Ryder, a young man who was destined to become Chief Justice in the Court of King's Bench, recorded in his diary putting on a 'blue flannel that has a very deep dye upon it', to ease his rheumatism. 'This is what Aunt Marshall recommended from her own and others' experience to be extremely good in any pains,' he wrote, but the significance lay, it would seem, not in the warmth of the flannel but in its colour.

Mrs. Delaney, friend of Swift and of Queen Charlotte, writing in 1743 about her godson's ague, sent his mother two *infallible receipts*. 1st. Pounded ginger, made into a paste with brandy, spread on sheep's leather and a plaister of it laid over the stomach. 2nd. A spider put into a goose-quill, well sealed and secured, and hung about the child's neck as low as the pit of the stomach. Either of these I am assured, will ease. . . .'

A current cure for rickets, to be found in the popular Boyle's *Family Receipts*, was to 'open a vein in both ears between the Junctures, mix a little Aqua-vitae with the Blood, and with it anoint the Breast, Sides and Neck: then take 3 ounces of the green Ointment, and warm a little of it in a Spoon, and anoint the wrists and Ancles as hot as it may be endured: do this for 9 Nights just before Bed-time: shift not the shirt all the time. If the veins do not appear, rub it with a little lint dipped in Aqua-vitae, or else cause the child to cry, and that will make the veins more visible and bleed the better.'

Although some of the traditional herbal cures which women had passed on through their daughters for generations, since medieval times, were sound enough and are still in use in modern medicine, others were the wildest invention born of the desperation of abysmal ignorance, for, as Macaulay once said: 'Nothing is so credulous as misery.'

Throughout the century, the influence of the Puritanical Anglican and Dissenting middle classes had a sobering influence on a large part of the population, but the early Hanoverian Courts contributed nothing and the moral tone was little better than that of the Restoration years. Lord Chesterfield remarked that 'the difficulties and dangers suffered by lovers and their ladies in the prudish reign of Queen Anne were in a great measure removed by the arrival of the Hanoverian monarch. King George I loved pleasures, and was not delicate in the choice of them.'

Before his accession, the King had divorced his wife, Sophie Dorothea of Celles, for her romantic love affair with Count Königsmark, and banished her for life to the desolate Ahlden Castle: and shortly after his arrival in England his mistress, Frau von Schulenberg, whom he created the Duchess of Kendal, joined him at Kensington Palace.

George II's complicated love life was faithfully recorded by Lord Hervey, and among his many mistresses was the Princesses' governess, the feather-brained, twice widowed Lady Deloraine, described by Sir Robert Walpole as having 'a weak head, a pretty face, a lying tongue and a false heart' and on another occasion more simply as a 'lying bitch', with 'most of the vices of her own sex, and the addition of ours, drinking'. She had a great influence on the King for a time and he liked to spend several hours with her each evening and 'talk bawdy', yet she remained in charge of the education and upbringing of the two younger princesses, Mary and Louisa, who were in their early teens, and held the King's attentions until after Queen Caroline's death, when he sent for his German mistress, Madame Walmoden, whom he created the Countess of Yarmouth, and Lady Deloraine, with an ill-grace, was obliged to fade from the scene.

The German Courts were small and dull, both George I and George II speaking little English and preferring Hanover, which they visited frequently, while the upper ranks of English society tended to form their own circle of fashion and culture, centred on their country houses and London mansions, many of which were being built in the new suburb of Mayfair.

England was at war during nearly the whole of the eighteenth century. King William had pursued the war with France until the Treaty of Ryswick, in 1697, which had seemed an effectual check on Louis XIV's attempted Catholic domination of Europe, but only three years later, on the death of the King of Spain, Louis XIV claimed the whole of the Spanish inheritance for his grandson, who was crowned Philip V of Spain. The following year the exiled James II died and Louis acknowledged his son as James III, the rightful King of England.

William prepared once more for war, forming the Grand Alliance between Austria, the Netherlands and England, to prevent the union of France and Spain and drive the Spanish from the Netherlands. Before he could go into action he died and during Queen Anne's reign John Churchill, later Duke of Marlborough, pursued the war to settle the problem of the Spanish succession.

It dragged on until 1713. The peace Treaty of Utrecht enabled the House of Bourbon to retain possession of both France and Spain, but Philip ceded his possession in Italy and the Netherlands to Emperor Charles of Austria, and England received Minorca and the strategic stronghold of Gibraltar, which gave us control of the western Mediterranean for our merchant ships. We also gained Newfoundland and the French colony of Acadia, which was renamed Nova Scotia. Our place was established as a significant European power.

Less than a year after George I's accession, there was a certain amount of Tory support for the Old Pretender's claim to the throne, but the 1715 Jacobite rebellion came to nothing.

George II succeeded his father in 1727 and Robert Walpole continued in office, supported by the great Whig landowners, until his dismissal in 1739 for refusing to take part in the next great European struggle to maintain a balance of power, the War of the Austrian Succession, in which King George II was mainly concerned for his Hanoverian possessions.

With the peace of Aix-la-Chapelle, in 1748, there was a temporary pause in the European struggle, but both in India and North America the French and English were in constant conflict and, by 1756, it was open battle again, with the outbreak of the Seven Years' War, when, in Europe, Maria Theresa of Austria now joined with France and Russia against Frederick of Prussia and George of England.

By the time it was over in 1763 George II had died and the young George III was on the throne. The war ended with the Peace of Paris and England not only victorious in Canada and India, but undisputed mistress of the high seas. The following year English ships were exploring the Pacific, and Captain Cook, in his travels from 1768 to 1771, was claiming all the new lands he touched—Australia, New Zealand and many of the islands of Polynesia—for the English Crown.

The first setback came in 1775, with the revolt of the American colonists against the trading and manufacturing restriction imposed upon them by Great Britain and the payment of a tax to help meet the costs of the war. On July 4, 1776, the thirteen colonies declared their independence. The war dragged on for seven more years, but in 1783 America's independence was finally acknowledged and Canada's boundary moved back to its present position.

Compared with modern warfare, the numbers of men engaged in these eighteenth-century wars were very small, even in relation to the far smaller population. Apart from the families who suffered bereavement, there was little effect on the economic development of the country, uninterrupted as it was by the long succession of victories.

For boys of the wealthy, the public schools came to favour again. At Eton, with the establishment of the house system, a far greater discipline was maintained. Harrow became fashionable and by 1718 had one hundred and four fee-paying students compared with only forty free scholars, and the segregation of rich and poor at these schools was rigid. At Eton only peers could be top of the form and at Winchester, the young Duke of Hamilton, as the senior in rank, become automatically head of the school. It was not long before the misnamed 'public schools' became almost entirely fee-paying, the curricula including Latin, Greek and English literature, with French, dancing and fencing as extras for those who wished to take them.

There was a certain amount of flogging, but most of it seems to have been inflicted by older boys upon their fags, and there is little evidence of cruelty on the part of the staff.

Many of the old grammar schools, which had already begun to decay after the Restoration, deteriorated still further during the eighteenth century. As prices rose endowments often became so inadequate that there were not enough funds to pay a competent staff. By 1795 Lord Chief Justice Kenyon declared that most of the ancient grammar schools had become 'empty walls, without scholars and everything neglected but the receipt of salaries', and in some cases headmasters corruptly pocketed the bulk of the endowment funds and employed a half-educated, inadequate master to do the work.

A large number of fee-paying day and boarding schools, for both boys and girls, run by private proprietors, came into existence throughout the century, some good, some tolerable, some appalling. The Dissenting Academies played an important part in the educational system, so far as boys were concerned, catering mainly for the middle classes of prosperous merchants and professional men: and the education they provided was in many ways far more suitable for the practical demands of the dawning Industrial Revolution than the traditional teaching of the aristocratic public schools and the universities, for the curricula included science, mathematics and geography as well as the Classics and living languages. In fact, towards the end of the century, they served as models for some of the fashionable public schools, such as Rugby and Oundle.

Middle class boys and younger sons of small squires were often apprenticed on leaving school to merchants, bankers, apothecaries, attorneys and brewers, paying premiums of anything from £20 to £100, but premiums rose steeply throughout the century and by 1800 some London merchants were asking as much as £1,000 to apprentice a boy.

It was against this background that the Charity School movement began in England. The eighteenth century was the Age of Elegance, the Age of Reason, the Age of the Whigs. It was the century when England was rapidly becoming a world power, the century which saw the beginnings of the industrial revolution and the enclosing of thousands of acres of common lands, which, with improved stock-breeding, resulted in more efficient agriculture but further impoverished thousands of peasants, already poor. It was an age when the division between the classes was never more rigid, but it was also the Age of Charity.

The bulk of the middle and lower middle classes were prospering on a rising and expanding market. They were for the most part devout church-goers, either to the Church of England or one of the many Dissenting groups, and they tended to be puritanical in their steadfast devotion to the principles of Christianity. They were sincerely distressed at the plight of the increasing numbers of the working classes and their deepening misery. Some felt a deep emotional pity. Others deemed it part of their Christian duty to do something for them. The realists argued that the increasing crime rate amongst the poor, whose children were brought up with an entire lack of moral standards, was a threat to the order and security of the country in general and their own comfortable way of life in particular.

The idea of eliminating poverty by way of increased

opportunities and higher wages did not enter into their reasoning, for the assumption that the unhappy lot of the poor was part of a divine purpose was a philosophy which had been instilled into them for generations.

There were two schools of thought concerning the way to help them. One was to establish working schools on the lines of the Tudor bridewells, those which had been founded, in association with the workhouses, when the Elizabethan poor laws had made each parish responsible for its own poor. In these institutions a few children, at the expense of the rate-payers, had been given apprenticeships in useful trades. This scheme, it was felt, would enable the youngest of children to earn a few pence each week and in time would give them the ability to be self-supporting and thus abolish pauperism. The other idea was that schools should be established in which children would be imbued with the tenets of the Christian faith, taught enough to be able to read their Bibles and Prayer-books, and thus come to understand that their lowly condition in the world was just their bad luck, and that if they behaved themselves and learnt to be more law-abiding they would have a better time in this world and also in the next. It was 'the great law of subordination'.

The first proposal was rejected, as being too costly, but the second was considered to have possibilities, for it was argued that it might serve an additional useful purpose by building up an even stronger body of Protestant believers to withstand the still formidable strength of Papacy, Jacobitism and the threat to the Protestant succession.

The existing schools for the poor at this time were the dame schools of the free endowed schools which had been founded by the beneficence of individuals. Dame schools were to be found in many villages and small towns, though by no means in all. In a century or more they had not changed. For a few pence a week a half-literate old man or woman, who was usually looking after a shop or business at the same time, would hold a school, usually in the cottage living room, teaching reading, sometimes writing, and occasionally, for an extra fee, a little rudimentary arithmetic. There were no standards and it was said that 'their only qualification for this employment was their unfitness for any other'. 'It's not much they pay me,' admitted one old woman, 'and it's not much I teach them.'

Of the endowed schools, Christ's Hospital had been rebuilt after the Great Fire and was serving as a model for similar but much smaller ventures.

John Evelyn, visiting the school in 1687, wrote that 'there were nearly 800 boys and girls, so decently clad, cleanly lodged, so wholesomely fed, so admirably taught, some mathematics, especially the forty of the late King's foundation, that I was delighted to see the progress some little youths of thirteen or fourteen years of age had made. I saw them at supper, visited their dormitories, and much admired the order, economy and excellent government of this most charitable seminary. Some are taught for the Universities, others designed for seamen, all for trades and callings. The girls are instructed in all such work as becomes their sex and may fit them for good wives, mistresses and to be a blessing to their generation. They sung a psalm before they sat down to supper in the great Hall, to an organ which played all the time, with such cheerful harmony, that it seemed to me a vision of angels. I came from the place with infinite satisfaction, having never seen a more noble, pious and admirable charity.'

During the Great Fire the school had fled to Islington and on their return it was found that the girls' ward had escaped undue damage. Nevertheless, it was decided 'to take down the old Ward over the South Cloister and to erect a large and convenient Ward over the same and some contiguous ground', and it was recommended that 'the girls be removed from the Ward in which now they are lodged into the great New Ward over the South Cloister and that more girls be taken out of the Town and Country to fill up the said Ward, which will hold above 70 girls. Also that they should have a Nurse to look after them distinct from the School Mistress'.

Here the girls remained until their school was moved to Hertford, in 1778, leaving the boys in full possession of the large complex of buildings until they moved to Horsham in 1902.

It was not until 1658 that the girls had been taught writing. The funds for this had been provided in the will of a benefactress, and at first they were taught by two of the boys, but in 1710 the committee ordered that 'the girls shall noe longer goe to the Writing School to learn to write, but that some conveniency shall be made in their own School for their Writing, and that the Writing Master shall send his servt. [the Usher] to instruct them at such hours as shall be thought most convenient.'

This was part of a tendency to separate girls from boys in schools of this kind all over the country at this time and after 1703 the girls dined in their own quarters instead of in the great hall with the boys.

King Edward's, Bridewell, was badly damaged during the Great Fire but alternative accommodation close by was found while the work of repairing and rebuilding was carried out. The chapel was re-opened in 1670 and by 1673 the apprentices were re-installed. There were about a hundred of them and they were now organized more on the lines of a school, with desks and forms, a master to teach them writing and reading, and smart blue uniforms. At the same time vagrants and other offenders, a disreputable band of common felons and prostitutes, were also brought back to the cells and the whipping post, and the public whippings of both men and women at the Bridewell was one of the sights of the City for the diversion of visitors.

Some of the governors saw the harm and folly in allowing destitute young apprentices to be brought up in such close proximity with the prisoners. Others would not agree with them and the argument went on between succeeding generations of governors all through the eighteenth century, while the number of prisoners increased and the number of apprentices fell away until by 1792 there was none left.

In the meantime many other schools for the poor had been founded, some to give an elementary education, some to provide also the means for an apprenticeship after leaving school.

In 1624 Sir William Borlase had founded the Borlase School at Marlow in Buckinghamshire, leaving provision for twelve pounds a year for a schoolmaster to teach twenty-four poor children to write, read and cast accounts. They were to be taken into the school between the ages of ten and fourteen and given two years schooling. Further provision was made to bind the boys as apprentices as well as for building alongside the school a workhouse and house of correction which was also to be used for the teaching of 'twenty-four poor women children . . . to make bone lace, to spin or to knit'.

The Red Maids school at Bristol with its 'one grave, painful and modest woman' was still going and scores more came into existence during the seventeeth and the early years of the eighteenth century, founded by benefactors and catering for local children. In 1706, for example, Elizabeth Gray founded a school at Risley, in Derbyshire, which at first was only for boys, the master teaching grammar and the classics and the usher spelling, writing, arithmetic and the Church catechism, but later she made provision for the extension of the school building to accommodate a mistress to teach girls 'to knit, sew and do other things proper for their education' and when she died, in 1720, she left money for the building of a separate school for girls, who were also to be taught to write and cast accounts.

The list is long and by the time Queen Anne came to the throne there were more than five hundred of these endowed schools throughout the country, mainly day schools, and either free or charging only a few pence a week. Excellent as they were in intention, there were not nearly enough of them and for the most part they were very small. The teaching, particularly in the girls' schools, was often hopelessly inadequate, for the teachers themselves were uneducated, so they did not touch the fringe of the problem of the thousands of poor children who were receiving no education at all.

In *Our Village*, Mary Russell Mitford describes a typical village school at Aberleigh. This had been endowed by Dame Eleanor Lacy, in 1563, for the instruction of twenty poor children and the maintenance of one discreet and godly matron, at a time when nearly the whole of the parish had belonged to the Lacy family. By the eighteenth century the parish had passed into other hands, but the Lacy family still retained the right to appoint the schoolmistress, while the Vicar and the parish officers chose the children, combating a great deal of ill-will in the process, from jealous canvassers. Miss Mitford recalled one schoolmistress, Dame Whitaker, who had been head nurse to two generations of Lacy children and then, having quarrelled with the lady's maid, had been banished to Aberleigh as village schoolmistress. She was fat, lazy and good-natured, much addicted to snuff and green tea, and even too indolent to scold the children when they deserved it. Under her misrule the girls not only learnt nothing but forgot what they already knew. The new shifts they were making for the Vicar's lady were mislaid. Books were torn. And the climax came when no sampler was prepared to carry round from house to house at Christmas time, as had been the custom for years, to display the girl's work. Dame Whitaker received so many complaints that she decided to make up her quarrel with the lady's maid and returned to her empty nursery.

Next came Dame Banks, the widow of Mr. Lacy's game-keeper. She was a complete contrast, thin, sharp-voiced and for ever scolding, but she was no better as a teacher. She was a 'well-intentioned, worthy woman, with a restless, irritable temper, a strong desire to do her duty and a woeful ignorance of how to set about it'. But just as she had driven the parish officers to the point of complaint, she fell ill and died.

Then came Mrs. Allen, nearer seventy than sixty, a charming, gentle but capable soul, who ran the school admirably. She had been in service all her life to a friend of the Lacys and was appointed to the school by them after her mistress had died, in order to provide her with a home and a living.

In many cases endowments which had been adequate at the time of the foundation of a school became insufficient as prices rose. Mrs. Elizabeth Montagu realized this when, in 1775, she was planning to establish a spinning, knitting and sewing school for girls on her Northumberland property. 'When I say establish, I mean for my life, for one cannot be charitable longer,' she said. 'Charitable institutions soon fall into neglect and abuse. I made a visit at Burniston to my Uncle Robinson's alms-houses. I gave each of the old people a guinea. I have sometimes sent them money: for what my uncle appointed nearly a hundred years ago is hardly a subsistence. Indeed, they would starve if they had not some helps.'

Various societies for the improvement of morals and manners had been organized towards the end of the seventeenth century but the one that became effective and was the driving force of the Charity School movement was the Society for Promoting Christian Knowledge, which was founded in 1698.

The benefactors of the endowed schools had been relatively rich. The founders of the Society for Promoting Christian Knowledge planned schools which, independent of the rates, should be supported by the voluntary subscriptions of the body of local people where it was thought the school was needed. At their first meetings, women were not allowed, in order to avoid any breath of scandal. The attitude to women taking any part in public affairs was so bigoted that it was considered better that wives should learn their husbands' views in the privacy of their own homes.

The purpose of the schools, said the S.P.C.K., was 'the Education of Poor Children in the Knowledge and Practice of the Christian Religion as Professed and Taught in the Church of England and for teaching such other things as are most suitable for their Condition.'

The thinking of the founders was to some extent influenced by the writings of John Locke who, in 1693, had published his *Thoughts Concerning Education*, which, he said, should, generally speaking, apply to girls as well as boys. 'Where the difference of sex requires different treatment, it will be no hard matter to distinguish.' True education, he said, was a conditioning of the mind rather than the acquisition of factual knowledge, which is true enough, but pursuing this line of thought to a fairly wild conclusion, he argued that the body should be conditioned as well as the mind and suggested that if boys and girls wore shoes which 'like those of the poor, let in water, they would never take cold, for the poor who are so used to wet feet take no more cold or harm by it than if they were wet in their hands'.

Thus the children of the poor, in their new schools, were to be conditioned to their station in life. So indoctrinated was the Church itself with this attitude to the poor that the Dissenter, Dr. Isaac Watts, the kindliest of men, said in all sincerity and solemnity that the purpose of the Charity schools was to teach children 'to know what their station in life is, how mean their circumstances, how necessary 'tis for them to be diligent, laborious, honest and faithful, humble and submissive, what duties they owe to the rest of mankind and particularly to their superiors'.

In an age of uncertainties and faltering values, when charity itself is deemed mere self-indulgence, and two and two hardly make four any more, one can but envy him his profound, complacent faith.

More brutally, the purpose of the schools was said to be 'to combat Popery and to teach the children of the poor to keep their stations'.

The boys were to be taught to read and write and cast accounts, the girls to read, perhaps to write a little, and to sew and knit. Where sufficient funds were available, the children were to be dressed in a distinctive uniform, the clothes serving to remind them, as Bishop Butler put it, 'of their servile state' and the fact that they were 'public objects of charity'. When they left school the money was to be paid for their apprenticeship to a craft or trade or to place them into service.

The S.P.C.K. organized the appeals for money and their solicitors recovered many charitable bequests in wills which in some way or other had gone astray. Endowed schools with diminishing assets often joined the scheme in order to be able to continue or extend their work, and some of the almost moribund grammar schools were also included. The procedure and practice in poorly endowed schools and schools supported entirely by public subscriptions being now almost identical, they were known collectively as Charity Schools.

The S.P.C.K. did not undertake to manage the schools or provide the finance, apart from the considerable sums their lawyers received from forgotten endowments and bequests, but they gave advice, organized schemes for raising money and were often successful in finding the right kind of teachers.

The procedure for founding a school was simple. The vicar of the parish or a few prominent people in the district, deciding that their parish needed a school for the poor, formed themselves into a committee, and having decided the amount of money they would need, sent out appeals to local residents for yearly subscriptions of single sums of money. These funds were vested in the trustees, who managed the schools.

During the early years of the eighteenth century subscriptions poured in and hundreds of small schools were founded which provided girls and boys with the rudimentary education promised, a Charity school uniform and an apprenticeship or placing out in service when they left. There were green children and blue, red ones and grey, with some girls in straw bonnets and others in muslin caps. By 1708 it was costing 9s. 2d. to clothe a boy and 10s. 3d. for a girl.

From the outset, the boys outnumbered the girls, but by 1707 sixty-nine charity schools had been established in London and its suburbs alone, teaching nearly 3,000 children, of whom about 800 were girls, and by the end of Queen Anne's reign there were 119 schools in the London area, teaching 5,000 children, of whom more than 1,300 were girls.

The movement spread throughout the whole of the British Isles and contributing to charity schools became a favourite form of benevolence and of easing one's conscience.

The S.P.C.K. had close connections with the Anglican Church, so that the majority of the schools taught the Anglican creed, but a few charity schools were founded by the Roman Catholics and the Dissenters, including the Quakers, in order to teach their own religious beliefs. In 1688, for example, George Fox recorded rather airily and vaguely in his journal:

'Returning towards London by Waltham, I advised the setting up of a school there for teaching children; and also a woman's school at Shacklewell, for instructing young ladies and maidens in whatsoever things were civil and useful in the creation,' but this is the first and last mention he ever makes of it in his diary, and it has been estimated that over ninety per cent of the charity schools were promoted under the auspices of the S.P.C.K. and the Anglican Church.

Children had to be between seven and twelve years of age and their parents too poor to afford any other form of education. Schoolmasters and mistresses had to be communicants of the Church of England, over twenty-five, sober and of good character, able to write a fair hand and satisfy the minister that they understood the principles of the Christian religion. They were usually given accommodation on the school premises and school hours were 7–11 and 1–5 o'clock in summer and 8–11 and 1–4 o'clock in winter. Their duties were to teach the children the catechism, good manners and behaviour, to prevent lying, cursing, swearing and the profaning of the Lord's Day, and instruct them in spelling and writing. Arithmetic was only for the boys usually and then only the bright ones, and it was limited to the four rules, which was deemed sufficient to equip them for the accounts they might have to keep in later life. The girls were to learn to read and to knit their stockings and gloves, to sew, make and mend their clothes. Some learned to write, a few to spin, but hardly any learnt arithmetic, which was regarded as a 'superior accomplishment'.

The master or mistress was enjoined to bring the children to Church twice on Sundays and Holy days, teach them to join in the public services and behave reverently. Prayers were to be said at school in the mornings and evenings and the children were enjoined to pray at home night and mornings and to say grace before and after meals.

A register was called morning and afternoon and truants were liable to be expelled.

Religious instruction was to stress humility and submission to their rank in life, and writing was to be taught only when the child could read competently. Then he was set to copy passages from the Bible, *The Whole Duty of Man*, or perhaps *Aesop's Fables*, these three books being, for many years to come, the Charity child's only reading matter in school.

In small villages where there were not enough children to justify the provision of a school, the master or mistress appointed would teach them at home, being paid by results and receiving 2s. 6d. when a child knew the alphabet, 2s. 6d. when he could spell, 5s. when he or she could 'read well and distinctly and say the Church Catechism' and 15s. more when he could write and cast accounts.

The training of teachers was a serious problem. Newcomers were advised to seek advice from others who had gained experience, and they were sometimes given leave to watch them at work and study their methods.

The story of the Charity schools of St. Leonard's, Shoreditch is typical of hundreds which were founded at this time. In September, 1705, a group of parishioners met in the Vestry House to discuss plans for a school for fifty boys, to be educated, clothed and apprenticed to a suitable trade or craft. Four years later they met to establish a girls' school on the same lines, though far fewer details of its organization have survived.

The parishioners represented the three liberties of the parish and the school places were allotted to the children from each liberty, in proportion to the amount each contributed. The first nine trustees for the boys' school, three from each liberty, were appointed from amongst the parishioners present at the first meeting, by taking names from a hat. They served for twelve months, after which they were elected each year. Each trustee could nominate one boy, if the other trustees approved, and anyone who contributed 20s. or more each year had the same right. For the rest, parents applied on behalf of their children and had to prove that they lived in the parish and were too poor to provide any other education for their child.

A room suitable for a school was found in Pitfield Street, Shoreditch, at a rental of £4 a year, and less than two months after the first vestry meeting the boys' school was opened 'to the glory of God', financed and maintained by guaranteed voluntary annual subscriptions, supplemented by occasional donations by donors in the sudden grip of a charitable impulse, and by collections at the Church door.

Trustees from each liberty visited the school once a week, to enquire into the boys' behaviour and to order any punishment deemed necessary, though it required the consent of all the Trustees before a boy could be expelled. At the monthly Trustee meetings they made arrangements for the apprenticeship of the boys nearing leaving age and also organized the quarterly 'Charity sermons' at the Parish church, to which all the parishioners of Shoreditch were invited, in order, it was hoped, that they would give generously to the offertory.

The boys' clothing was regarded as school property and the coat, cap, bands, shirts and shoes were renewed each year, but it was stressed in the school rules that parents must send their children to school neat, clean and well-brushed, and that if, as not infrequently happened, they appropriated the clothes, particularly the shoes, which they probably sold, the child would be expelled.

The salary of the first schoolmaster at St. Leonard's was £31 a year, but he was given a payment for every boy who was apprenticed, which was made either by the boys' parents or his new master. By 1754 this payment was 8s. 6d. and the boy was presented with £3 for clothing, on leaving school.

One of the school rules, which many a schoolmaster would like to see in operation today, was that 'if any parent, Nurse or any other Person abuse the Master or any of the Trustees, for giving due Correction to their Children for their Faults, their Child shall be expell'd the School and have no more benefits whatever'.

The expulsion rate was very high at St. Leonard's. During the first hundred years of its existence less than a third of the boys managed to run the course and get themselves apprenticed. Some were expelled for bad language or truancy, others because they were too dull or too disinclined to cope with the education offered them. A number were taken away by their families and put to work to earn some money, and one boy, on the principle that the sins of the fathers shall be visited on the children, was expelled because his mother was an habitual drunkard.

In January 1709 the subscribers had their first meeting to found the St. Leonard's Girls' School for forty girls. Three trustees were chosen to serve for the first twelve months and the minister was asked to reserve forty places for the girls in church. By February 24 an eleven year lease of a house in Pitfield Street had been taken for them, at a rent of £5 a year, but from March, 1709, until October, 1715, no more trustee meetings were held.

By this time there were fifty girls in the school, being taught reading and sewing and a little writing.

In 1722, when the lease of their house expired, the trustees decided to build a school in the Kingsland Road to house the boys' and girls' school under one roof, with accommodation for the master and the mistress. There were fifty boys, dressed in coats of light grey with brass buttons, and fifty girls in deep blue. And a singing master was appointed, who taught in both schools.

The girls were completely re-clothed at Whitsuntide, given additional clothing at Michaelmas and Christmas, and on leaving school were given a Bible and Prayer-book and a present of £1 towards their equipment for service.

Probably the earliest of the London charity schools for girls was the one established for a hundred girls in the parish of St. James's, Westminster in October, 1699, by the rector, Dr. William Wake, who afterwards became Archbishop of Canterbury.

The Grey Coat school in the parish of St. Margaret's, Westminster, was founded as a charity school for forty boys in 1698, a house being taken for them in Broad Sanctuary and the Master bidden to 'study and endeavour to win the love and affection of the Children, thereby to invite and encourage them rather than by correction to force them to learne. . . .'

School hours had been made long to prevent the boys being

sent out to beg, either by their parents or the women with whom many had been boarded out by the overseers, but these children from the murky corners of old Westminster—Cabbage Lane, Rogues' Acre, Dirty Lane, Long Ditch, Pick Pocket Alley, Bandy Leg Walk—were for ever playing truant, their parents or guardians complaining that they could not afford to be without their services for so long each day.

The old Elizabethan workhouse had become too small for the parish and in 1700 a new one was opened in Petty France. The Grey Coat governors decided that if they could obtain the old workhouse building at a pepper corn rent they could take in both boys and girls, feed, clothe and provide for them entirely and at the same time overcome the truancy problem.

The property belonged to Westminster Abbey and terms were soon arranged, whereupon the trustees set to work to equip and prepare it for forty boys and twenty girls. They had not much money and the furniture was sparse. Records give details of the making of the beds and bedding and the buying of straw for palliasses, for there were no feather beds for the Grey Coat children. They had wooden platters, trenchers, porringers and spoons and for the sixty children only five combs and two brushes were provided. But they had plenty of food—cheese, butter, pease, oatmeal, beef, turnips, bread and beer—and were well clad, the boys in leather breeches and grey coats, the girls in plain grey dresses, worn over leather bodices, and white caps: and within a few years they were given white linen aprons and white tuckers.

In 1706 Queen Anne granted the hospital a royal charter, which enhanced the dignity of the governors and encouraged donations, but made little difference to the children.

Once or twice a sick child was taken to Queen Anne to be touched for the King's Evil and the Queen recommended two little girls who had been orphaned during the War of the Spanish Succession to be admitted to the hospital, but the promised donation towards their upkeep seems never to have been paid.

In 1709 the girls were given their own mistress to teach them

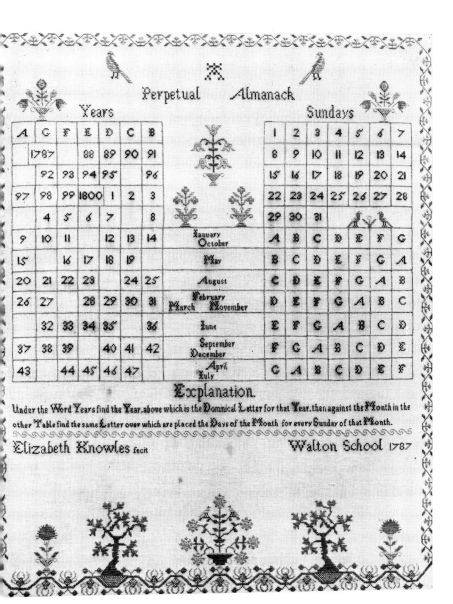

5. A schoolgirl's eighteenth-century sampler, in the form of a perpetual calendar. Such test-pieces in embroidery, involving the alphabet, figures and names, were typical.

6. *Above:* Portrait of Mary Robinson (Perdita) 1758–1800 by G. Dance.
Above right: Mde Frances D'Arbly, better known as Fanny Burney (1752–1840).
Right: St. Leonard's Charity School, Shoreditch, in the London Borough of Hackney.

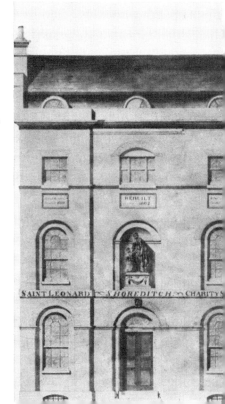

to read, sew, knit and spin. She was a Mrs. Kitson and she insisted on a salary of £10 a year and to be allowed sheets on her bed. But the next year, when she asked for an increase of salary to £15 a year, she was dismissed and a less demanding Mrs. Higner appointed in her place.

The income from donations fluctuated and at times life became very spartan. There were complaints about the food. The girls' hair was sold to periwig makers to raise funds. They were set to spinning and a stall was taken at Spitalfields to display their work for sale to the Spitalfield weavers, but by 1734 it was decided that the money earned by this means was so little and the hindrance to education so great, that spinning was abandoned and twenty-four spinning wheels were sold for a pound.

Another famous school was Archbishop Tenison's, founded in Lambeth in 1706. The first schoolmistress, Mary Davies, had charge of twelve poor girls between the ages of eight and fourteen. Each child was 'new cloathed' and given a Bible and a Book of Common Prayer, and the curriculum included reading, writing, spinning, knitting, plain sewing and marking. In a somewhat gentler manner than at St. Leonard's, parents were asked to 'forbear coming to the School on such occasions that the Mistress may not be interrupted or discouraged in the Exercise of necessary Discipline', adding that any complaints of undue severity could be made to the Trustees at their quarterly meetings.

A few years later, it was found that all was not going well at the girls' school at Christ's Hospital. At the Visitation of April, 1715, the treasurer had to complain about 'the unruly and disorderly carriage and behaviour of the Girls' which he attributed to the incompetence and neglect of the headmistress. And after a stormy session with her and her husband, she was sacked.

In 1703 the S.P.C.K. suggested that the Charity School children might meet once a year and walk in procession to some Church, to take part in a special service. The first rally was in Whitsun week of 1704 in St. Andrew's Church, Holborn, and as their numbers increased they met for many years at the larger Christ Church, Newgate Street. They were also kept well to the fore at time of national rejoicing, such as the peace with France after the Treaty of Utrecht in 1713, when a service of thanksgiving was held at St. Paul's. On that occasion four thousand of them lined the processional route, perched on especially built scaffolding. Queen Anne herself invited the Grey Coat children, including her two little protegées, and they seem to have been given special treatment, with seats allotted for them in Fleet Street and special orders that they were to be given 'small beer and bread and cheese before they started, and buttock of beef and strong beer on their return'.

By 1782 the Charity Children's annual service was being held in St. Paul's and it was one of these services which inspired Blake to write:

> 'Twas on a Holy Thursday, their
> Innocent faces clean
> Came children walking, two and two
> In red and blue and green. . . .'

Neither the boys nor the girls were as angelic as the poet's vision and in the girls' schools all manner of punishments were devised to maintain discipline. At Greenwich school the committee of ladies decided that 'Shame might have a better effect on the Minds of their Own Sex than Fear' and suggested punishments that 'may excite their Modesty' rather than 'their Dread of Corporal Punishment'. For 'high crimes' such as profanity, lying or pilfering, the culprit was dressed in a fool's coat and made to sit in the middle of the schoolroom for an hour, and pilferers were also sent publicly, in their fool's coat, to ask forgiveness of the person they had wronged, 'which they do with great Reluctance, but . . . rather do than be turned out of the School'.

In William Law's school a girl was given a shilling for saying the catechism and sixpence for repeating by heart the morning and evening prayers, and with these gifts she was commended and exhorted 'to go on in her duty': but any girl found lying, cursing, swearing or stealing from her companions had to 'stand chained a whole morning to some particular part of the room by herself' and then 'kneel and confess to God before them all'.

Under some endowments, rewards were given for regular attendance. At Blewbury, for example, each child was given sixpence a week for forty weeks in the year, but fined a penny for every day's absence. No excuse was accepted and by this means 'the School (was) kept pretty full without much trouble'.

The most difficult problem with which the trustees had to contend in the management of the subscription Charity schools was that the income, relying on the whims of subscribers, fluctuated. When a subscriber died, even if he had contributed regularly, his family may not have been inclined to continue the gift. Often there were grave shortages or even deficiencies in the school accounts. Hackney Parish Schools, which had been founded in 1714, were forced to close down between 1734 and 1738 because of lack of funds, while the Charity School at Highgate was closed altogether after the group of 'noble ladies' who had first organized it grew weary of the project and turned their benevolent hearts to another form of charity.

Expenses were little enough. As late as 1815, the expenses of the St. Leonard's school for girls were only £204 19s. 8d., which included the salary of the mistress, writing master, teacher of psalmody and secretary, the clothing of the girls, books and printing, rewards and donations to girls on leaving school, coals, rent, furniture and sundries. Nevertheless, as the first flush of charitable enthusiasm faded, all kinds of methods had to be devised to raise money. A few schools asked for a small payment of a copper or two a week. At Preston, for example, each of the nineteen girls gave one shilling a quarter. At Ewhurst the Vicar hired out two palls for funerals, one for 1s. and a superior one for 2s. 6d., and gave the proceeds to the Charity School. But the most usual method of appeal was to place effigies of charity children outside churches or at the school door, close to a collecting box, in the hope of catching the sympathy of passers-by.

In 1703 Captain Thomas Coram of the merchant service, returning from America, was appalled to see the dead body of an abandoned baby lying on the roadside, and even more shocked when he was told that this was the usual fate of many unwanted children, while those who survived their abandonment long enough were often snatched by thieves and brought up as criminals or prostitutes. Anyone finding an abandoned child and taking it to one of the all too few workhouses was invariably accused of having been responsible for it in some way, while of the babies who were brought in by the constables, very few survived their first few months of workhouse life.

Coram set to work to rouse public indignation. Addison supported him with a special article in the *Guardian*, appealing on behalf of the unwanted, abandoned child, but it was not until 1739 that the Captain had raised sufficient funds and obtained the charter for the foundation of the Foundling Hospital, for he had to overcome many objections. It was alleged that since most of the children were illegitimate, the establishment of the hospital would encourage vice and the numbers of foundlings would increase, a line of thought which has found echo in the arguments for and against contraception. During the first years, dozens of foundlings arrived at the hospital, brought by carriers from all over the country, until at last it could take no more and had to make a rule that only the illegitimate children of mothers who had hitherto been of good character, and had been deserted or betrayed, could be admitted: and if, at a later date, the mother found herself able to support the child, she could have it back.

The foundlings were given the usual elementary education of reading, writing and instruction in the Church catechism. The boys were taught some elementary arithmetic, in preparation for apprenticeship, and the girls to sew and knit and help in the domestic work of the hospital, to equip them for domestic service or apprenticeship to a dressmaker, but the trustees were at pains to let it be known that the children 'would not be educated to as high a standard so as to put them on a level with the children of parents who had the humanity and virtue to preserve them and the industry to support them'.

Neither the children nor anyone else was to be allowed to forget that they were foundlings, a staggeringly cruel concept for a Christian institution. As Dr. Watts said of the children in all the charity schools: 'There are none of these poor who are, or ought to be, bred up to such an accomplished skill in Writing and Accounts as to be qualified for superior posts; except here and there a single Lad whose bright Genius and constant Application and Industry have outrun all his Fellows.'

The poor must be kept firmly where they belonged, at the bottom of the social ladder.

Chapter Nine

THE DECLINE OF THE
CHARITY SCHOOL MOVEMENT

BY 1727 THERE were charity schools in every county of England, in most of the counties of Wales and throughout Scotland and Ireland. In England and Wales there were 1,389 schools teaching 22,024 boys and 5,830 girls, in Scotland and Ireland some 226 schools teaching 4,150 boys and 1,058 girls: but by the middle of the century the movement had lost its impetus and by 1760 it was abundantly clear that it was not going to develop in the way that the promoters had hoped.

There were many reasons for this, political, economic and social. From the outset, the charity schools had had many critics. At a time when the population was declining, and with it the supply of cheap labour, it was argued that the schools were wasting the time of children who would be better employed in remunerative work and accustoming themselves to the fact that unremitting toil was what life was intended to hold for them. Moreover, despite the attempts of indoctrination of servility and submission, there was a real danger that they would be educated above their station and one day refuse to do the work which made life so much more comfortable for their betters. Over and over again it was stressed that the function of the poor was to provide manual labour which it was their duty to perform for the good of the country. Any scheme of social improvement, such as the charity schools, which would unfit them for this work, must therefore be discouraged, as it would upset the economic order of things.

Bernard de Mandeville, the Dutchman who settled in London as a doctor and wasted his talents on amoral and carping criticism of many social matters, published in the 1720s an essay on charity schools, in which he said, with sardonic realism, that 'poverty and ignorance were the only means of ensuring that an adequate supply of labour for the hard and dirty work of the land would be available'.

'Going to school in comparison to working is idleness,' he argued, and the longer children continued in an 'easy sort of life, the more unfit they will be when grown up for downright labour both as to strength and inclination. . . . To make the society happy and people easy under the meanest circumstances it is requisite that great numbers of them be ignorant as well as poor. Knowledge both enhances and multiplies our desires and the fewer things a man wishes for, the more easily his necessities may be supplied.'

Mandeville was convinced that the poor, after being educated, would look upon 'downright labour' with contempt, and said that instead of going to school and wasting time, they could learn all they needed to know at Church.

He also had sharp things to say about the trustees of the charity schools, so many of whom were small shopkeepers and tradesmen, suggesting, probably most unfairly, that the sole motive of their interest was to give themselves an opportunity to assert their little authority over the schoolmasters and obtain the contracts for school clothing, food and equipment.

The political objection to the charity schools came from the Whigs, who were obsessed with the idea that many of the school teachers, under the influence of the Anglican Church, which was regarded as a stronghold of Toryism, were Jacobites and would encourage a spirit of subversiveness amongst the children and opposition to the Hanoverian succession.

In 1716 the Whigs began an attack on the charity schools in Parliament, by introducing the Close Vestries Bill, a reform which 'sought virtually to disestablish the clergyman from his immemorial participation in local government . . . and to place in a completely subordinate position the Churchwardens who were the most ancient officers of the parish.'[1] At the same time, they wanted to transfer the right of appointing masters and mistresses of the charity schools in the parish to an elected lay body. The Church resisted and the charity school trustees pointed out that the schools were supported not by the parish but by voluntary subscriptions, and it was the subscribers who had the right to appoint the teachers and nominate the children. If the management were passed to an elected body, the subscriptions would fall and the schools disappear.

The Bill passed the Commons but was thrown out by the Lords. Dudley Ryder, at this time a law student at the Middle Temple, noted in his diary as early as January, 1716, that at his club at the 'Change they were lamenting the mischief that is like to come to the nation by the means of the charity schools that are erected about London especially, which are most of them in the hands of the Tories and the clergy. If a law was made that no charity or free schools should have clergymen for their masters it might be of great service to reform them.' In October of the same year he recorded that on the way to his grandmother's funeral, 'I went in the coach with Cousin Marshall. We had some discourse about the Bill that was brought into the House of Commons the last session and carried in that House for the regulating vestries. He says that that Bill was designed chiefly against the charity schools which it would very much have discouraged if not totally stopped.'

Almost inevitably there were stories of the misappropriation of funds by certain school trustees, sometimes by intent, sometimes through inefficiency. Gradually an increasing body of opinion felt that the children should do something more useful with their times than attending school. 'In a free nation where slaves are not allowed, the surest wealth consists in a multitude of the laborious poor,' said Mandeville brutally.

In 1719 the S.P.C.K. sent a circular letter to the trustees of

[1] Webb, S. and B., *English Local Government from the Revolution to the Municipal Corporation Act. The Parish and the County*, 1906, p. 255. Quoted in *The Charity School Movement*, M. G. Jones, C.U.P., 1938.

the schools urging them 'to use their utmost Endeavours to get some kind of Labour added to the Instructions given to the Children in the Charity Schools; as Husbandry in any of its Branches, Spinning, Sewing, Knitting, or any Employment to which the particular Manufacturers of their respective Countries may lead them; this will bring them to an Habit of Industry as well as prepare them for the Business by which they are afterwards to subsist in the World, and effectually obviate an Objection against the Charity Schools that they tend to take poor Children off from those servile Offices which are necessary in all Communities and for which the wise Governor of the World has by His Providence designed them.'

Opinion was turning to the point of view that the charity children should work for wages as the workhouse children in their working schools had been doing for many years. The workhouse children were kept by the rates. One of the earliest had been opened in 1689, in Bishopgate Street, where pauper boys and girls from the surrounding parishes had been placed by the church wardens and maintained and taught. The girls had a workroom and a ward over the chapel: and by 1729 there were a hundred and twenty-nine of them, fully occupied in spinning jersey. Workhouses were soon being established all over the country and in all cases the children were given industrial occupation. In Buckinghamshire the girls were taught lace-making. At Wisbech they made yarn for the Norwich weavers. At Colchester they span and carded wool. At Luton all the inmates, eight boys and thirteen girls, between the ages of three and twelve, plaited wheat-straw for the straw hat industry. The Spitalfields children wound raw silk for throwing.

Gradually the two forms of schools, the voluntary and the rate-aided, tended to merge. Workhouse children continued to provide cheap, industrial labour, but also attended the charity schools to receive a little education, in some cases before they were old enough for industrial work. Charity school children began to do part-time industrial work. As we have seen, at the Grey Coat girls' school, the girls were taught, for several years, to spin yarn and their work was offered for sale to the Spital-field weavers.

Abuses very quickly followed. At Artleborough, a charity school which had been established in 1705, to teach a few children to read, had become a school of industry by less than a generation later. At first the mistress took the profits of the children's work for her own fees. Later she took 2d. a week from the spinners' earnings, 1½d. a week from the knitters' and 1d. a week from those who learned to read. Then two bene-factors made these payments to the mistress, so that the children could keep all their earnings, which varied between a 1s. and 2s. 6d. a week.

The parents, delighted to have an additional source of income, encouraged their children to spend ever longer hours at school, until some were going from five or six in the morning until eight or nine at night. The raw material, jersey and yarn, came regularly from Northampton and Wellingborough, and the spun yarn was collected and taken to Coventry for manu-facture.

This was no isolated case. In villages near Luton and Dunstable there were straw-plaiting schools where it was rare for anything to be taught but the complicated patterns of the various plaits. At one time there were three plaiting schools in one street alone in Berkhamsted. At the plaiting school at Frithsden, children worked from eight in the morning till four in the afternoon, with a short break for a dinner of bread and lard. They went home to tea and then on to another plaiting school in the nearby village of Potten End: and sometimes they were taught in the dark, to accustom them to working without looking at the plait. Weekly markets for the straw plaits, each twenty yards long, were held at Berkhamsted, Tring and Hemel Hempstead, where they were bought by the agents of the Dunstable and Luton hat-makers.

Towards the end of the eighteenth century, straw-plaiting succeeded lace-making as a cottage industry in this part of the southern midlands, as fashion, both for men and women, became simpler, and it was considered to be quite profitable, though many complained that it 'made the poor saucy and caused a dearth of indoor servants'

In places the labour of the workhouse children relieved the rates and in others the parish began to contribute to the maintenance of the charity school, and it was difficult to draw the line between the children's section of the parish workhouse and the original charity subscription school.

In some respects the residential working-charity schools, with a partial endowment, which came into existence before the middle of the century, gave a child more protection. The report on Stroud Workhouse, published in 1723, makes this point. 'Parish Officers are now too eager to get rid of them; they place them out so young, with little money, to sorry masters, that 'tis little better than murdering them. But where Children are put into a way of contributing to their own maintenance and may be kept in these Houses at little or no Charge to the Parish, till they are old enough for Trades or Services, it can hardly be supposed that Officers will then be so monstrously cruel as to go on in the old Road of sacrificing them.'

The S.P.C.K., as it saw what was happening, regretted their earlier advice to train the charity school children to some form of industrial occupation, but by then it was too late. Moreover, by the middle of the century, with increasing medical knowledge, the death rate was falling and the population rising rapidly. There were now thousands of poor children throughout the country, and particularly in the teeming slums of London, for whom the numbers of the charity and industrial schools were quite inadequate. They grew up in ignorance, squalor and lawlessness, under a vicious penal system in which, as late as 1769, there were a hundred and sixty offences for which the penalty was death or transportation to the American colonies, while minor offences were punished by fines, flogging or the humiliation of the pillory and the stocks.

There was a note of desperation in the charity sermon preached by William Sharpe in 1755, on 'The Amiableness and Advantage of making suitable provision for the Education and Employment of Poor Children', for he laid more stress on the practical advantage than the amiableness. 'If Compassion cannot move you, let Consideration or Interest prevail with you. For neglect this poor Man's numerous family, leave them to follow their own Imagination, and to make the wretched shift they can, and experience the sad Consequence. They will grow up soon into publick Nuisances; infect your Families with Vice and Violence, break in upon your Comfort and Security. Take the same persons under your patronage, teach them what is right—and hear how you will be repaid. They will be serviceable to you in many Ways by themselves and by their Examples; Industry, Security, Good Order and Good Manners will get ground amongst you; your City will be stocked with honest, laborious, ingenious Artesans, some of the most useful members of a Community, Wealth will increase.'

But he did not specify whose wealth.

As the eighteenth century progressed it was becoming increasingly difficult to raise subscriptions for the charity schools and the decline had already become noticeable when William Sharpe preached his sermon. With the failure of the South Sea Company in 1720, after a nation-wide mania for overseas investment, thousands of people of the middle classes as well as the wealthy lost large sums of money, some being almost ruined. Taxes to pay for the War of the Austrian Succession and then for the Seven Years' War, from 1756 to 1763, steadily increased, and only a generation later came the French Revolution, followed by the Napoleonic Wars.

The Church of England was doing little to help the charity schools during the middle years of the century. The bishops were appointed by the Crown and the government, who distrusted the loyalty of the Church and the ordinary run of clergy. This meant that the bishops were often out of touch with the parish priests. The old sympathy between the Church and the Crown, which had existed in Queen Anne's day, disappeared with the Hanoverians, and although George I had contributed £50 a year to the charity schools, there was no genuine goodwill.

Clergymen had grown lax in their duties and often did no

more than conduct the Sunday services. They did little parish visiting and if they troubled to catechize the children in their charity schools at all, it was a formal, impersonal business, conveying as little to the children as the learning by rote implanted in them by incompetent teachers.

Moreover, things were going badly wrong at many of the residential charity schools. At the Bridewell, the number of children was still declining, as an increasing number of criminal offenders were crowded into the cells of the fast decaying building, but such apprentices as there were were rapidly acquiring a reputation for appalling violence and lawlessness.

At the Grey Coat Hospital, conditions had deteriorated disastrously. Dishonest masters left tradesmen's bills unpaid and in the 1730s, when the Governor took an inventory of the contents of the hospital, there were only 49 beds for a hundred children and only eight chairs. The cook slept in a cupboard and the laundry maids on the floor of the ironing room. The boys washed in a wooden trough outside the building and the girls wherever opportunity or inclination presented themselves.

Both boys and girls were flogged unmercifully and at one time the matron was arrested and only after much difficulty allowed out on bail, but it was under the mastership of the dishonest Boorden that the fortunes of the school reached their lowest point, and when his wife was appointed matron they were 'free to do evil with both hands earnestly'. They stole the children's food and the linen supplies for their clothing. In 1773 an apprentice from Christ's Hospital broke in one evening and murdered and robbed the infirmary nurse. Many boys ran away and eight were expelled at one time for smashing the windows in protest at the bullying they endured. On another occasion the girls tried to set fire to the building, telling the governors later that they were constantly flogged and half starved.

A new master was appointed but he was no improvement on Boorden and there were more riots and violence and more expulsions: and matters did not improve until after 1804, when the Dean and Chapter of Westminster refused to renew the lease of the Hospital to the overseers, from whom the Governors had held it, and granted a new lease direct to the Board, reserving to themselves the right of nominating children.

The Dissenters had only a few charity schools for their own children and the Quakers, who were to establish many excellent schools in the nineteenth century, had none at all during the early years of the eighteenth century, for amongst the Friends there was as yet little conviction that the poor amongst them needed schooling. Not until 1779 was Ackworth, near Pontefract, founded for members of the Society 'not in affluence'. The first fee, for board and tuition, was eight guineas a year, and by 1781 the school had 310 boys and girls from all over the country. As Ackworth was four days' coach ride from London, this was a considerable achievement. Both boys and girls learnt reading, writing, English grammar, arithmetic, history and geography, and the girls were also taught reading and knitting and were expected to clean their classrooms, make the beds, clean the shoes, and keep their own, the boys' and the household linen in order, while both girls and boys helped in the kitchen work.

By this time a slow change was coming over the face of England, as the inventions of Watt's steam engine of 1765, Arkwright's spinning machine of 1768 and Crompton's mule of 1776 were put to practical use and the first stage of the Industrial Revolution dawned, with the establishment of factories using steam-driven machinery, to replace the old days of hand-work. Very soon, thousands of English children were entering the factories when little more than infants, with no preliminary schooling at all. Several people hit on the idea of opening schools for them on Sundays, which were their only free days. Mrs. Catherine Cappe and the Reverend Theophilus Lindsey opened a Sunday school at Catterick in 1763 and Hannah Ball at High Wycombe from 1769 until her death in 1792. In 1780 Robert Raikes established his first Sunday school in Gloucester, since the nearby farmers and other property owners had complained that the child factory workers, on their one free day, were apt, not surprisingly, to run wild and do damage.

Robert Raikes' Sunday schools attracted not only the children but their parents as well, and sometimes entire families would walk miles each week to attend them, carrying their Sunday dinners with them. They spent all day learning the three R's and absorbing religious instruction, and five years later Raikes was able to write with pleasure of their 'sense of subordination and of due respect to their superiors'.

A few years later, around 1796, Joseph Lancaster opened a school, in his father's house in Southwark, for the children of mechanics. Here boys and girls were taught reading, writing and arithmetic for about 4d. a week. The numbers fluctuated between over a hundred during the summer to fifty or sixty in winter. He was not a rich man, but had recently joined the Quakers, who helped him financially, so that by 1801 he was able to offer free schooling to the children of the very poor, as well as a free dinner.

Andrew Bell, a Church of England clergyman who had served as a missionary in Madras, faced with the problem of a lack of teachers, had devised the system of appointing senior pupils as monitors to take charge of some of the classes. In 1797 he had published an account of this system, in which the teacher taught the monitors and the monitors the children, and Lancaster adopted the system in his own school. It had its drawbacks, but at a time when there were so few teachers and no training facilities, it also had advantages, and Lancaster's school was so successful that by 1810 the Royal Lancastrian Society was formed, for the founding of more schools. Bell, however, was a strong Anglican and bitter arguments followed, the Church of England anxious lest the education of the young be taken away from their influence. In 1811, therefore, the National Society for Promoting the Education of the Poor in the Principles of the Church of England throughout England and Wales was formed, taking over control of the charity schools still under the care of the S.P.C.K., and in 1814 the

Royal Lancastrian Society was re-formed as the non-sectarian British and Foreign School Society.

All the old arguments about the evils of teaching the poor were raised yet again, but by this time the French Revolution had sounded a warning to all those who underestimated the intelligence and potential power of the working classes. From the attitude that education might do a great deal of harm, 'as it would enable them to reach everything that would tend to inflame their passions', there was a change to the point of view that 'ignorance might give birth to disastrous eruptions'. The idea now was to teach them a little, reaffirm that their place in life had been ordained by an inscrutable Providence, and trust to luck that they would behave with a sweet reasonableness. A little education would form 'many beneficial habits of an indelible nature—habits of submission and respect for their superiors'—and religion should do the rest.

There were very few books for children at the beginning of the eighteenth century. In the dame schools the horn books were still in use till the end of the century, for they were very cheap, costing only about a penny or twopence, and they were almost indestructible, outlasting two or three generations of small readers. Elsewhere, as printed books became cheaper, they gradually took the place of the horn books, and chapmen would include a few little books for children in their packs. At first these were purely instructional but gradually they became more amusing. Publishers gave up their expensive tooled leather bindings and began to issue little books of sixteen to thirty-two pages, bound in stiff paper and with wood block illustrations. Rhyming alphabets were popular and early in the 1740s Newberry published for 3d. 'A Little Lottery Book for Children Containing a new method of playing them into a Knowledge of the Letters, Figures, etc. embellished with about fifty Cuts, and published with the approbation of the Court of Common Sense.' This they followed, in 1744, with 'A Little Pretty Pocket Book intended for the instruction and amusement of little Master Tommy and pretty Miss Polly.'

Older children were not specifically catered for yet. They

7. *Above:* Campden House School, Kensington, as it was in 1792.
Below left: Mary Godwin, later Mrs. Wollstonecraft.
Below right: Charlotte Brontë.

8. Frances Mary Buss, 1850–94, founder and first Head Mistress of North London Collegiate School.

Dorothea Beale, 1831–1906, Princ of Cheltenham Ladies' College.

The 'Giant Stride' in the Gymnasium at the North London Collegiate School, 1882

THE GYMNASIUM OF THE NORTH LONDON COLLEGIATE SCHOOL FOR GIRLS.

read *The Pilgrim's Progress*, *Gulliver's Travels* and *Robinson Crusoe*. Some tackled Tom Jones and Humphrey Clinker, but Foxe's *Book of Martyrs* was a favourite gift for a child, with James Janerway's *The Conversion and the Holy Exemplary Lives and Joyful Deaths of Several Young Children* running a close but daunting and depressing second.

The first translation of the *Arabian Nights* appeared in 1704 and by 1707 the packmen were distributing the stories from them. Perrault's fairy stories—*Cinderella, Red Riding-Hood* and the *Sleeping Beauty*—were translated and put into circulation, along with the old English stories, *Guy of Warwick, The Seven Champions, Robin Hood* and *Dick Whittington*: and *Aesop* and *La Fontaine* were constantly being reprinted.

By the 1760s publishers were realizing that there was a large and growing market for children's books, particularly amongst the increasingly literate middle classes, and they produced numbers of stories, some obviously inspired by *Robinson Crusoe*, but mostly tales of magic and mystery, ghosts and hob-goblins, fairies and witches. Newberry's gay little books covered with gilt embossed paper, and known as the gilt books, included *Christmas Box, New Year's Gift* and *Goody Two Shoes*.

But there was a strong body of opinion which disapproved of stories of fantasy for children.

Mrs. Sarah Trimmer was a cultured woman who moved on the fringe of Dr. Johnson's literary circle. She was the mother of many children and was deeply interested in the problem of educating the children of the poor, particularly those who showed intellectual promise: and she deplored the way in which so many of the charity schools had been turned into small factories. Seeing that the charity school children had very little reading matter, except the Old and New Testaments, which they mainly learnt by rote and probably could not understand, Mrs. Trimmer wrote simple lesson books for them and abridgements of the Old and New Testaments, which were published for her by the S.P.C.K. Another writer of children's books at this time was Anna Barbauld, daughter of a Dissenting parson who kept a boarding school for boys. She received the same Classical education as her father's pupils and married a Dissenting minister who also opened a boarding school. Besides helping her husband run the school she wrote devotional pieces compiled from the psalms and *Hymns in Prose for Children*. Later, with her brother, she prepared *Evenings at Home for Children*, a collection of stories, articles and moral and improving dialogues, all of which were full of information and good principles.

Romantics like Charles Lamb were appalled at such stern offerings for the young. 'Knowledge must come to a child *in the shape of knowledge*,' he wrote to Coleridge, 'and his empty noddle must be turned with conceit of his own powers when he has learnt that a horse is an animal, and Billy is better than a horse, and such like; instead of that beautiful interest in wild tales which made the child a man while all the time he suspected himself to be no bigger than a child. . . .'

This outburst was prompted by an announcement by John Marshall that his children's books had been 'entirely divested of that prejudicial nonsense (to young minds), the Tales of Hobgoblins, Witches, Fairies, Love, Gallantry, etc.'

Lamb was infuriated. 'Damn them!' he said. 'I mean the cursed Barbauld crew, those blights and blasts of all that is human in man and child.'

Yet there was much good in them. Mrs. Barbauld's prose had a lyric quality. 'The sheep rest upon their soft fleeces, and their loud bleating is no more heard amongst the hills. Darkness is spread over the skies, and darkness is upon the ground, every eye is shut, and every hand is still.' Mrs. Trimmer, in *The History of the Robins*, pleaded for kindness to animals, at a time when they were mostly treated with the most callous brutality, as did that other popular writer, Thomas Day, in his *Sandford and Merton*, which, ludicrously didactic as it now seems, was widely read in its day.

During these last years of the eighteenth century and the early years of the nineteenth, Hannah More and her sisters were working amongst the poor children of Gloucestershire. Hannah, born in 1745, was the fourth of five daughters of a

Gloucestershire schoolmaster. When she was twelve years old she was sent to the boarding school which had just been opened by her eldest sister, and while she was still in her teens she was writing poems and plays. She came to London for a few years, joining the literary circle of the Blue Stockings, which included Dr. Johnson and David Garrick, and Garrick staged one of her plays at Drury Lane, but in early middle age she tired of the social round of London and retired to a cottage in Somerset to write. Her work included *Strictures on the Modern System of Female Education*, in which she deplored the amount of time given to music in most fashionable schools, leaving little time for solid acquisitions, adding: 'I love music, and were it only cultivated as an amusement should commend it.'

She made a great deal of money from her books and poems and after her elder sister had given up her school all five sisters lived together at Barley Wood, near Cheddar, where, encouraged by William Wilberforce, they devoted the rest of their lives to helping the poor of the surrounding villages and establishing Sunday schools and industrial schools for the children and their parents.

Cheddar was so remote that there were no schools at all in the thirteen surrounding parishes and no resident clergyman. The one incumbent, wrote Hannah, 'is intoxicated six times a week, and very frequently is prevented from preaching by two black eyes, honestly earned by fighting' and she found that in one of the parishes the only Bible available was used to prop up a flower pot.

With great courage the sisters made their preliminary survey. 'In Cheddar there lived more than two thousand people in the parish, almost all very poor; no gentry, a dozen wealthy farmers, hard, brutal and ignorant. . . . We went to every house in the place and found such a scene of the greatest ignorance and vice. . . . A great many refused to send their children unless we could pay them for it, and not a few refused because they were not sure of my intentions, being apprehensive that at the end of seven years. . . . I should acquire a power over them and send them beyond sea. I must have heard this myself in order to have believed that so much ignorance existed out of Africa,' reported Hannah.

Though farmers feared lest their ploughmen should become better educated than themselves and some revived the old bugbear of seditious teaching, the sisters developed their plans and rented a house, appointed 'the excellent Mrs. Baber' as schoolmistress, and opened their first Sunday School at Cheddar in 1789. Within ten years, they had established and were controlling a dozen schools in the neighbouring parishes—Sunday schools where the children learnt to read the Bible, industrial schools where on weekdays girls were taught sewing, knitting and spinning and 'such coarse work as may fit them for servants', and evening schools where adults learnt to read.

The sisters did not consider that writing was a necessary accomplishment for the poor, and in 1823, by which time poor children were generally being given a somewhat wider elementary education, Hannah, now an old woman, wrote to Wilberforce deploring the fact. 'Happily my own schools go on in the old-fashioned way,' she said. 'I taught the teachers their alphabet thirty years ago and they continue pious, faithful and soberminded.'

Chapter Ten

PRECEPT AND PRACTICE

UDLEY RYDER, BORN towards the end of the seventeenth century, was the son of a Nonconformist linen-draper of the City of London who, like so many prosperous City Dissenters at this time, had chosen to live in the rural retreat of Hackney. The Ryder home was close to the church and the Black and White House, which had become the home of the Vyners after the death of Mrs. Perwich: but it was now once more a young ladies' boarding school, kept by Mrs. Hutton.

Dudley had received his education in one of the Hackney Dissenting academies. As a Nonconformist, he was barred from Oxford or Cambridge, so he had been sent to Edinburgh, where he studied law, and later to Leyden, returning to England to read at the Middle Temple. In 1754, already knighted, he became Chief Justice in the Court of King's Bench and was made a Privy Counsellor, but in 1715, when he was only twenty-four, he was diffident and shy, doubting his ability as a lawyer and desperately anxious to acquire the polish of manners and conversation of the sophisticated men about town, whom he met every day in the Temple and surrounding coffee houses.

For men of intellect these were stirring times, not only in politics, but also in the realms of literature and science. The system of government by party had begun half a century earlier and by 1679 the names of Whig and Tory had been adopted, but it was only in 1694 that the party system was properly organized. The following year saw the liberation of the Press, with the end of the licensing laws, and the birth of English journalism, for within a few months, in addition to the outpourings of the political pamphleteers, notably Swift and Defoe, appeared a number of small newspapers, little more than news-sheets, but far wider in scope than the old news-letters.

Until this time there were no magazines, while books were far from being easily available. The only two important collections were at Oxford and Cambridge. Private libraries, even those of the clergy, were mostly small, and Macaulay said that 'an esquire passed among his neighbours for a great scholar if Hudibras and Baker's Chronicle, Tarleton's Jests, and the Seven Champions of Christendom lay in his hall window among the fishing-rods and fowling-pieces'.

Republication of books was very slow. The last folio of Shakespeare was not published until 1688 and the first octavo edition did not appear until 1709, nearly a century after his death.

In London there was no circulating library and people who could not afford to buy books had to content themselves with a brief glimpse at one of the booksellers' shops in St. Paul's Churchyard.

It was the work of Addison and Steele and the publication of the *Tatler* in 1709, the *Spectator* in 1711 and the *Guardian* in 1713 which promoted a love of English literature amongst the English middle classes and stimulated the publishers to extend their lists beyond the sermons and pamphlets, ballad broadsheets and occasional romances which had hitherto been their main concern. At the same time the seventeenth-century rationalism of Locke, with his treatises, *An Essay Concerning Human Understanding*, *Thoughts Concerning Education*, and *On the Conduct of Human Understanding*, was being logically developed into eighteenth-century concepts of the value of education, and the seventeenth-century discoveries of William Gilbert, William Harvey, William Hooke, Robert Boyle, John Napier and, above all, Isaac Newton, with his brilliant contribution towards the scientific understanding of the universe, were preparing the way for the work of Joseph Priestley, John Dalton, Humphry Davy, Michael Faraday, James Watt, Richard Arkwright and William Hargreaves later in the eighteenth century.

Dudley Ryder's diary, begun in 1715, not only reveals, with extraordinary intimacy, the thoughts of a young man during the Augustan Age of literature and the dawn of the Age of Reason, but sheds light on the education and way of life of some of the prosperous ladies of Hackney.

The first relevant entry is on August 21, 1715, when he was home for the weekend and came across his friend, young Mr. Hudson, who was feeling lonely. 'I told him he must find out a way to get some of the ladies at the school to visit him now and then, and I promised to assist him. . . . So we went together to the back gate and there they were.' And they behaved very much as girls do today. 'He after a little time of silence spoke to them . . . and they seemed very much inclined to have a correspondence with him, but they told him Mrs. Hutton was coming and desired he would go and come again half an hour afterwards. I came home and stayed longer at supper than half an hour, that when I came they were gone. However, Mr. Hudson called to them at their window and asked them to come down. They told him they could not but seemed very much inclined to it.'

The next day, Dudley walked with Mr. Hudson in his garden and discussed ways of getting to know the girls. He confessed to his diary that he was ashamed of himself, yet he could not keep away. A day or two later he was recording: 'As I came home went to the back door of the schoolhouse in the field and there found Mr. Hudson, Milbourn and Gould at the door. The girls were at first very merry at dancing but presently comes the schoolmistress and reproved them very severely, for their having held discourse with a man and entertaining them upon a wall. One of the Lancashire girls talked very smartly to her again. However, the mistress was very angry and took away from thence. . . .'

This seems to have put Dudley off chasing girls for good,

but they appear to have made quite a stir in Hackney amongst the less serious-minded young men.

The Black and White House had been built in 1570 but Sir Thomas Vyner added to it considerably, so it must have been quite a large establishment when Mrs. Hutton opened a school there. In the window of the large drawing room were the arms of James I, Charles I, the Princess Elizabeth and her husband, the Prince Palatine, and also of the Vyners. After Mrs. Hutton retired, the Ryder family moved into it, and when the historic old house was pulled down, in 1796, the material went to the building of the little houses in Bohemia Place.

Dudley's diary covers less than two years of his life but in it emerges the commercial attitude to marriage, which was as widespread amongst the prosperous middle clases as the landed gentry. On October 11, 1715, he called on his cousin Watkins, who had just finished another courtship, as the lady's mother thought her daughter too young to be married. The young lady had been recommended to him by some friends, whereupon he had written to the mother and asked leave to call on them to discuss terms.

Dudley's brother William was anxious to find a wife and he and Dudley discussed William's affair with Mrs. Walker, but Dudley considered that she had 'nothing at heart but a man with a good fortune and was determined to make the best of her market', so he suggested Mrs. Gifford, and William was taken with the idea. 'I promised to go to-morrow and see her father's will' wrote Dudley hard-headedly in his diary.

He seems to have been unlucky in his women-folk, for few of them appear to have had any but the most elementary education and were feather-brained and silly. 'Received a letter from Aunt Stevenson. She writes very carelessly and sometimes obscurely that I don't well know what she means,' he complained.

On Friday, November 11, he 'went to Mrs. Hudson with mother and sister to breakfast. The conversation turned entirely upon the manners, behaviour, way of living, clothes, dress, etc. of their neighbours and though at the same time they were blaming others for prying into the secrets of families and talking about others.'

Yet this was the day, as he recorded later in the entry for November 11, that the Jacobites of the 1715 rebellion reached as far south as Lancaster. Nobody seemed in the least concerned and the invasion was not even mentioned at the breakfast party.

On Twelfth Night he went to Aunt Bickley, to make merry with his cousin Ryder and Mrs. Lloyd, the young woman who lived with his aunt, and with whom at the time he was infatuated. After an afternoon and evening at cards, during which he managed to kiss Mrs. Lloyd 'very much', 'we at 11 o'clock sat down together to the fire and had a pretty brisk conversation in which I maintained the chief part with Mrs. Lloyd. Cousin Ryder sat silent all the while excepting a few observations and reflections which she would make upon (what) I said, taking notice of anything that looked like a satire upon the Sex. They are both of them unacquainted with the world and have seen little of polite conversation and are therefore suspicious and mighty jealous of their honour and very captious at anything that seems to reflect upon their sex.'

Later he decided that Mrs. Lloyd 'wants something of good breeding', no doubt because he felt she had been too permissive during the afternoon's junketings. 'Cousin Ryder has good sense, but has not the talent of conversation, says very little, reads much and delights mightily in books of gallantry, romances and tragedies but her great defect is in her ignorance of mankind.'

On May 3, 1716, he went to his brother's. 'There were two ladies. Drank some tea with him. He was extremely free with them in talk and action. He was merry and tumbled them about and did abundance of things that looked rude, but yet I find such a familiarity is extremely taking with the generality of women, though all the wit and humour lies in nothing but external familiar notions and actions.'

By now he had decided that 'young women should be kept at a proper distance and not allow themselves in too close and near a correspondence with our sex. Their beauty or other less qualifications grow familiar before matrimony and we grow tired and weary of them before they have gained the effect of them.'

Mrs. Lloyd must have scared the life out of him and by now he had taken a fancy to a Mrs. Marshall, but his cousin Billio told him that 'Mr. Baker, the dissenting parson, knows her very well and talked of her as one he was extremely intimate with and had kissed very often. This indeed was the most powerful antidote against my love I have yet met with.'

Old Mrs. Ryder seems to have been a great trial to them all. On Sunday, July 8, Dudley wrote: 'My mother grows extremely peevish and fretful, that she is angry at everything and my father can scarce say or do anything but she immediately snaps him up and takes it all in an ill sense.'

After dinner that day he went with his sister to see Aunt Billio. 'Mother went part of the way with us but she went in so scandalous a gown that I could not help taking notice of it to her and in such a manner as made her a little angry and she would not go.'

He was sorry afterwards that he had spoken harshly to her, but said that 'my mother is very much to blame in wearing clothes that make her friends blush for her and ashamed of being seen in her company.'

Fashions were certainly inclined to be outrageous at this time but Mrs. Ryder was a year or two out of date, for it was in July, 1713 that Addison wrote his article ON NAKED BOSOMS in the *Guardian*, begging that henceforth they be covered.

Mrs. Ryder probably never read Addison, but Dudley certainly did, and amongst all his criticisms of women, most of which were justified, the saddest is that concerning his brother Richard's wife. After being alone with her for an hour, he said: 'She is a person of very good natural parts and sense but not having been used to reading her knowledge is confined within the compass of a very few things, that it is very difficult to maintain a conversation with her for any time.'

And this complaint is repeated time and again by writers of

these years on women and their education. A few years later, William Law was saying much the same thing. In 1729 he published his little book *A Serious Call to a Devout and Holy Life*, in which one chapter is devoted to a criticism of the lack of proper education for girls. 'The right education of this *sex* is of the utmost importance to human life,' he says. 'There is nothing that is more desirable for the common good of all the world. For though *women* can't carry on the *trade* and *business* of the world, yet as they are *mothers*, and *mistresses* of families that have for some time the care of the education of their children of both sorts, they are entrusted with that which is of the greatest consequence to human life. For this reason, *good* or *bad* women are likely to do as much good or harm in the world, as good or bad men in the greater business of life.'

He complains that the majority of middle-class women lacked intelligent conversation. Having been treated like idiots for generations, they tended to have become idiots. They were bred up to the marriage market and to make themselves as physically attractive as possible, and there, for most of them, the rigorous part of their training ended. All the rest was the acquisition of accomplishments.

William Law felt that it was all a terrible waste of good potential material, for he thought that, generally speaking, there is 'a finer sense, a clearer mind, a readier approbation, and gentler disposition in that sex, than in any other.' And he blames it mainly on a society which seemed to prefer its women to be 'poor and gaudy spectacles of the greatest vanity', so many 'painted idols, that are to allure and gratify men's passions', and not on the nature of women themselves.

He illustrates his points with an account of his imaginary Matilda, typical of many a mother of the time, and her three daughters. When the eldest girl ventured to say that 'she thought it was better to cover the neck, than to go so far naked as the modern dress requires', she was reduced to tears by her mother's angry reprimand. Matilda half-starved the girls to keep them slim and regarded the appearance of a pimple as a mortal sin. If they looked bright and healthy, she took steps to make them assume the pale and languid look, which was considered so much more feminine and alluring, ready to weep and swoon at the least provocation and hardly able to 'bear the weight of their best clothes'.

The eldest girl went into a fashionable decline and died in her twentieth year, and 'when her body was open'd, it appear'd that her *ribs* had grown into her liver, and that her other *entrails* were much hurt, by being crush'd together with her *stays*, which her mother had order'd to be twitch'd so strait, that it often brought tears into her eyes, whilst the maid was dressing her'.

The youngest girl ran off with a handsome gambler and we are never told what happened in the end to her and the second sister, but it is safe to assume that they came to no good.

Law's ideal woman is Eusebia, the pious widow and her five daughters, whom she brings up to a pretty bleak and negative existence, training them 'to all kinds of labour that are proper for women, as sewing, knitting, spinning, and all other parts of housewifery: not for their *amusement*, but that they may be serviceable to themselves and others, and be saved from those temptations which attend an idle life'.

Academic education did not enter into this discourse. The girls are to be brought up to behave modestly, 'look for nothing, claim nothing, resent nothing . . . go through all the actions and accidents of life calmly and quietly, as in the presence of God, neither seeking vain applause nor resenting neglects or affronts, but doing and receiving every thing in the meek and lowly spirit of our Lord and Saviour Jesus Christ.'

If they can manage all this, those who marry will make their husbands happy, while those who were 'not inclin'd, or could not dispose of themselves well in marriage would know to how live to great and excellent ends in a state of virginity'.

There were many educational theorists during the eighteenth century, the one who probably made the most impact being the French philosopher Rousseau. He advocated a closer study of the child by the teacher. He disliked the established order of things and maintained that 'every thing is good as it comes from the hands of the Almighty, every thing degenerates in the hands of man'. He was all for the simple life of the noble savage, though presumably without the noble savage's less attractive habits. In urging that children's upbringing should be simpler, he was a pioneer who must be applauded, but he suggested a personal freedom in all things which, taken to its logical conclusion, could lead only to anarchy.

And what about the girls? He had nothing for them at all. He treated his wife with callous indifference and abandoned their five children to a foundling hospital. 'Girls should avoid abstract studies and works of genius,' he said impertinently, and 'should be early accustomed to restraint . . . they must be trained to bear the yoke from the first.' 'Cunning is the natural gift of woman . . . she should early learn to submit to injustice and to suffer the wrongs inflicted on her by her husband without complaint.'

The only constructive thing he has to say to girls is that they should avoid restricting clothes, as 'it is not a pleasant thing to see a woman cut in two like a wasp', but this piece of advice neither his fellow countrywomen nor the English, who followed French fashion closely, were to heed for another three or four decades, when, after the French Revolution, they took to the flimsy, loose muslin dresses introduced by the Merveilleuses during the early years of the Directory. In France, it was Napoleon who put an end to this fashion for semi-nakedness, and in England it was the exceptionally cold winter of 1799 that made women think again and put themselves into scarves and shawls: and within a few years they were back to tight stays and long drawers, to increasing layers of petticoats, mittens and muffs and enveloping poke bonnets.

The Court of George III did little to stimulate an interest in the provision of education for girls. The King's father, Frederick Prince of Wales, had married Augusta of Saxe-Gotha when she was seventeen. Against the wishes of George II, who disliked both Augusta and his own son, her governess Madame Rixlieven, came to England to be with her for a time, but the King soon insisted on her being sent home again. After the birth of their first child and the bitter quarrel concerning the place of its birth the Prince and Princess of Wales were ignominiously turned out of St. James's Palace, but the Prince was very popular with the people and might have done them good service if he had lived to be King, for he was a cultured man and in contrast to his father, who never read a book and did not care for 'bainting and boetry', a voracious reader and a patron of the arts.

In the family circle and amongst close friends he spoke French but he loved the English language and English literature and shared with the Princess a love of music, playing the cello in the village orchestra at Cliveden, their country home. He was a generous patron of English and French painters and became a discriminating collector. He was also interested in theology and philosophy, and although he attended the Anglican Church regularly he grew weary of the lack of inspiration in the clergy of the middle years of the eighteenth century, preferring the Methodists to the Anglican bishops: and he sometimes went secretly to hear John Whitfield preach.

Deploring 'a great depravity of morals diffused throughout the country', he was a great family man and took infinite delight in the careful upbringing of his children. At Cliveden, where there was an open-air theatre, he arranged private theatricals for them and they were coached by James Quin, the foremost actor of the day before the advent of David Garrick. They enjoyed concerts, ballets and masquerades and sometimes the Prince himself conducted an orchestra on the long terrace. They played cricket and baseball together, but the Prince also took immense care with their education, the boys having tutors under the control of Lord North, and the girls their governesses. The princes had a strict régime mapped out for them, from 7 o'clock in the morning, when they rose, until bedtime between 9 and 10 p.m., but three times a week, at half past four, the French dancing-master attended, to teach both the Princes and Princesses dancing and deportment, and on Sundays, after prayers at 9.30, it was a rule that 'the eldest Princes and the two eldest Princesses, are to go to Prince

George's apartments, to be instructed by Dr. Ayscough in the Principles of Religion till 11 o'clock'.

There were nine children, five boys and four girls, though Prince Frederick died before the last daughter was born. Augusta, the eldest of the family, was very intelligent and her father's close companion. Prince George, the future George III, was serious minded and an intelligent talker, but inclined to be mentally lazy, and he was very slow in learning to read. Yet his father gave him every encouragement. 'You can't imagine how happy you made me yesterday,' he wrote to him, on one occasion, in an undated letter. 'Any mark of a sincere, or a sensible feeling heart gives me much more joy than any sign of wit or improvement in your learning which I daresay will come along in time. . . .'

However, in 1751 'poor Fred' fell ill and died, leaving George to become Prince of Wales when he was only twelve. The Whigs at once advised the King to change the young prince's tutors. Lord Harcourt and Dr. Hayter were appointed to take charge. Horace Walpole said that Harcourt was 'a civil, sheepish peer' who was 'in need of a governor himself' and Princess Augusta said of Hayter that he was 'a mighty learned man, but he did not seem very proper to convey knowledge to children'. He lacked that 'clearness that she thought necessary'. Their incompetence led to endless arguments, quarrels, enquiries, dismissals and new appointments, but during these years neither the Prince nor his brothers learned very much, and by the time the Prince of Wales was twenty he admitted to Lord Bute that 'through the negligence, if not wickedness' of those who should have been responsible for his education he had not acquired the degree of knowledge and experience that might have been expected of a young man of his age. By the following year George II was dead and he had succeeded as George III, shortly afterwards being married, by the choice of his mother and Lord Bute, to the worthy but dull seventeen-year-old Charlotte of Mecklenburg, although he was deeply in love with Lady Sarah Lennox.

The Court was conducted with more seemliness than during

the reigns of the first two Georges, but Queen Charlotte was so occupied with the upbringing of her thirteen surviving children that it was dreary, domestic and very frugal. The seven princes left the family circle for their separate establishments as soon as they could get permission from their reluctant father and the necessary funds. Prince George's love affairs, as Prince of Wales, as Prince Regent, and as George IV, have been amply documented. The Duke of York brought disgrace on himself and was obliged to retire temporarily from his office of Commander-in-Chief of the army, after his liaison with the disreputable Mary Anne Clarke and the shady business of selling commissions, in which she had involved herself: and later he made a childless marriage. The details of the private life of the Duke of Cumberland were said to be so scandalous that they could be only whispered in polite society, though they were probably grossly exaggerated. The Duke of Clarence lived in 'blameless irregularity' with Mrs. Jordan and their ten illegitimate Fitzclarences and the Duke of Kent lived for twenty-seven years with Madame St. Laurent, but after the Princess Charlotte died in childbirth and the Dukes took a step nearer to the succession, both hurriedly shed their partners, in order to make orthodox marriages to suitable German princesses.

The six daughters of George III were strictly brought up with governesses and as they grew older they were kept securely within their parents' Court, spending their time in reading, needlework, card games and conversation. They met no one outside the Court circle and neither the King nor the Queen could bear the thought of any of them leaving to be married. The King was said to have burst into tears every time the subject was mentioned, and at one time, when the behaviour of the three eldest princes seemed particularly outrageous, the girls were not even allowed to write to them, though the brothers and sisters were devoted to each other all their lives.

In 1786, when Princess Elizabeth, the third daughter and the artist of the family, was sixteen, she retired to a cottage on Kew Green for a time, suffering from an undiagnosed illness, which resulted in the secret birth of a daughter. The father was believed to have been George Ramus, one of the King's pages. She may have been married to him, but after she returned to the family circle she never saw him or her daughter again, and the King apparently knew nothing about the affair.

The Princess Royal was the unhappiest of the princesses, having always been repressed and brow-beaten by her mother: and not until she was thirty was a marriage arranged for her with Prince Frederick of Württemberg. Even then there was doubt of its legality, for the fate of his first wife, a sister of the unfortunate Caroline, Princess of Wales, was not entirely certain. After running away with her lover, she had given birth to an illegitimate daughter. Prince Frederick brought her back and clapped her into gaol, and there she was said to have died, but there were strong rumours that she had escaped and was living in hiding with her Russian lover.

Princess Augusta had a long love affair with one of the royal equerries, Major General Sir Brent Spencer, and throughout all his long absences abroad on foreign service they remained devoted, but he died in 1828, at the age of sixty-eight, by which time Princess Augusta was sixty and still unmarried.

Princess Amelia, the youngest of the sisters, had for years been desperately in love with another equerry, who was twenty-seven years older and apparently rather half-hearted about the romance, but she died of tuberculosis, when she was only twenty-seven.

Princess Sophia had all her life had a passion for yet another equerry, General Thomas Garth, described by Greville as a 'hideous old Devil old enough to be her father', and in her early twenties she retired from Court to give birth to his son, again without the King's knowledge. After that, her ardour seemed to wane. The General remained at Court until his death in 1829 and she occasionally saw her son, until, after his father's death, he tried to blackmail the royal family into giving him an annuity in exchange for incriminating evidence of his parenthood. As there was little secrecy by then about the affair, his attempt failed and he disappeared, leaving Sophie to a lonely old age of spinsterhood and blindness.

At forty, Princess Mary, the family beauty, married her cousin, the Duke of Gloucester, to whom she had been engaged for years, but after a short time he became aggressively jealous of her devotion to her parents, both of whom were mortally sick by now, and he is said to have ill-treated her.

It was still a man's world and against this Court background it is not surprising that the position of women remained subservient and that there was no change in the provision of their education beyond equipping them for the marriage market, yet there were one or two boarding schools at this time which were outstandingly better than the general run of such establishments.

The More sisters' school at Bristol was particularly successful and here, in the early 1760s, arrived the beautiful little Mary Darby, who later was to achieve fame as Perdita Robinson. She was born in Bristol in 1758. Her parents were both educated and she tells us, in her memoirs, that her grandmother had been a keen botanist and had prepared medicines for the maladies of the peasantry. Before she was seven, Mary had been taught to read. She could recite several long poems and had already had two years teaching with various masters, including a music master, after her father had given her one of 'Kirkman's finest harpsichords'.

She was happy at Martha More's school and her father was prosperous, but this state of contentment was not to last. Her father was asked to establish a whale fishery off the coast of Labrador and 'to civilize the Esquimaux', who, it was optimistically forecast, would ultimately be able to run the fishery for the benefit of the company: and he departed for two years. By this time the family had moved into a larger and more elegant house and Mary was hopelessly spoiled. She no longer boarded at the school but lived at home, in the greatest luxury, with a 'bed of crimson damask' and dresses of finest cambric. 'To sing, to play a lesson on the harpsichord, to recite an elegy, and to make doggerel verses, made the extent of my occupations', she said.

But then things began to go wrong. The letters from America grew fewer and then stopped. Father had taken a mistress. And worse still, the fishery business had failed and he had fallen badly into debt. He gave a bill of sale on the Bristol home and Mrs. Darby and the children were turned out.

Eventually they had a letter from Mr. Darby, summoning them to London, where he had recently arrived. Mary was now nearly ten years old and her brother a year or so younger. Their father said he had decided to put the children to school and that he would pay for their mother to live in respectable lodgings close by.

Thus Mary ended up at a school in Chelsea—a very different establishment from Martha More's. 'The mistress of this seminary,' wrote Mary later, 'was perhaps one of the most extraordinary women that ever graced, or disgraced society; her name was Meribah Lorrington. She was the most extensively accomplished female that I ever remember to have met with; her mental powers were no less capable of cultivation than superiorly cultivated. Her father . . . had been the master of an academy at Earl's Court . . . and early after his marriage, losing his wife, he resolved on giving his daughter a masculine education. Meribah was early instructed in all the modern accomplishments, as well as in classical knowledge. She was mistress of the Latin, French and Italian languages; she was said to be a perfect arithmetician, and possessed the art of painting on silk to a degree of exquisite perfection.'

Unfortunately, she drank.

'All that I ever learned I acquired from this extraordinary woman. In those hours when her senses were not intoxicated, she would delight in the task of instructing me. She had only five or six pupils, and it was my lot to be her particular favourite. She always, out of school, called me her little friend, and made no scruple of conversing with me (sometimes half the night; for I slept in her chamber) on domestic and confidential affairs. She confessed she drank because of loneliness and grief for her dear husband.'

Mary stayed at the Chelsea school for a year or more, while her mother boarded with a clergyman's family close by. She worked hard and acquired a taste for books and literature which never left her. She and Mrs. Lorrington read to each other after school hours and Mary wrote more poetry. But then, because of 'pecuniary derangements', Mrs. Lorrington had to give up the school.

The manners of Mrs. Lorrington's father, said Mary, were 'singularly disgusting, as was his appearance; for he wore a silvery beard which reached his breast; and a kind of Persian robe which gave the external appearance of a necromancer. . . . He was one of the Anabaptist persuasion, and so stern in his conversation that the young pupils were exposed to perpetual terror. . . . Added to these circumstances, the failing of his daughter became so evident, that even during school hours she was frequently in a state of confirmed intoxication. These events conspired to break up the establishment.'

Not long afterwards, poor Meribah died of drink in the Chelsea workhouse.

Mary was sent to Mrs. Leigh's Boarding School at Battersea, which was cheerful and comfortable, but Mr. Darby was now back in America and neither the school fees nor the money to support his wife arrived, so Mary, now nearly fourteen, was taken away. Her mother, faced with the problem of supporting herself and her children, took the only course open to a respectable woman. She rented a house in Little Chelsea, furnished it for a young ladies' boarding school, engaged some teachers and announced herself in business. Before long they had ten or twelve pupils and in a modest way were prospering. Mary taught English and also looked after the girls' clothes and superintended their dressing and undressing by the servants, as well as reading to them 'sacred and moral lessons on saints' days and Sunday evenings'.

Then, only eight months later, Mr. Darby turned up again and with maddening lack of logic berated his wife 'beyond the bounds of reason' for tarnishing his name by daring to open a school, a public mode of revealing to the world her unprotected situation which could only serve to damage his conjugal reputation.

Under his 'positive command' she had to give up the school and return to London, where she took lodgings in Marylebone, while father set himself up in Green Street, Grosvenor Square, with his mistress. Mary was put to school at Oxford House, Marylebone, and it was here that she began to show her outstanding dramatic gifts and develop her beautiful speaking voice.

Mr. Darby departed yet again for America, with a new Labrador scheme, bidding his wife farewell with the words: 'Take care that no dishonour falls upon my daughter. If she is not safe at my return I will annihilate you.'

The rest of Mary's story is an example of the desperate plight into which women could be driven by the conventions of the times. Her father was in money troubles again and his allowance variable and uncertain. The dancing master at Oxford House was also ballet master at Covent Garden and introduced her to David Garrick, with a view to her going on the stage. Garrick saw Mary's possibilities and she and her mother moved to Chancery Lane, where Garrick began to coach her, but Mrs. Darby was worried about allowing her to adopt a profession which was barely respectable and mortally afraid of her husband's threat. Mary was beautiful, still only fifteen, and had many admirers. Before she took the irrevocable first step on to the stage, her mother persuaded her to accept the proposal of Mr. Robinson, who seemed a young man of considerable fortune and many rich friends, and was articled to a lawyer. Mrs. Darby must have been as green and inexperienced as her daughter, for when Robinson insisted that the marriage should be in secret, because his father might be angry at his marrying before he had completed his legal training, she agreed. It was enough to see the wedding ring on Mary's finger, the badge of respectability which would satisfy her father.

The marriage was a disaster. Robinson proved to be the illegitimate son of a wealthy merchant who had given him a start in life but refused any more help when he ran into debt. He neglected Mary and squandered what was left of his money. While they were on the run from their debtors, their daughter was born, and when Robinson was caught, arrested and taken to lodgings at the King's Bench prison, Mary and the baby went with him. For the next nine months they remained there, Mary doing all the work of cooking and cleaning their quarters, and when Robinson managed to get his release they had practically no money and Mary tried to support them all by writing. 'Alas, how little did I know either the fatigue or the hazard of mental occupation,' she said. 'I feel in every fibre of my brain the fatal conviction that it is *destroying labour*.'

One day she chanced to run into Brereton, an old Drury Lane friend, who suggested that she should consider the stage again. Garrick had retired by now and Sheridan had just taken over the management, but he was willing to give her a chance. Again Garrick coached her and in 1776, still only eighteen years old, she made her début as Juliet to Brereton's Romeo. She was an instant success and for the next year or two she enjoyed the gay and fashionable life, moving into a house in Covent Garden, but still supporting her husband, who by now was quite indifferent to her, amusing himself in his own way, with gamblers, prostitutes and all the drunken riff-raff of the town. At last, in 1779, when she was twenty-one, Mary was commanded to perform before the King and Queen and other members of the royal family, including the Prince of Wales, who by now was seventeen. The play was *The Winter's Tale*, and as Perdita she stole the heart of the young Prince. In great secret, and using the Earl of Essex as his messenger, he wooed Perdita, and at length, after several clandestine meetings at Kew, she succumbed. The Prince set her up in a house in Cork Street and she left the stage. When he was eighteen, he was granted a separate establishment in a wing of Buckingham Palace and they were constantly seen together, Perdita, magnificently dressed, riding in a coach which had cost the Prince nine hundred guineas.

The idyll lasted for little more than two years. When the

Prince came of age, he was granted an income of £63,000 a year and his debts, to the tune of £30,000, were settled for him: and as he was about to take up his abode in Carlton House he abruptly dropped Perdita for a new love.

Perdita herself was heavily in debt to tradespeople by now and in the end the Prince's friend, Charles James Fox, arranged an annuity of £500 for Perdita and she departed to France for a time, but eventually, with her daughter and her mother, she settled in a little house in St. James's Place. When she was only twenty-six she became an invalid, after a severe attack of rheumatic fever, but she was able to supplement her income by writing of all kinds—novels, plays, poems and articles. She achieved a modest success but in 1794 was complaining that 'my mental labours have failed through the dishonest conduct of my publishers. My works have sold handsomely, but the profits have been theirs.'

She was not the first woman writer to suffer that trial. Hannah Woolley had had similar trouble nearly a century earlier. But Perdita battled on. In 1800 she undertook to write a series of satirical odes for the *Morning Post*, taking the name of Tabitha Bramble, but her health was failing fast, and she died before they were completed.

Chapter Eleven

MORE EIGHTEENTH-CENTURY
BOARDING SCHOOLS

THROUGHOUT THE EIGHTEENTH century dozens of small boarding schools for 'young ladies' were opened throughout the country and there was a particularly large crop in London and the suburbs. As early as 1711 an advertisement appeared in the *Spectator*, announcing that 'Near the Windmill in Hampstead is a good Boarding School; where young Gentlewomen may be boarded and taught English, French, Dancing, Musick and all sorts of Needlework.'

The curriculum was nearly always the same. It was the conditions which varied—from the spartan and squalid to the comfortable and even luxurious.

Mrs. Montagu, writing to her sister in 1773 said: 'I am glad you intend to send my eldest neice [sic] to a boarding-school. What girls learn at these schools is trifling, but they unlearn what would be of great disservice—a provincial dialect, which is extremely ungenteel, and other tricks that they learn in the nursery. The carriage of the person, which is of great importance, is well attended to, and dancing is well taught. As for the French language, I do not think it is necessary, unless for persons in very high life. It is rarely much cultivated at schools. I believe all the boarding-schools are much on the same plan, so that you may place the young lady wherever there is a good air and a good dancing-master.'

On another occasion she wrote: 'called on my pretty neice at Chelsea, who I had the pleasure of finding in perfect health, with a little addition of embonpoint extremely becoming. . . .

I found fault with her stays, which lift up her shoulders; and they say they had your leave to get others, but I could not understand why they had neglected to do so. I was pleased to find my neice perfectly clean and neat, tho' I called on ye Saturday, which is usually the eve of cleanliness. I remember at Mrs. Robartes', at Kensington, the girls used to be so dirty, sometimes one could not salute them.'

Susan Sibbald went to a school at Bath—Belvedere House—which was kept by the three Misses Lee. This seems to have been one of the better kind. Although from the front it looked shut and confined, with the Venetian blinds perpetually drawn, at the back, where the girls spent most of their time, there was a 'wide and splendid view'. The girls' day was carefully mapped for them and in addition to the inevitable needlework and dancing, they learned a little French and geography. They slept several girls to a room but they had separate beds and a mistress slept with them. 'There was no want of good living at Belvedere House,' she says in her memoir 'generally roast beef on Mondays; on Tuesdays and Fridays roast shoulders of mutton, a round of beef on Wednesdays; Thursdays boiled legs of mutton, and stewed beef and pickled walnuts on Saturdays. Then two days in the week we had "choke dogs", dumplings with currents [sic] in them, other days rice or other puddings; but after the meat not before, as was the case in some schools. A few of the girls remained a few minutes after the others had gone up to the schoolroom and had a glass of port wine each, for which an extra charge was made.'

But the fascinating thing about these memoirs is the description of the mealtimes, which have the flavour of the medieval nunnery. The girls had to eat in silence. 'If a young lady wished to be helped a second time, she leant forward and put her right elbow on the table. If little meat and more vegetables were desired, the hand was extended, the thumb and forefinger meeting, and on the plate being brought, the teacher could point out who it was for.'

A fashionable London boarding school was in Queen Square, Bloomsbury, founded by Mrs. Dennis. Mrs. Thrale was sent here for a time, as a child in the 1750s, and refers to it as the Great School in Queen Square, where Mrs. Dennis and her brother, the Admiral Sir Peter Dennis, said 'I was qualified, at eight years old, for teacher rather than learner; and he actually did instruct me in the rudiments of navigation, as the globes were already familiar to me.'

In 1761 Fanny Burney and her younger sister Susannah were sent there for a short time, during their mother's last illness, but when Mrs. Burney died they were brought home again to Poland Street, and although Susannah and the eldest sister were later sent to school in Paris, for Fanny the brief spell at Queen Square was the only school she ever knew.

Mrs. Thrale's daughter, Cecilia, was educated there and Boswell's daughter Veronica, for he called her 'Our Queen Square daughter'. Another pupil was Esther Milner, who became the wife of Thomas Day, the eccentric author of *Sandford and Merton* and several other works. A few years earlier, being a fervent disciple of Rousseau, he had chosen two girls, a twelve-year-old, flaxen-haired orphan from a charity school at Shrewsbury, whom he named Sabrina, and Lucretia, a brunette from the Foundling Hospital in London, and taken them both to France, where he planned to discover and discipline their characters, strictly on the lines advocated by Rousseau, and marry the one whom he decided had shaped the better. But he very soon ran into trouble. The girls quarrelled and proved altogether too much for him. Then they both took smallpox and he had to nurse them. When they recovered, he was only too thankful to bring them back to London. Lucretia, altogether intractable, he apprenticed to a milliner on Ludgate Hill. Sabrina he reserved for further experiments, but she tried Thomas's patience beyond endurance, for she could not conquer certain 'weaknesses'. One can hardly blame her. For example, she flinched when he dropped melted sealing-wax on her arm. She started and screamed when he fired pistols at her garments, though he had assured her they were not loaded. When he told her 'secrets' she divulged them to the servants. The last straw was when she outraged his principles by 'wearing thin sleeves for ornaments'. He packed her off to boarding school for three years, with a £50 a year allowance, and then, with a dowry of £500, married her off to a barrister.

After that he moved to the literary circle at Lichfield and proposed first to Honora Sneyd and, when she rejected him, to her sister Elizabeth. Elizabeth told him to go back to France for a time and acquire some French graces and manners, but when he returned to display them to her she just laughed. However, with Esther Milner, whom he married when he was thirty, he had eleven happy years, for they had much in common, Esther having a literary bent. She was writing essays and poems while still a schoolgirl in Queen Square, and when Day's life was cut short in 1789, by a fall from a horse, she was so heart-broken that only two years later she died herself.

There seems to have been a strong literary tradition at the school in Queen Square, for the poems of another pupil inspired David Mallet to write: *The Discovery; Upon Reading some Verses by a Young Lady at a Boarding School*, in which Apollo's messenger

> Looked up at Queen's Square the north-east side
> A blooming creature there he found
> With pen and ink and books around,
> Alone and writing by a taper. . . .

In 1786 Sophie v. La Roche, that indefatigable German sightseer, obtained permission to visit the school, during her stay in London. By this time it was run by four spinster sisters called Stevenson and occupied Numbers 24 and 25 in the square. There were 220 pupils and the fees were more than a hundred guineas a year. 'A liveried attendant led us from the pretty hall into the visitors' room where the damask draperies, fine lustres fitted to the wall, mirrors and two sofas, in every way resembled the interior of a wealthy home,' wrote Sophie. Then she was taken to watch a dancing lesson. The girls ranged in age from six to sixteen, and as Sophie entered they all rose and bowed. They were dressed in white, with red, blue, green or violet girdles and neat white caps. And the dancing master was teaching minuets and folk dancing to six couples at a time, while the rest of the school watched.

Yet with all the expensive trappings removed, basically the teaching and training of the school seems to have offered nothing new. Sophie compared it with Madame de Maintenon's St. Cyr and felt that, on the whole, the French girls were livelier and more easily amused than the English girls, 'who are inclined to pensiveness and more enduring passion'.

A few years later, during the 1790s, this school was maintaining its prestige and was known as the Young Ladies Eton. One of its pupils was the mother of Frances Power Cobbe, and in her autobiography Frances recalls much that her mother had told her about it. The mistress by this time was Mrs. Devis, a highly intelligent woman who published for her pupils an English grammar and also a geography textbook. The girls were taught history, which included some of Mrs. Trimmer's 'Sacred History', and they learnt to speak French with a very good accent, as well as to read it, and to play on the harpsichord. But above all they were trained in manners and decorum—how to enter and leave a room, how to sit and how to rise. In the back of the school building a coach was permanently kept, so that the girls could practice ascending and descending from it 'with calmness and grace and without any unnecessary display of ankles'.

They also practised the art of greeting acquaintances in the street and the drawing room, of paying and receiving visits and writing letters of compliment and thanks.

Every girl was dressed in the full fashion of the late eighteenth century and her mother, like all her school fellows, wore hair powder and rouge when she entered the school at fifteen, the rouge costing five guineas a pot. And Frances Power Cobbe, writing in 1894, deplores the demeanour of the 'abrupt speaking, courtesy-neglecting, slouching, slangy young damsel who may now carry off the glories of a University degree' compared with the grace of the women of her mother's generation.

After Mrs. Devis died the school became less fashionable and with diminishing numbers occupied only one house again, but it did not close until the 1850s. Then the elegant Queen Anne and even earlier houses, from numbers 22 to 28 in the north-eastern corner of the square, were demolished for the building of the National Hospital, and the mahogany doors and stair-cases, marble chimney pieces and painted ceilings were sold as scrap.

Returning to Sophie v. La Roche, visiting London in 1786, she went to see Christ's Hospital, but the girls had moved to Hertford by this time. Educationally all was well at Hertford. After the governors' visit in 1783 they had made a very satisfac-tory report on the reading, writing, ciphering and general appearance and behaviour of the girls. The only trouble was that there was so little interest in giving impoverished girls the kind of education that the school offered, since it was of so little material benefit to them at this time, that they were having difficulty in filling the school. The rule that girls had to be daughters of freemen of the City of London had to be relaxed and places offered to other London girls. Even so, presentations were often returned to the governors unused, and it was not until the next century that the status of the school was raised to its present high standard and the numbers enlarged.

Nevertheless, it was during the 1780s that the Freemasons established their school in London—the Royal Freemasons' School for Female Children—for the maintenance and educa-tion of the orphans and daughters of poor Freemasons. The first building, a handsome Georgian house, went up in 1788 in Elizabeth Place, off the Westminster Bridge Road, but when this part of London was rebuilt, during the mid-nineteenth century, a new school, designed by Philip Hardwicke, was opened in 1852, in St. John's Hill, Wandsworth Common, a red brick, Gothic building, with an impressive central clock tower.

From Christ's Hospital Sophie went to look at the Foundling Hospital, which by now had been established for nearly half a century. 'The girls were playing all kinds of games on one side of the large lawns, the boys on the other; they looked bright and attractive and very healthy,' wrote Sophie. 'The elder girls had laid the tables in very pretty, spacious dining-rooms; everything was white and spotless; other girls did the waiting; the meal only consisted of one course of mutton boiled with barley, but it was so well prepared, and served in such quantities, that with their good bread and mug of beer besides, the children could not want anything better.'

'We were also shown over the bedrooms, where the beds were so cleanly, the air so pure and everything looked so nice, that I fancied they were symbols of the nation's best characteristics.'

Sophie was inclined to see everything in the best possible light and was nothing if not overwhelmingly polite, but she was an honest observer and it seems that the Foundling children were in better shape and a good deal cleaner than the young ladies at Mrs. Robartes' school at Kensington.

Mrs. Sherwood, whose best remembered book today is *The Fairchild Family*, was born in 1775, the same year as Jane Austen, at Stanford in Worcestershire. She was the daughter of the Rev. Dr. George Butt, who in 1784 was appointed one of the chaplains to George III, and she was brought up in a literary circle, with a house full of books. Mary was always very close to her brother Marten and her younger sister Lucy, but her mother Martha Butt, was difficult, having a grievance and 'mental humiliation' which stayed with her all her married life. Dr. Butt had been very much in love with the beautiful Mary Woodhouse, who had died young. The motherless Martha, Mary Woodhouse's cousin and companion, was plain, dumpy and pock-marked, but with a considerable fortune, and her father had forced her into a marriage with George Butt, who was not unappreciative of her handsome dowry.

Though Mary was indulged by her father, her mother brought her up very strictly. Her food was of the plainest, a great deal of it being dry bread and cold milk. Like Susan Sibbald, when she did her lessons she had to stand in stocks, wearing an iron collar round her neck and a back board strapped to her shoulders. At first Dr. Butt taught his son

Latin, but Mrs. Butt, feeling that her husband was not giving enough time to the boy's education, learnt the language herself and taught both Marten and Mary.

The children's first reading was the usual *Robinson Crusoe*, Sarah Fielding's *Little Female Academy*, in which even the fairy stories had a high moral tone, and *Aesop's Fables*, but Mary began making up stories of her own by the time she was six, and even before she could write. She used to follow her mother round the house and beg her to write them down for her, which Mrs. Butt very sensibly did: and before long Mary was reading all the books in her father's library.

In 1788 the family moved to Kidderminster. Marten was sent to Mr. Valpy's School at Reading, but the girls, apart from going once a fortnight to the Assembly Rooms for dancing lessons, were still taught at home by their parents. Mrs. Butt disliked Kidderminster and its society and became something of a recluse, so that Mary and Lucy, always very fond of each other, spent hours together, inventing stories and trying their hands at poems and plays. But when Mary was seventeen she was sent to the Abbey School at Reading.

The old abbey, with its beautiful garden and ruined church had been used as a girls' school for many years. It was run by Mde Latournelle, an Englishwoman who had married a Frenchman, and who was now helped by a much younger woman, Madame St. Quintin, an old pupil of the school who had been left destitute and returned as a teacher. Later she was married to M. St. Quintin, a French emigré, who had fled to England during the Revolution, had arrived in Reading to stay with Dr. Valpy, and had become a teacher both in Dr. Valpy's school and at the Abbey.

Mary arrived at the school rather late on a Sunday evening. Term had not yet begun and M. and Mme St. Quintin were still in London, but Mme Latournelle welcomed her and made her sit down by the fire to warm herself before going to bed. She was a woman of the old school, said Mary, hardly under seventy, and by this time acting mainly as housekeeper, but she was very active, although she had a cork leg. She received

Mary in the wainscotted parlour, 'the wainscot a little tarnished, while the room was hung around with chenille pieces
representing tombs and weeping willows. A screen in cloth-
work stood in a corner, and there were several miniatures over
the lofty mantelpiece.'

There were about sixty boarders at the school and Mary slept
in a large room with five other girls, but each had a bed to
herself, and as the daughter of a distinguished father she was
privileged to be a parlour boarder, which meant that she had
her meals with the staff in the parlour.

She was called early the next morning, before it was light,
and when she reached the parlour she found Mde Latournelle
making tea by firelight and three teachers sitting on three
chairs by the fire. From her first glance at these ladies, Mary
made up her mind that she would learn nothing from them.

'The first was a little simpering Englishwoman, very like a
second-rate milliner of those days; she taught spelling and
needlework. The second was a dashing, slovenly, rather handsome French girl, who ran away with some low man a few
months afterwards. The third a Swiss, and though plain and
marked with the small-pox, had some good in her.'

But Mary enjoyed her breakfast, for never before had she
been allowed to eat toast and butter, nor had her mother ever
let her sit close to a fire. When M. and Mme St. Quintin
arrived, she was pleased with Madame but scared of Monsieur
and his foreign ways, until after their first interview; and when
she told him she knew Latin he took her into his own class and
either he or his young assistant, M. Malrone, taught her every
day.

Discipline was very light for the older girls of the senior
class and after their morning lessons in M. St. Quintin's study
they had the rest of the day to themselves, while supper in the
parlour was usually a gay affair, with several guests. Many of
them were French refugees and the conversation was mainly in
French, during which they chattered of politics and literature
and exchanged all the gossip from Paris and London.

After the first summer holidays, which Mary spent with Mrs.

Valpy on the other side of the green, she found that two new masters had arrived at the school, Monsieur Pictet, who had been a secretary to Catherine of Russia, and his son. The father gave Mary special teaching in French, which she enjoyed, and lessons in philosophy and metaphysics which bored her but which she endured because she liked the old man.

After the Christmas holidays, Lucy joined her at the Abbey School for the last year, and by this time the school had been enlarged to include an old house at the back of the Abbey. It was now divided into a junior school, under the care of Madame Latournelle and her teachers, and the senior school, who took lessons from Monsieur Le Quintin and the Pictets.

Jane Austen and her sister Cassandra were sent away to school when they were very young, to make room in the rectory for the six brothers and the pupils which Mr. Austen took in to augment his income. At first they went to a school at Oxford run by a Mrs. Cawley who was a connection by marriage to Mrs. Austen. Jane Cooper, their cousin, who was a year or two older, was also at this school, but it was not a happy place, for the widowed Mrs. Cawley was 'a stiff-mannered person'. After a few months she moved the school to Southampton, and here Jane and Cassandra both caught diphtheria and were very ill. Cousin Jane was very worried about them but Mrs. Cawley was quite unmoved. As their condition grew worse, Jane Cooper wrote home. Mrs. Cooper and Mrs. Austen hurried down to Southampton and took their children away—and only just in time, for Jane Austen very nearly died. Unfortunately Mrs. Cooper caught the infection and died, but when the Austen girls were better all three children were packed off to the Abbey School at Reading. Jane was only seven and Cassandra nine, so this was well before Mary Sherwood's time, but Mde Latournelle was established there and the school was as pleasant and the discipline as light as it was ten years later: and young as they were, the three girls were allowed out to dine at an inn with their respective brothers, Edward Austen and Edward Cooper, and their friends, on the few occasions when they happened to be passing through Reading.

Very little is known about Jane and Cassandra's education, but they left Reading about 1787, by which time some of the boys had left home and there was more room for them at the Rectory. They presumably received the rest of their education at home, from brothers, parents and visiting tutors, but Jane always maintained that she had received very little orthodox education and, like Lady Mary Wortley Montagu before her, once said that if a woman 'has the misfortune to know anything' she 'should conceal it as well as she can'.

During her last months at the Abbey School Mary Sherwood had noticed that Mme St. Quintin was often in tears and her husband absent for increasingly long periods, leaving most of the teaching to the Pictets.

The sad truth was that M. St. Quintin was an inveterate gambler, and this state of affairs was not helped by the fact that also living in the town was Dr. Mitford, the friend of both St. Quintin and Dr. Valpy. Dr. Mitford, a doctor without a practice, had already gambled away his wife's handsome fortune and was living on the proceeds of a lucky win with a lottery ticket he had bought for his small daughter Mary, which produced £20,000.

Mary Sherwood had left Reading in the summer of 1793, the year that the news of the execution of Louis XVI had brought such sorrow and alarm to the French emigrés, and within a few months she had begun to write her first published story *The Traditions*. Perhaps she had read about Jenny Bickerstaff in the *Tatler*, but she had no intention of being thought a 'literary lady' and did her work secretly. However, her father came upon it, quite by chance, and was so pleased with it that he encouraged her to finish it. At this point came the news from Reading that M. St. Quintin was in dire financial troubles. Dr. Butt suggested that Mary's book, hardly yet completed, should be published by subscription for the benefit of the distressed schoolmaster. Her cousin, Dr. Salt, prepared the manuscript for the printers and the results enabled M. St.

Quintin and his wife to leave Reading and set up up a new school in Hans Place, off Sloane Street, Chelsea. Everyone was delighted, except for one dour clergyman who called on Dr. Butt to foretell the amount of evil which could well follow the publication of Mary's 'crude girlish fancies', for she was not yet nineteen. He belonged to the school of thought which deplored novel reading amongst young women which, as the *Spectator* once warned, 'along with chocolate, and especially in the month of May, were thought to "inflame the blood".'

No one took any notice of the clergyman and the following year, by which time the Butts had left Kidderminster and were back in Stanford, M. St. Quintin visited them to report that the sales of *The Traditions* had been so successful that he and his wife were now comfortably settled in Hans Place, with a growing number of pupils.

That was the year that Dr. Butt died suddenly of a stroke. Mrs. Butt, always inclined to parsimony, now began to count every penny and decided that they must move to a dreary little house at Bridgnorth. While the move was being arranged, Mary went to stay with her godmother for a time and they visited M. and Mme St. Quintin at their new school in Hans Place.

Back in Bridgnorth Mary and Lucy had their time well filled, for they were both writing, and Mary completed her novel *Margarita*, which she sold for £40. They also took charge of the Sunday school and soon had their full complement of thirty-five girl pupils which, with the old schoolmaster's thirty-five boys, was all the little building would hold.

In 1799 Mary and her brother paid a visit to Gloucestershire and a friend took them to call on Hannah More, who at that time was living in Pulteney Street, Bath. The house, said Mary, was large and handsome and the door was opened by a foot-man. They first met the four other sisters, who said that Hannah was not well, but after a time they were taken upstairs to a drawing room which was next the presence chamber. There was another delay before they were led into a dressing room where the great lady sat in an arm chair, 'in due invalid order', and 'looked at them out of a magnificent pair of dark eyes'. She was very gracious to their friend, Mrs. King, and also to Marten: and when she was told he was a clergyman, she gave him some 'excellent advice, her sisters gathering up her words carefully, in a rather Boswellian fashion', but of Mary she took very little notice.

On her return to Bridgnorth, Mary completed her story *Susan Grey*, which she had written and read aloud, chapter by chapter, to the elder girls of her Sunday school, saying later that she believed it to be 'the first narrative allowing of anything like correct writing, or refined sentiments expressed without vulgarisms, ever prepared for the poor, and having religion for its object'.

It was very soon after this that she married her cousin, Henry Sherwood, whose regiment was soon ordered to India, and here they remained until 1816, Mary continuing to write her children's books and helping to run the army orphanage and girls' school.

While she had been at the Abbey School Mary Sherwood had, on one occasion, seen little Mary Russell Mitford, then about four years old, a precocious child, taught by her mother and nurse and spoilt by her father. She could read by the time she was three and in 1798, when she was ten years old, she was sent to the St. Quintins' new school at 22 Hans Place, where they now had about twenty boarders.

When the St. Quintins had first left Reading, Miss Rowden, an old pupil of the school who had been helping them, stayed on with Mde Latournelle, but shortly after Mary Russell Mitford arrived at Hans Place, Miss Rowden came there too, Mde Latournelle having presumably retired.

M. St. Quintin taught French, history, geography, and as much science as he was master of, or as he thought it requisite for a young lady to know, and Miss Rowden, with the help of masters for Italian, music, dancing and drawing, directed the general course of study, while Madame St. Quintin sat dozing in the drawing room with a piece of needlework or in the library with a book in her hand, to receive the friends of the young ladies or any other chance visitors.

It was in many ways a good school. The house was new and freshly painted, overlooking the pleasantly laid out central garden of the square, and had its own large garden at the back. There was plenty of space for exercise in bad weather and Hyde Park close at hand for longer walks. The food was good and the atmosphere happy. The teaching was intelligent and in most of the girls it instilled a genuine love of reading and literature.

Miss Rowden was apt to speak in superlatives about all her pupils, but in later years Mary Mitford wrote: 'Fanny Rowden surely does not mean to assert that all who have breathed the air of 22 Hans Place must be female Solomons. If she do, Heaven help her! Don Quixote, when he took his fair nymphs of the inn for the daughters of the governor of the castle, did not make a greater mistake.'

Mary was short, plain and plump when she arrived at school, but she had a sweet smile and a beautiful speaking voice. She was very bright, and undeniably smug, but she was also lovable and doted on her parents. She was a worker and was soon hard at it, absorbing French, Italian, history, geography, astronomy, music, singing, drawing and dancing. And after a year or two, when she saw Miss Rowden reading Virgil, she asked to be taught Latin as well.

'I have just taken a lesson in Latin,' she wrote home, 'but I shall in consequence, omit some of my other business. It is extremely like Italian, that I think I shall find it much easier than I expected.'

Her father, showing that frequently expressed horror of a woman learning Latin, wrote back: 'Your mother and I have had much conversation concerning the utility of your learning Latin, and we both agree that it is perfectly unnecessary, and would occasion you additional trouble. It would occupy more of your time than you could conveniently appropriate to it; and we are more than satisfied with your application and proficiency in everything.'

Notwithstanding, the Latin lessons continued.

The school year was divided into three terms and there were festivals before each breaking up, with prize giving at midsummer and the performance of a play or ballet at Easter and Christmas.

Most of the girls' schools staged plays and Hannah More had written *Search After Happiness* for her sisters' Bristol school, followed later by her *Sacred Dramas*, as being more suitable than the plays 'not always of the purest kind', which were sometimes performed by the girls. Dr. Erasmus Darwin, the doctor, sage, botanist and poet of Lichfield, thoroughly disapproved of these amateur theatricals, saying that 'the danger consists in this, lest the acquisition of bolder action and a more elevated voice, should annihilate that retiring modesty and blushing embarrassment to which young ladies owe one of their most powerful external charms.'

But this was no kind of talk for M. St. Quintin and Mary acted in *Search After Happiness* and also danced in the ballets from time to time, under the tuition of M. Duval the dancing master, but she had no ear for music and in 1802 was writing home that she was much obliged to her parents 'for saying I need not learn dancing, as it is really my aversion'. In the same letter she said: 'I am glad my sweet mama agrees with me with regard to Dryden, as I never liked him as well as Pope. Miss Rowden has never read any translation of Virgil but his, and consequently could not judge of their respective merits. . . .' And it is a relief to read in another letter that this erudite fifteen-year-old sends 'a thousand thanks to my dear darlings for the cake, puddings, letters, sweets, etc.', even if they did make her overweight.

She left school at the end of 1802, when she was fifteen, an age when most girls were considered ready to come out into society. She returned to Reading and began to write poems and essays in a leisurely sort of way, but by 1820 her father had run through all his money again. They had to move from their pretentious mansion to a small cottage, where Mary was faced with the prospect of being obliged to keep them all by her writing. In 1823 appeared the first volume of *Our Village*, to which another four were added during the next ten years. In these essays she rather belied the zeal for learning she had shown by her letters home during her schooldays.

The English teacher, she said, was coarse and common compared with the delicate, gentle French mistress—a better sort of nursery-maid; one who from pure laziness would rather do things herself than take the trouble to see that they were done by another. Under her fosterage our evil habits throve apace: she put away, and hid, and lied for us, till we became the most irregular and untidy generation that ever trod the floor of a schoolroom and matters were not put right until the French mistress left, after the peace of Amiens, and in her place came a 'Tall, majestic woman, between sixty and seventy, made taller by yellow slippers with long slender heels, such as I have never seen before or since. She wore a long train and her face was almost invisible, being concealed between a mannish kind of neckcloth, that tied in her chin, and an enormous cap, whose wide flaunting strip hung over her cheeks and eyes,—to say nothing of a huge pair of spectacles.' She devoted herself untiringly to the training of the girls, and 'having the fidgetty neatness of a Dutch woman', soon set about curing them of their untidy habits, by throwing away possessions that had been left lying about, including a skipping rope which 'nearly overset her by entangling with her train' and was tossed out of the window.

The climax came when sundry objects found scattered around, 'bonnets, old and new, with strings and without, pelisses, tippets, parasols, unmatched shoes, halves of pairs of gloves, books tattered or whole, music in many parts, pin-cushions, petticoats, thimbles, frocks, sashes, dolls, portfolios, shuttle-cocks, play-things, work-things, trumpery without end' were collected in a vast heap, sorted out and pinned to the persons of the owners, 'after the manner of Mr. Lancaster's punishments'.

As they stood in the classroom, hopelessly encumbered, the drill sergeant arrived to give them an hour's exercises before the dancing master came for their dancing lesson. He asked for an explanation but Madame's English was not up to the occasion and the drill sergeant spoke no word of French. When he at last gathered that the girls were in disgrace he declared, disapproving of anything French, that 'it made his blood boil to see so many free-born English girls domineered by a natural enemy and he could not drill them with their encumbrances', so the exercise ended in disorder and a triumph for the girls.

Then Miss Rowden came to teach English. 'Miss R. to whom poor Madame took so unfortunate an aversion, was one of the most charming women that I have ever known,' wrote Mary. She loved her even more than Madame and for the last two years of her school days, Miss Rowden had special charge of Mary's education. Yet Mary complained that she worked her hard, so that instead of spending her spare time 'in the full enjoyment of my dearly beloved idleness, I found myself, to my unspeakable discomposure, getting by rote (an operation which I always detested) sundry tedious abridgments of heraldry, botany, biography, mineralogy, mythology and at least half a dozen "ologies" more, compiled by herself for my express edification. I gave her fair warning that I should forget all these wise things in no time, and kept my word; but there was no escaping the previous formality of learning them. O! dear me! I groan in spirit at the very recollection. I was even threatened with Latin grammar.'

Yet she recalled with happiness and gratitude those private lessons when Miss Rowden introduced her to Pope's *Homer*, Dryden's *Virgil* and *Paradise Lost*: 'and Miss R. compensated in another way for the pain and grief of my unwilling application!' said Mary, 'she took me often to the theatre; whether as an extra branch of education, or because she was herself in the height of a dramatic fever, it would be invidious to enquire'.

The average number of girls at the school was twenty. Sometimes it rose to thirty, but seldom more, 'principally because the house would not, with a proper regard to health and accommodation—points never forgotten by our excellently intentioned governess—conveniently contain a greater number.'

And they dispensed with parlour boarders after the escapade of one of the older girls. Having reached the age of seventeen, her guardians, not knowing what to do with her, kept her on at Hans Place as a parlour boarder. Moved from the schoolroom to the drawing room, in that transition stage when 'learning has been cast aside and knowledge not come', she became idle and lonely, 'silly beyond her usual silliness', and after a few weeks of secret confidences with one of the other boarders, accompanied by closetings, note-writings and eager whisperings, she slipped secretly away one moonlit night for Gretna Green.

That was the last of the parlour boarders, the school company consisting of 'young ladies sent up from the country for "improvement": the desperately naughty and the hopelessly dull, banished from home to be out of the way, and to try what school would do—or the luckless daughters of the newly wealthy, on whom the magic air of a London seminary was expected to work as sudden a transformation as the wand of Cinderella's fairy godmother.'

There were also some foreign girls at the school. Mary mentions a beautiful Italian girl, an Anglo-Portuguese Jewess, the daughter of a crack-brained Austrian, straight from Vienna, a young Russian countess and two French girls, one of whom, orphaned in the Revolution and cared for by a wealthy aunt living in London, turned out to be the greatest dunce in the school, though in many ways she was intelligent enough and a beautiful dancer. She always laughed at the English awkwardness 'with two left legs' and ended up as a famous beauty at the Court of Napoleon.

After Waterloo, the St. Quintins left Hans Place and returned to Paris; and in 1816, shortly after the Sherwoods had come home from India, they paid a visit to France, where Mrs. Sherwood says they stayed with Miss Rowden, 'who had accompanied M. and Mme Quintin back to Paris, where they had opened a school for English girls'. And amongst their pupils who was destined for future fame was Fanny Kemble.

A few months before Mary Russell Mitford arrived at Hans Place, Bobbin, the youngest daughter of Arthur Young, was sent to school at Campden House not far away. This was an early seventeenth-century house, a smaller version of Holland House, with a wide entrance porch, deep-bay windows and turrets, and it stood on the west side of what is now Church Street, Kensington. Queen Anne had lived here for a time before her accession, with Prince George of Denmark and their small son, Prince William, but by the latter part of the eighteenth century it had become a girls' school, although it was eventually to become a private residence again.

For Arthur Young and Bobbin the choice of this school was disastrous. In his journal for 1791 Arthur Young wrote: 'This year, so fatal to every worldly hope, which overturned every prospect I had in life, and changed me almost as much as a new creation, opened in the common manner by my going to London to attend the meeting of the Board [of Agriculture]. I brought my dear angelic child with me, who went to school in January, in good health, but never in good spirits, for she abhorred school. Oh, what infatuation ever to send her to one. In the country she had health, spirits, and strength, as if that were not enough with what she might have learned at home, instead of going to that region of constraint and death, Camden [sic] House.[1]

'The rules of health are detestable, no air but in a measured formal walk, and all running and quick motions prohibited. Preposterous! She slept with a girl who could hear only with one ear, and so ever laid on one side; and my dear child could do no otherwise afterwards without pain; because the vile beds are so small that they must both lie the same way. The school discipline of all sorts, the food, etc. etc. all contributed. She never had a bellyful of breakfast. Detestable this at the expense of 80 l a year. Oh! how I regret ever putting her

[1] M. Betham Edwards, editor of Arthur Young's *Autobiography* (Smith, Elder and Co., 1898) suggests that 'Camden' House may have been a school in Camden Town, but on p. 323 Arthur Young spells it correctly as Campden House.

there, or to any other, for they are all theatres of knavery, illiberality and infamy. Upon her being ill in March I took her away to my lodgings in Jermyn Street, where Dr. Turton attended her until April 12, when I carried her to Bradfield.'

Bobbin seems to have been suffering from tuberculosis, though the disease was never diagnosed. Doctors prescribed all manner of conflicting diets and treatments and she was stuffed with medicines till at last she wrote to her father that 'having had so much physic I am right down tired of it', but he replied begging her to take all that was given her and to do all she could to get well, for 'I am now paying your school the same as if present'.

This news cannot have been much comfort to her but in any case it was too late, for a week or two afterwards she died, killed, so her father alleged, by the appalling conditions of the school and the attentions of five doctors.

A girl who survived the school was Jane Berry, who married Bobbin's brother, and another was Maria Fagniani. Maria was born in 1771, a daughter of the Marchesa Fagniani and begotten, in a casual manner, by the future Marquis of Queensberry, but wished on to George Selwyn, who seems to have been in no position to deny any responsibility for her. When the Marchesa and her husband returned to Italy, this affectionate old rake brought the child up at Selwyn House in Cleveland Row, doting on her and lavishing every care and attention. When she was six or seven years old, he sent her to school at Campden House, though he could hardly bear her out of his sight and was constantly visiting her.

Conditions seem to have been just as bad as when Bobbin Young arrived there a few years later, for he was constantly worrying about her, thinking that she looked pale and thin. Miss Terry, the mistress, wrote to reassure him. 'She is this minute engaged in a party of high romps,' she protested. 'Miss Terry is sorry that Mr. Selwyn is so uneasy. The dear child's spirits are *not* depressed. She is very lively, ate a good dinner; and behaved just like other children.'

However, Maria did not stay there long, for the grand-parents were asking her mother awkward questions about her whereabouts and she was escorted to Italy to meet them. Yet she was soon back in George Selwyn's care, despite the fact that before she was ten years old her marked resemblance to the Marquis of Queensberry could not be denied. She did not go away to school again, and having been willed fortunes by both George Selwyn and the Marquis—Old Q—became a highly eligible heiress and married the third Lord Hertford.

Mary Somerville, born in 1780, who attained such distinction as a mathematician and scientist that she was regarded as one of the most remarkable women of her time and was elected to the Royal Society, gives a grim picture of her schooldays in Scotland. 'At ten years old I was sent to a boarding-school kept by a Miss Primrose at Musselburgh, where I was utterly wretched,' she said. 'A few days after my arrival, although perfectly straight and well made, I was enclosed in stiff stays with a steel busk in front, while, above my frock, bands drew my shoulders back till my shoulder-blades met. Then a steel rod, with a semi-circle which went under the chin, was clasped to the steel busk in my stays. In this constrained state I, and most of the younger girls, had to prepare our lessons. The chief thing I had to do was to learn by heart a page of Johnson's Dictionary; not only to spell the words, give their parts of speech and meaning, but as an exercise of memory to remember their order of succession. Besides I had to learn the first principles of writing, and the rudiments of French and English grammar. The method of teaching was extremely tedious and inefficient. Our religious duties were attended to in a remarkable way. Some of the girls were Presbyterians, others belonged to the Church of England, so Miss Primrose cut the matter short by taking us all to the kirk in the morning and to church in the afternoon. . . .' One of their favourite play-time games was 'Scotch and English', 'in which each party tried to rob the other of their playthings. The little ones were always compelled to be English, for the bigger girls thought it too degrading.'

Chapter Twelve

WOMEN LEARNED AND ROMANTIC

A WOMAN OF genuine scholarship who in her day was considered one of the most learned students of Anglo-Saxon and the early Teutonic languages in the country was Elizabeth Elstob. Like Mary Astell, she was born in New-castle, the daughter of a prosperous merchant, but her father died in 1688, when Elizabeth was five years old, and her mother three years later, leaving Elizabeth under the guardianship of her father's brother, a Prebendary of Canterbury. Her brother William, ten years older, went from Eton to Cambridge and was destined for the Church, while Mary lived with her aunt and uncle at Canterbury.

Her mother had been an educated woman and had already begun to teach her small daughter Latin and inspire her with love of languages, but at Canterbury her uncle, 'no friend to Women's learning' would not allow her to continue these studies, 'notwithstanding her repeated requests that she might, being always put off with that common vulgar saying that one tongue is enough for a Woman'.

We know very little of her education in Canterbury, but after a good deal of persuasion on her part, and she was a tenacious child, she was allowed to learn French, and for the rest she seems to have been self-taught. Yet by the time she was nineteen and ready to join her brother at his living of St. Swithin's in the City of London she was already familiar with several languages.

For the next thirteen years she lived in great contentment with him, giving most of her time to scholarship. In 1708 she translated Mlle de Scudéry's *Essay on Glory*, in 1709 she published her translation of *An English Saxon Homily on the Birthday of St Gregory*, in 1713 a pamphlet entitled *Some Testimonies of Learned Men in Favour of the Intended Edition of the Saxon Homilies* and in 1715 her *English–Saxon Grammar*.

By the few Anglo-Saxon scholars competent to judge her work, it was acclaimed for its accuracy, and to the City vicarage came many learned men, including Ralph Thoresby, the antiquarian and diarist, for her brother was also a writer and antiquarian and had become one of the earliest members of the Society of Antiquaries.

But in 1715 William died of tuberculosis, leaving Elizabeth at thirty-one with no money, a pile of debts and the prospect of having to earn her own living. She was in the middle of her most important work, a translation of *Aelfric's Sermons*, which she hoped to publish by subscription, but no patronage was forthcoming for so erudite a work and no help from her uncle in Canterbury, who shortly afterwards died. By 1718 she had to disappear from London to avoid imprisonment for debt, changing her name and ending up destitute in Worcestershire, where it seems probable that she survived by becoming a servant in some large household.

It was Mrs. Sarah Chapone, wife of a Gloucestershire clergyman and a friend of Mrs. Delaney who, some ten or eleven years later, discovered the almost forgotten scholar in her obscurity and managed to bring her plight to the notice of Queen Caroline. At first the Queen thought of giving her an allowance of twenty pounds a year, but then said that 'as she is so proper to be the mistress of a boarding-school of young ladies of higher rank, I will instead of an annual allowance send her one hundred pounds now, and repeat the same at the end of every five years'.

This she did but in 1737 she died and the bounty ceased. Nevertheless, it gave Elizabeth, by now nearing fifty and in poor health, the chance to establish herself in a little school in Evesham. It was not the kind of school Queen Caroline had envisaged, for it was a day school and her pupils paid her only fourpence a week, but she was happy with them and a good teacher.

Living only a few miles away, at Campden, was George Ballard, a tailor and stay-maker by trade but an antiquary by inclination, and a student of Anglo-Saxon. He had long respected the work of the Elstobs and when he learnt of Elizabeth's whereabouts he wrote to her, suggesting she should do some more Anglo-Saxon translations.

She asked him to visit her. 'You will see a poor little contemptible old maid generally vapou'd up to the ears, but very cheerful when she meets with an agreeable conversation,' she wrote.

At their first meeting Ballard was twenty-nine and Elizabeth fifty-two, and the friendship brought her much happiness. For the first time for years she was to meet someone with common interests who respected her for her past achievements and brought her back to the notice of her antiquarian friends of the past. She was able to help him with his famous work *Memoirs of Learned Ladies*, on which he had already embarked, but the meeting came too late to inspire her to any further work of her own.

'I must acquaint you that I have no time to do anything till six at night, when I have done the Duty of the day,' she wrote to him, 'and am then frequently so fatigu'd that I am oblig'd to lye down for an hour or two to rest myself and recover my Spirits.' And on another occasion, she said: '. . . when my School is done my little ones leave me incapable of either reading, writing or thinking, for their noise is not out of my head till I fall asleep, which is often too late.'

Mrs. Chapone tried to secure for her the headmistress's post at a charity school which Lady Elizabeth Hastings was about to open, work which would be 'less precarious and fatiguing', with an annual income and a patroness who would be charitable if Elizabeth became too ill to run the school, but the scheme did not materialize. Someone else was appointed and Elizabeth herself had had doubts about her ability to fill the post, as she felt she was not sufficiently competent in 'the two Accomplishments of a good House-wife, Spinning and Knitting'.

At last she became too crippled with rheumatism to run her school any longer and her friends sent her to Bath for a time. The cure seems to have given her some temporary relief and it was here that she met a doctor who told her, as she later wrote to Ballard, that 'mine is a wrong employment to hope for any encouragement in, if I cou'd teach to make Artificial Flowers, a bit of Tapistry, and the like I shou'd get more than I shall by instilling the Principles of Religion and Virtue, or improving the Minds of Young Ladies, for those are things little regarded.'

Shortly after this Mrs. Delaney obtained for her the position of governess in the household of the Duchess of Portland and here, after nearly a quarter of a century of poverty and insecurity, Elizabeth established herself in reasonable contentment for the last fourteen years of her life. It was an unlikely end to so promising a youth and a sad waste of her talents, but grinding penury had blunted her susceptibilities and she became devoted to her small charges. It saddened her that she now had little opportunity to see the friends who had been so good to her, but her social status in the Duchess's household was diminished to servitude. 'I have less time than I ever had in my life to command,' she wrote to Ballard, and, at another time: 'Alas, my acquaintance and interest is reduced to a very narrow compass.'

George Ballard was in failing health. In 1750 he had been given a clerkship at Magdalen College, Oxford and was working hard on his *Memoirs of Learned Ladies*. In one of her last letters to him, before his death in 1754, a note of bitterness creeps in, for Elizabeth had come to realize that, even in a great and enlightened household like that of the Portlands, the idea of a woman engaged in serious intellectual work was not approved. 'I am sorry to tell you the choice you have made for the Honour of the Females was the wrongest subject you could pitch upon,' she said. 'For you can come into no company of Ladies and Gentlemen, where you shall not hear an open and vehement exclamation against Learned Women, and by those Women who read much themselves. . . .'

Two years later, in 1756, Elizabeth Elstob died. This was about five years after Mrs. Montagu, in vastly different circumstances, had moved into her splendid house in Hill Street, Mayfair. Born in 1720, she was the daughter of a wealthy Yorkshire squire. Her mother had been educated at Mrs. Makin's school and having thoroughly digested Mrs. Makin's observation that 'the barbarous custom to breed women low is grown general mongst us', saw to it that her daughters received the best education available, from governesses and tutors.

Elizabeth Montagu's childhood home was an enlightened and cultured household and she also spent part of the time at the home of her learned grandfather at Cambridge, where he trained her to listen carefully to the conversation of the divines, scholars, philosophers and travellers who came to his house and afterwards tell him all she could remember of it.

In 1742, when she was twenty-two, she made a marriage for love with Edward Montagu, for they were both sufficiently wealthy for material concerns and marriage settlements to be of little account. Edward Montagu, several years older than his wife, was a distinguished mathematician, but his wealth came from his Yorkshire estates and coal mines: and although the death of their only child was a bitter grief, the marriage was happy for thirty-three years, Edward Montagu dying in 1775 and Elizabeth surviving him until 1800.

The county society of Yorkshire she described as 'ignorant, awkward, absurd—for the most part . . . drunken and vicious', but at her husband's Berkshire estate near Newbury she found the society more congenial. The Montagus also had a London home in Dover Street, but Elizabeth Montagu, sharp-witted and observant, found too many people in London society with heads 'full of powder and very empty of thought', while party politics she hated, alleging that they were 'pursued for the benefit of individuals, not for the good of the country'.

During the first years of her married life she lived in the

social swim, however, dividing her time between the usual visits to country houses and spells at Tunbridge Wells and Bath. Yet she always found the most happiness in her books and her letter writing. After the move to Hill Street, in 1751, the pace of social life quickened for a time. On Christmas Eve of 1752, for example, she reported that 'the Chinese room at Hill Street was filled by a succession of visitors from eleven in the morning till eleven at night'. But her interest in high society, with all its vacuities and gossip, its profligate intrigues, its hypocrisy and lack of culture, was beginning to pall, and less than two years later she was writing of London parties where 'cold scraps of visiting conversation' were served up 'with the indelicacy and indifference of an ordinary, at which no power of the mind does the honours; the particular taste of each guest is not consulted, the solid part of the entertainment is too gross for a delicate taste, and the lighter fare insipid.'

By the time she was thirty-five she was heartily sick of it all. Going 'wherever two or three fools were gathered together, to assemblies, dinner parties, card parties and visiting days' had lost its charm and there came the night when 'she did not bother to go to Lady Townshend's ball' despite 'the new pink silver negligée which lay ready for her', preferring to spend the evening in reading and study.

Card playing in particular was an abomination, and many people in London society were ruining themselves. At the Duke of Richmond's as many as eighteen card-tables would be set for playing, night after night, in the gallery of his house near Whitehall, with supper and wine to follow, 'for the consolation of the half-ruined and congratulations of the lucky gamblers'.

Elizabeth Montagu decided to give her own kind of parties, to which only her specially selected friends would be invited, and where there would be intelligent and cultured conversation, with positively no card playing.

Conversation parties of a kind were already being held by a few hostesses, but as Sarah Scott, Elizabeth's sister, said: 'they were for the most part terrible things . . . the principal speakers are always those to whom one is the least inclined to attend. Every day in the week would be as much taken up with these parties, if cards did not conquer even the love of talking.'

Elizabeth Montagu's parties were different, for as she once explained to David Garrick: 'I never invite fools to my house.' The company of cultured men and women was so well selected that they were at once successful. At first she gave breakfast parties but soon changed them to after dinner gatherings, where about twenty guests met to discuss the literature and events of the day. A few of her friends copied the idea and Boswell, writing of them, said that 'about this time, it was much the fashion for several ladies to have evening assemblies, where the fair sex might participate in conversation with literary and ingenious men, animated by a desire to please'.

The nucleus of the group of friends comprised Mrs. Montagu, Mrs. Vesey, Mrs. Carter, Mrs. Boscawen, Lord Lyttelton, the Earl of Bath, Horace Walpole and Mr. Stillingfleet.

Mrs. Vesey was not particularly intellectual but a greatly loved, intelligent and charming woman, who had the knack of bringing people together, at her house in Clarges Street, and encouraging them to talk. She was married to the Rt. Hon. Agmondsham Vesey and, according to Mrs. Piozzi, she loved Mrs. Montagu almost as much as she hated her husband.

Mrs. Carter, who was never married, the 'Mrs' being a courtesy title, was the daughter of a Kentish clergyman and probably the most erudite woman of the circle, and she and Mrs. Montagu were known as Mind and Matter. She was an untiring student from her childhood days and suffered all her life from the headaches caused by drinking green tea and taking snuff, in order to keep awake to study. She mastered Latin, Greek, Hebrew, French, Italian, Spanish, German, Portuguese and Arabic, studied astronomy, geography and ancient history, played on the spinet and the German flute, was an excellent needlewoman and a splendid cook.

'The learned Mrs. Carter,' recorded Boswell, 'at that period when she was eager to study, did not wake as early as she wished, and she therefore had a contrivance, that, at a certain

hour, her chamber-light should burn a string to which a heavy
weight was suspended, which then fell with a strong, sudden
noise: this roused her from sleep, and then she had no difficulty in getting up.'

She published numerous translations and several volumes of
poems, as well as contributing to the *Gentleman's Magazine* and
the *Rambler*, but her most distinguished work was the translation from the Greek of *All the Works of Epictetus Now Extant*,
which appeared in 1758. Dr. Johnson had a profound respect
for her scholarship, and of another eminent Greek scholar he
once said that 'he understood Greek better than anyone he had
ever known except Elizabeth Carter'. 'A man is in general
better pleased when he has a good dinner on his table than
when his wife talks Greek,' he said on another occasion. 'My
old friend, Mrs. Carter, could make a pudding as well as
translate Epictetus from the Greek and work a handkerchief as
well as compose a poem.'

She was said to read and write for eight to twelve hours
every day and in between times fit in ten miles walking. And
she was much given to romantic friendships with other women,
to retirement from the social treadmill of London and enjoyment of the simple life. At twenty-two she was writing to the
nineteen-year-old Miss Talbot: 'Miss Talbot is absolutely my
passion; I think of her all day, dream of her all night, and one
way or other introduce her into every subject I talk of.'

Eighteen years later, when she was forty, she was writing to
Mrs. Montagu: 'I longed for you extremely the other night at
Reading,' for the ruins of the old Abbey in the moonlight had
stirred her romantic heart. Then there was Mrs. Vesey, whose
letters she read while sitting on the seashore in the 'soft melan-
choly light of this fair autumnal moon', in a mood of that
'pensive kind of tranquillity which has such an inexplicable
union with the tenderest feelings of the heart', while Mrs.
Vesey, like some star-crossed lover, was gazing, by appointment, at the same moon though many miles away.

The friendship with Miss Talbot lasted for many years, for
in 1763, when Elizabeth Carter was in France with Mrs.

Montagu, Miss Talbot, feeling a little neglected, gently chides her that she 'is fallen in love with another woman. . . . A pretty gentleman you will come home indeed.'

Mrs. Boscawen, the fourth woman of the little group, was the wife of the Admiral, welcomed at the parties for the 'strength of her understanding, the poignancy of her humour, and the brilliance of her wit'.

The term 'Blue Stocking' was first used by the friends during the 1750s. The story goes that at one of these parties the absent-minded Benjamin Stillingfleet arrived in blue worsted stockings instead of the customary black silk. 'Such was the excellence of his conversation,' says Boswell, 'and his absence was felt so great a loss, that it used to be said: "We can do nothing without the blue stockings"; and thus, by degrees, the title was established.'

Mrs. Montagu, writing to Dr. Monsey in 1757, mentioned that 'our friend Mr. Stillingfleet . . . is so much a man of pleasure he has left off his old friends and his blue stockings, and is at operas and other gay assemblies every night.'

Hannah More went to the Blue Stocking parties before she retired from London, as well as Dr. Johnson and Boswell, Sir Joshua Reynolds and David Garrick, and Garrick on at least one occasion enraptured them all with recitals from Lear and Macbeth.

In 1769 Elizabeth Montagu published anonymously her *Essay on the Writings and Genius of Shakespeare, Compared with the Greek and French Dramatic Poets, with some remarks upon the Misrepresentations of M. de Voltaire.* This was first attributed to Lord Lyttelton and acclaimed by Reynolds, Cowper and others as a brilliant piece of criticism, but Johnson, before the authorship was known, rejected it as of little value. And later, when it was common knowledge that it was the work of Mrs. Montagu, he offended her mortally by saying that there was not 'one substance of true criticism in her book . . . none showing the beauty of thought, as formed by the human heart'.

It was a very hard pill to swallow but, with commendable forbearance, she continued to invite him to her parties.

After more than thirty years in Hill Street, Mrs. Montagu moved to the new mansion she had built for herself in Portman Square, and here the Blue Stocking parties were larger and more elaborate, but by this time many of the original circle were dead and the guests were less carefully chosen. They were never the same as in the Hill Street days, for some of the old sparkle and spontaneity had gone. Fanny Burney who in 1778, when she was only twenty-six, achieved sudden fame with the publication of *Evelina*, described one of the breakfast parties at Montagu House. It was sumptuous, gorgeous, over-crowded. 'In splendour of company, banquet and locality, it could not be surpassed: and hundreds were there.'

But Mrs. Montagu was in failing health and her eyesight was troubling her. The Blue Stocking parties became rarer and gradually faded away: but they were not forgotten, and although there were plenty to laugh at them, there were many more who hankered after an invitation to their gatherings, for they had proved beyond doubt that women, even without the benefit of a formal education at a public school and university, were equally as capable of erudition as men.

It was a first, faltering step towards emancipation, but there was a very long journey still ahead.

Fanny Burney, as we have seen, had little formal education after the few months in Queen Square. In King's Lynn, where she was born, in 1752, her mother was one of only three women who could read with ease and enjoyment, while her stepmother, whom Dr. Burney married in 1766, was one of the remaining two. And even in London only a very small number of women could be described as educated and cultured. When Mr. Seaton from Scotland, who married Fanny's eldest sister, called one day and found her out, he was enchanted to discover that Fanny was capable of intelligent conversation: for 'except you and your sister, I have scarce met with one worthy of being spoke to', he said. 'In England I was quite struck to see how forward the girls are made—a child of ten years old will chat and keep you company with the ease of a woman of 26—But then, how does this education go on? Not at all; it absolutely stops short. If I had gone into almost any other house and talked at this rate to a young lady, she would have amused me with gaping and yawning all the time, and would not have understood a word I have uttered. . . . The truth is, that young women here are so mortally silly and insipid that I cannot bear them.'

Yet Fanny was by no means independent and she was terrified when she turned down her first proposal, lest her father should insist on her accepting the man. 'To unite myself for life to a man who is not infinitely dear to me is what I can never consent to do, unless, indeed, I was strongly urged by my father,' she confided to her diary, but happily Dr. Burney was 'too indulgent to require me to give my hand without my heart'.

Daughters were still regarded as the property of their parents, to be disposed of in marriage as they wished, and it was only the girls fortunate enough to have kind and understanding parents who were allowed a choice in the matter. Dr. Johnson explained to Boswell that girls had to be subjected to this tyranny and the strictest supervision, for chastity in women was of the utmost importance, since all property was dependent on it: and Mrs. Delaney justified the system by insisting that happiness depended not on married love, but on 'riches, honours and length of years'.

Fanny Burney's first novel *Evelina* was published anonymously in 1778, and although everyone who read it was entranced by it, no one thought it could have been written by a woman. When the truth was known, Fanny feared she might 'lose her reputation', but she need not have worried. Women writers were being accepted and she achieved fame not only in London, where she was warmly received by the literary circle of the Blue Stockings, but throughout all Europe.

It was in 1786 that, through an introduction to Queen Charlotte by Mrs. Delaney, she was summoned to Court to become second keeper of the robes. She went with strong misgivings, which were more than justified, for she hated the empty formality of Court life, the interminable card playing and the bickerings and petty jealousies of the German women at Court, Mrs. Schwellenberg being a particular thorn in the flesh. After five years of mixing the Queen's snuff, helping her on and off with her elaborate clothes and jewellery, during which she invariably tied the hairs at the back of the Queen's neck in with her necklace, she was allowed to retire, and the following year was happily married to the French emigré, General D'Arblay.

While the Blue Stockings were amusing themselves with their evening parties in London, two other women, with similar literary and intellectual interests, and tied by a romantic friendship, had settled down in a cottage in Wales, to live the simple life of study and retreat and communion with nature which had been extolled not only by Rousseau, but the English poets, Pope, Thomson and Gray.

They were Sarah Ponsonby and Eleanor Butler, who were to become famous as the Ladies of Llangollen. Sarah Ponsonby was orphaned at seven and brought up by a stepmother for a few years, but when the stepmother also died Sarah was left destitute, for her inheritance had been lost to a half-brother. At the age of thirteen, therefore, she was handed over to the care of her mother's cousin, Lady Betty Fownes, who had married Sir William, squire of Woodstock, a few miles from Kilkenny: and the next she knew was to find herself at Mrs. Parke's Boarding School in Kilkenny, where she was happy enough in the acquisition of the usual accomplishments of drawing and fine needlework.

Eleanor Butler at this time was twenty-nine, a descendant of the illustrious James Butler, first Duke of Ormonde, who had supported Charles I and the Restoration. The second Duke had been impeached by George I for his Jacobite sympathies and the gaunt, grey castle of Kilkenny, first built for Strongbow's son-in-law, the Earl of Pembroke, where Ormondes had lived since the fourteenth century, was now inhabited, in a state of muddled and tarnished grandeur, by an impecunious Catholic branch of the family, of whom Eleanor was the youngest of three daughters.

Her mother, descended from a sister of Strongbow, was

a stronger character than her husband and was ultimately responsible for the restitution of the family titles and fortune. She sent the two elder girls to the fashionable convent of the Blue Nuns in Paris, for their education. Eleanor, several years younger, plain and unwanted and overshadowed by the birth of the long-awaited brother and heir a year later, spent a childhood which was nearly as lonely as Sarah's, until she was eventually sent to the English Benedictine Convent of Our Blessed Lady of Consolation at Cambrai for a year or two, where she seems to have been very happy. There were seldom more than eight or ten boarders at these convents and the Cambrai house, though not so fashionable as the Blue Nuns in Paris, had a high reputation for education. It gave Eleanor an abiding interest in literature and at the same time, owing to the liberal views on religion held by so many French writers at this time, a marked distaste for priests and Irish popery.

Back in Kilkenny, Eleanor found life at the castle dreary and lonely and her only real pleasures were reading and study, for her two sisters were both married, as well as her brother, who had turned Protestant and won an heiress, as a preliminary to winning back the Ormonde titles. At twenty-nine Eleanor found herself an old maid, too well educated to have anything in common with most of the other women of Kilkenny, and too plain, poor and masculine-looking to attract a husband.

Sarah and Eleanor met when Lady Betty Fownes wrote to the castle, asking Eleanor's mother to keep an eye on little Sarah while she was at school at Mrs. Parke's, and from that time a warm friendship sprang up between Sarah and Eleanor, despite the disparity in their ages.

On Sarah's part it began probably as schoolgirl hero-worship. For Eleanor it went deeper, but it brought them both much happiness, for Sarah shared Eleanor's love of literature and they had many interests in common.

When she was eighteen Sarah left Mrs. Parke's School and returned to live with the Fownes, who divided their time between Woodstock and their town house in Dublin. She was happy with Lady Betty, who, probably as a mental escape from her irritable husband, was said to be killing herself with the working of vast cross-stitch carpets and gros-point chair seats: but after a year or two there was trouble with Sir William. He was gout-ridden, bad-tempered and hankering after the heir which Lady Betty had failed to produce. Thinking that her health was declining faster than it actually was, he fancied he might soon be free to marry again. He was only in his early fifties and still might have an heir. His choice for a second wife fell on Sarah and he accordingly began to make advances well ahead of the time propriety might demand. Sarah, sincerely fond of Lady Betty, was genuinely shocked and distressed.

In a secret correspondence, she confided her troubles to Eleanor, who was equally unhappy at Kilkenny, for her mother was now pressing her strongly to enter a convent, where she would be out of the way and no longer an embarrassment to her family. To Mrs. Butler the plan had added advantages, for by offering her daughter to the Church it would square her conscience for having allowed her son to turn Protestant. Also Eleanor's inheritance, guaranteed by her brother's marriage settlement, which she would automatically forfeit, after the preliminary dowry had been paid to the convent, would help the family finances.

Eleanor resisted with all the strength she could command, but at last, confiding their letters to a trusted servant, she and the unhappy Sarah made their plans to run away, hoping to find some rural retreat where they could live together in peaceful seclusion.

Late on a night of March, 1778, when the household was all in bed and asleep, Sarah Ponsonby, dressed in men's clothes and armed with a pistol, crept downstairs and climbed out of a parlour window, where a trusted labourer was waiting to guide her to the place where Eleanor had arranged to meet her. Eleanor, having crept unobserved from the castle, had changed into men's clothes and ridden over to the barn unaccompanied. The runaways planned to make their way to Waterford and take a boat to England. They travelled all through that wet and windy night, but either they missed the packet or it never sailed, for they were forced to spend the whole of the next day and night sheltering in a barn.

As soon as they were missed, both families went in search of them, and they were discovered through the barking of Sarah's little dog Frisk, whom she had brought with her on the venture. Lady Betty arrived first, bundled them into her coach, and they all set off for Woodstock again, but they were intercepted by the Butlers who, despite Eleanor's protests, insisted on carrying her off to her brother-in-law's house at Borris. Here she was kept as closely guarded as a prisoner, while arrangements were made to transfer her to the convent in France.

Sarah had caught a chill after the night in the barn and was very ill for a time. Agonized letters came from Eleanor and at last, after much anxious pleading, Sarah was allowed to drive over to Borris, for one last farewell with Eleanor before she was shipped off to France. It gave them a chance to make fresh plans. A day or two later Eleanor managed to escape from Borris and make her way to Woodstock where, with the help of an accommodating housemaid, she stayed for a day or two, hidden from the rest of the family. When she eventually showed herself, Sir William, righteously indignant, asked the Butlers to take her away again, but they refused to have anything more to do with her.

Then Sarah announced her intention 'to live and die with Miss Butler' and there was now nothing anyone could do to dissuade them or prevent them from leaving Woodstock together.

With the housemaid, Mary Carryll, they set off and reached as far as Wales. They had very little money—perhaps £250 to £300 a year between them and a little ready cash—but after a few weeks wandering they came across a small Georgian cottage, with four acres of land, near Llangollen, which they were able to rent for just under twenty-three pounds a year. And here at Plas Newydd they were to live for the rest of their lives, Eleanor dying in 1828 and Sarah surviving her for only three years.

They lived in considerable style, enlarging and altering the cottage, and gradually transforming it into a *ferme ornée* which, though hardly an improvement, was in the current romantic taste for the Gothic. They maintained a gardener, a footman and a kitchen maid to help Mary Carryll, who did the cooking. They were hard pressed for money and often in debt. They appealed to their families for money and allowances which they asserted were legally theirs, and all too frequently met with disappointments, but they weathered the storm with loans and gifts. They made ever more improvements, establishing a vegetable garden with asparagus and strawberry beds; they planted peach trees, built a dairy, kept cows and chickens, planted their garden with a multitude of flowering shrubs and perennials, and lived off their small estate with as much romantic enjoyment as Marie Antoinette and her ladies playing at milkmaids and shepherdesses at the Trianon. They walked for miles, they gardened, they read and studied, taught themselves languages, kept journals and wrote innumerable letters. And Sarah netted purses. On one occasion, when she had written to her wealthy relative Lord Bessborough for money, he sent her £50 but begged her not to send him another purse, 'for I have, I believe Twenty by me, which are not of any use'.

They established themselves amongst the local gentry and the charm of their establishment brought them many visitors, both old friends and new. Queen Charlotte asked to see a plan of their cottage and garden. Harriet Bowdler, sister of Thomas Bowdler, who edited the bowdlerized 'Family Shakespeare' and herself a writer and educationist, became a close friend. Later the poetess Anna Seward, the 'Swan of Lichfield', who was much given to passionate friendships and particularly adored Sarah, was a frequent and much loved visitor, and also into their circle came Mr. Chappelow, the parson who was so able a botanist and naturalist, and the Piozzis, for some years after Mrs. Thrale had married Signor Piozzi they settled down in her native Wales.

In July, 1790, Sarah and Eleanor were deeply affronted by a

paragraph in the *General Evening Post*. 'Miss Butler and Miss
Ponsonby have retired from society into a certain Welch Vale,'
it began. 'Both Ladies are daughters of the great Irish families
whose names they retain.'

There followed an account of their first and later escapes
from their families, which the *Evening Post* described signi-
ficantly as 'elopements', and the note ended by saying: 'Miss
Butler is tall and masculine, she wears always a riding habit,
hangs her hat with the air of a sportsman in the hall, and
appears in all respects as a young man, if we except the petticoats which she still retains.

'Miss Ponsonby, on the contrary, is polite and effeminate,
fair and beautiful. . . .

'They live in neatness, elegance and taste. Two females are
their only servants.

'Miss Ponsonby does the duties and honours of the house,
while Miss Butler superintends the gardens and the rest of the
grounds.'

The insinuation was obvious and caused an epidemic of
speculation about any women who chose to live together, preferring each other's company to that of such men as their
parents had chosen for them as husbands.

In the case of Eleanor and Sarah the description was true in
many respects but not entirely accurate, for Eleanor was
inclined to be stocky and both wore the same masculine-
looking riding habits, which was a quite usual dress in the
country about this time. Mrs. Montagu, writing in 1778 from
Tunbridge Wells to her sister-in-law, said: 'Minouet dancing
is just now out of fashion; and by the military air and dress of
many of the ladies, I should not be surprised if backsword and
cudgell playing should take place of it. I think our encampment
excellent for making men less effeminate; but if they make our
women more masculine, the male and female character, which
should ever be kept distinct, will now be more so than they
have been.'

Women such as Harriet Bowdler and Anna Seward maintained that men gave their affection to their children and their

men friends, but their love for wife or mistress was usually only transitory, while in the case of an arranged marriage it may never have existed at all. Romantic friendships between women were justified by a community of interests in the arts which the men of their acquaintance did not share.

Throughout the long friendship of Sarah Ponsonby and Eleanor Butler, though there were suggestions that Sarah, so much younger and gentler, sometimes may have regretted leaving Ireland and her friends, they maintained a deep affection. They survived the buzz of scandal touched off by the *General Evening Post* and it was soon forgotten. Eleanor suffered financially, for even after the Ormonde estates and titles were restored to her brother, she benefited hardly at all, and her mother ignored her in her will, but they continued to receive a succession of distinguished guests, which included Southey, Wordsworth and Sir Walter Scott, while Byron sent them a complimentary copy of *The Corsair* and Prince Puckler Muskau declared them to be 'the most celebrated Virgins in Europe'.

They blazed the trail for women who wanted to live independent lives, but this was possible only because they had no absolute need to earn their own living. For women who had no means at all, the story was very different. With little or no education, the only alternative to a marriage which, all too often, was distasteful, remained the drudgery of the ill-paid governess or companion, domestic service or the factory.

Yet the most moving—and ultimately the most effective—call for women's freedom from the tyranny of prejudice and for a proper education came from Mary Wollstonecraft.

She was born in Essex, in 1759, the second of six children. Her drunken father ran through a fortune and left the children to bring themselves up as best they could. Little is known of her early education. She was probably taught by her mother, but from the time she was very young she read, studied and thought for herself, and at nineteen she went out into the world to earn her living in the only way open to a gentlewoman. She went to Bath for a time, as a companion; she taught at a school at

Newington Green: she became governess to Lord Kingsborough's family, in Dublin and Bristol.

During these years she gained a first-hand knowledge of the glaring injustices of the eighteenth-century world, created by the inequality of the sexes and of the classes. In 1784, four years after her mother's death, she helped her sister run away from a brutal husband, and in 1787 she published her *Thoughts on the Education of Daughters*. 'Would men but generously snap our chains, and be constant with rational fellowship instead of slavish obedience, they would find us more observant daughters, more affectionate sisters, more faithful wives, more reasonable mothers—in a word, better citizens,' she said.

The following year she became literary adviser to her publishers, which gave her the opportunity to meet many of the liberal thinkers of the day, including Tom Paine, and in 1790, in answer to Burke's *Reflections on the French Revolution*, she wrote her *Vindication of the Rights of Man*, followed in 1791 by her *Vindication of the Rights of Woman*, which she dedicated to Talleyrand.

In suggesting that women had the same rights as men, in the same way as the poor had the same human rights as the rich, she went farther than any woman writer had ever gone before and raised a storm of shocked protest.

She did not pull her punches. In her dedication to Talleyrand she declared that 'modesty, the fairest garb of virtue, has been more grossly insulted in France than even in England, till their women have treated as *prudish* that attention to decency which brutes instinctively observe'.

She did not deny that women had domestic duties in the ordering of their household and the training of their children in their early years, but pointed out that subjection and lack of education prevented them from carrying them out efficiently. Woman, she said, must be in a position to advance the human race instead of retarding it. She did not even claim that women were intellectually, physically and morally the equal of men, but argued that being weaker physically and mentally, and not superior morally, the way in which they were brought up to subordination to their husbands hindered the development of their physical, mental and moral capacities.

She attacked the system of education which directed the one aim of girls to catching a husband and poured scorn on Dr. Gregory's advice in his book *A Legacy to a Daughter*, in which he suggested that a languishing delicacy was more attractive in a girl than any signs of robust health and enjoyment of life. She despised women who 'glory in their subjection' and described a woman of fashion she had known 'who was more than commonly proud of her delicacy and sensibility. She thought a distinguishing taste and puny appetite the height of all human perfection, and acted accordingly.' She 'reclined with self-complacency on a sofa, and boasted of her want of appetite as a proof of delicacy that extended to, or perhaps, arose from her exquisite sensibility'.

'Women are everywhere in this deplorable state,' she said, 'for, in order to preserve their innocence, as ignorance is courteously termed, truth is hidden from them, and they are made to assume an artificial character before their faculties have acquired any strength. . . . Taught from their infancy that beauty is woman's sceptre, the mind shapes itself to the body, and roaming round its gilt cage, only seeks to adore its prison.'

Even worse than Dr. Gregory's advice were the sermons to women of the Rev. Dr. James Fordyce, who also advocated a faltering and timid weakness to promote a sexual attraction, but plumbed the depths of profanity by suggesting that piety was always a touching sight to a man and gave a pleasing composure to the face and figure. Piety was, in fact, of cosmetic value, for the 'beauties of holiness seem to radiate about her'. And the very thought of such deviousness gave Mary Wollstonecraft a 'sickly qualm'.

Dr. Fordyce was all for timidity and ignorance and was one of the many writers who cautioned women to hide carefully any good sense and knowledge they may have happened to possess. A husband must be left to assume that his wife married him because her physical and mental weakness were unable to resist him. It was an outrage to a woman's modesty to confess a strong and enduring love to any man, even her husband, and he advised a wife 'never to let her husband know the extent of her sensibility or affection'.

Rousseau had no justification for discussing women and marriage, for although he broke his wife's heart by his brutal handing over of their children to a foundling hospital from the time of their birth, she was a kitchen maid with so low an intelligence that she was practically an imbecile, unable to read after months of teaching, nor to add up or tell the time, and for days on end he did not bother to address a word to her. Yet he wrote a great deal of nonsense about the education of women, saying amongst other things, that it was to be deplored, since it would make them less subservient to men. Mary Wollstonecraft's reply to this was that she did not want women to have power over men but over themselves.

And 'granting that woman ought to be beautiful, innocent and silly, to render her a more alluring and indulgent companion;—what is her understanding sacrificed for? And why is all this preparation necessary only, according to Rousseau's own account, to make her the mistress of her husband, a very short time? For no man ever insisted more on the transient nature of love.'

She disapproved of the existing boarding-schools for girls, quoting from Day's *Sandford and Merton*: 'We encourage a vicious indolence and inactivity which we falsely call delicacy —we breed them to useless arts which terminate in vanity and sensuality,' and added comments from her own experience.

'In nurseries and boarding-schools I fear girls are first spoiled; particularly in the latter. A number of girls sleep in the same room and wash together. And though I should be sorry to contaminate an innocent creature's mind by instilling false delicacy or those indecent prudish notions which early cautions respecting the other sex naturally engender, I should be very anxious to prevent their acquiring nasty or immodest habits; and as many girls have learned very nasty tricks from ignorant servants, the mixing them thus indiscriminately together is very improper.

'To say the truth, women are in general too familiar with each other, which leads to that gross degree of familiarity that so frequently renders the marriage state unhappy.'

In general she did not approve of boys going away to school either, thinking that children are best brought up in the atmosphere of a home created by loving parents.

For the education of both boys and girls she advocated the establishment of day schools, which should be national rather than private establishments, so that teachers were free to teach what, as educationists, they considered it proper for the children to know, instead of being obliged to teach them what their parents wished them to know, and produce results to please the parents who were paying for the education.

This national system of day schools should be for both sexes and all classes, for she maintained that co-education would produce higher moral standards, bring about a better understanding between men and women and result in happier marriages.

She stressed the importance of women's economic independence and foresaw a time when they would be able to enter the professions, particularly medicine, thereby anticipating Sophia Jex-Blake and Elizabeth Garrett by more than half a century: and she also claimed the right of women to stand for Parliament, at a time when the echoes of Dr. Johnson's sentiment that 'portrait painting was an improper employment for a woman and the public practice of any art, and staring in men's faces was very indelicate in a female' had hardly had time to die away.

A later assessment of Mary Wollstonecraft and her writing was that she was 'one of the forces that helped to mould the nineteenth century' but at the time of the publication of *A Vindication of the Rights of Woman* her book was called shameless. Hannah More thought her a 'disgusting and unnatural character' and Horace Walpole referred to her as a 'hyena in petticoats'.

In 1792 she went alone to Paris, during the Terror, to collect material for her unfinished *Historical and Moral View of the*

French Revolution. There she met Captain Gilbert Imlay, an American timber merchant, and fell deeply in love. In May, 1794, she bore his daughter, Fanny. She adored Imlay, and forgetting that in some characters the burden of adoration induces an unreasoning tedium, was prostrated when he deserted her.

Back in England, she tried to commit suicide from Putney Bridge, but was rescued. Shortly afterwards she resumed her friendship with William Godwin. For a time they lived in separate establishments, but when Mary became pregnant they forgot their theories and married. Their daughter Mary, who was to become the wife of Shelley, was born on August 30, 1797, but a few days later, at the age of thirty-eight, her mother died.

Writing of her in later years, Mary Godwin said: 'Open as day to melting charity, with a heart brimful of generous affection, yearning for sympathy, her life had been one course of hardship, poverty, lonely struggle and bitter disappointment'.

Chapter Thirteen

INTO THE NINETEENTH CENTURY

URING THE EARLY years of the nineteenth century, although many more small boarding-schools for girls came into existence, there was little improvement in the manner of their training and education. In 1808 Thomas Broadhurst who, with his wife, conducted a girls' school at Bath, wrote his *Advice to Young Ladies on the Improvement of the Mind*, in which he congratulated his readers that they were fortunate enough to live in a time when there were more opportunities for their education, a proof that they were now held in 'higher estimation than when the case was otherwise', but warns them against 'any display of literary attainments; since of all objects that are disagreeable to the other sex, a pedantic female, I believe, is the most confessedly so'.

In the same year, the son of John Bowdler, who was a lawyer, worried perhaps by Mary Wollstonecraft's predictions, announced that there was no need to trouble girls with any more education than they were already receiving, for it might tempt them to try to enter professions of a higher status 'than the order of the world will permit them to engage in'.

Elizabeth Sewell has given us a vivid description of her schooldays, first in the Isle of Wight and then at Bath. She was born in 1815, the second of four sisters. Her elder sister went to Miss Crooke's school at Newport in the Isle of Wight when she was three and a half, Elizabeth and the two younger sisters when they were four. Miss Crooke was strict and quick-tempered and the children were terrified of her, though their mother never knew it.

They were taught to read and spell, to write and cipher. They learned Pinnock's Catechism of History and Geography, and they parsed sentences. Using Mrs. Trimmer's *Selections*, they read portions of the Old Testament, the Gospels and the Acts of the Apostles every day and the older girls had French, music and drawing lessons from visiting masters.

At first the sisters were day girls but when they were a little older all four boarded at Miss Crooke's, sharing a bedroom with a fifth small girl. '. . . the wretchedness of the large bedroom, the two blocked-up windows, with a third which we were forbidden even to look out of, on pain of paying half a crown; the great worm-eaten four-post bedsteads, without an atom of curtain or drapery; the deal tables for washing-stands, with the jugs holding rain-water, in which wonderful specimens of entomology disported themselves; the two or three old chairs, which, with our trunks, were the only seats—it makes me shudder to look back upon it all, for there was nothing to cheer us, all was dreary and hopeless', wrote Elizabeth in her autobiography. 'The touch of the coarse sheets, on the first night of going back to school, and the sight of the large horn lanthorn, put upon the floor in the centre of the room, as our only light whilst undressing, were as chilling and depressing to the mind as to the body. In this large room we used to sit in the winter mornings learning our lessons until we were called down to a breakfast of milk and water, with an allowance of three pieces of thick bread and butter, but—except on rare occasions—no more, however hungry we might be.'

In very cold weather they were allowed to stand in front of the schoolroom fire for a few minutes, but that was their only taste of direct warmth, for after that they were sent to their seats for the rest of the day.

Lessons went on from morning till night, and for the slightest fault the girls had to learn extra lessons, such as long lists of French idioms, for a punishment, and if they had had a particularly unlucky day they were doing their punishment until 8 o'clock bedtime and even in to the next day. For greater faults the punishments were more ingenious and for telling a lie the child had to stand in a corner of the schoolroom for hours, wearing a long black gown with a piece of red cloth, cut in the shape of a tongue and emblazoned with the word LIAR, tied round the neck and hanging down in front, an ignominy which struck real terror into many an unfortunate small girl's heart.

Elizabeth Sewell's father was a solicitor, but this was a school of mixed social classes, including the daughters of shopkeepers and farmers. However, when Elizabeth was nearly thirteen, her mother decided to send her and her elder sister Ellen to a small school of only twelve pupils, which was run by Miss Aldridge and her sister at Camden Crescent, Bath.

The teaching at this school was poor, said Elizabeth. 'The French master was an indifferent one, and professed to teach Italian also which I question if he was at all competent to do. We had a second-rate dancing mistress, a fairly good sentimental singing master ... a very inferior drawing master ... and a music master with a great reputation, a violent temper, and an amount of conceit and vanity which made him tell us that he slept in white kid gloves to keep his hands white.'

Elizabeth, who confessed to having little talent for either music or drawing, was as frightened of him as she had been of Miss Crooke. Arithmetic was carefully taught, but it was only from the English master that she learnt anything of lasting value.

These were all visiting teachers and only Miss Aldridge and her sister lived at the school with the girls. They were kind and good but seem to have been ineffective. For Elizabeth those two and a half years at Bath were years 'of most rapid growth for good and evil', she confessed. 'Much that was wrong went on at our Bath school unknown to our governesses; not so much actions as conversation, involving feelings and principles in which were to be found the germs of life-long motives and actions; but we were not a bad set of girls in many ways.'

When Elizabeth was fifteen and Ellen seventeen they came home from Bath to undertake the education of the two younger sisters, who rejoiced at the news that they were at last to leave Miss Crooke: and it was during these years that Elizabeth began to write the stories which won her a modest fame, although only a year or two earlier she had startled a young woman visitor by declaring that 'women had no business to write'.

While Elizabeth and her elder sister were still at Miss Crooke's School, the four eldest Brontë sisters were sampling school life at Cowan Bridge, an establishment which, as the result of a charitable scheme, had been opened a few months earlier for the daughters of poor clergymen.

The fees were £14 a year, the rest of the money for clothing, board, lodging and education being raised by subscription. The curriculum as described in the prospectus seemed comprehensive enough and good value for the money, offering an education in languages, needlework and music, which would equip the young ladies to earn their livings in later life as governesses or teachers. The Rector and Theological lecturer was the Rev. W. Wilson, M.A. Elocution and Ventriloquy were taught by the Rev. Edward Wilson, Housekeeping and Domestic Economy by the Rev. R. Wilson, M.A. and Arithmetic and Dressmaking by Mrs. W. Wilson. This looks as though it were very much a family affair, but the Rev. Ian Blythe undertook Latin, Greek and Philosophy, Miss Jane Thompson English reading and Poetry, while Miss Finch, the singing mistress, was also the scourge mistress, having been engaged for a trifling remuneration, explained Mr. Wilson, 'to assist me in regulating the DISCIPLINE of the College'.

The school was opened in January, 1824. Maria was ten and Elizabeth nine when Mr. Brontë took them there in July of that year. Charlotte was eight when she followed them a few weeks later and Emily, who had been kept at home to recover from whooping cough, was only six, when she arrived in the November. She was the school's forty-fourth pupil. The eldest girl was twenty-two, there were eleven girls in their teens, ten between ten and twelve and only four under ten, of whom three were Brontës and Emily the youngest in the entire school.

The building which had been taken over for the school had low ceilings and stone floors, windows which were either not made to open or so difficult to open that they were always kept shut, narrow winding passages and primitive sanitation.

The girls were called by their surnames and the uniform was a buff nankeen dress with short sleeves and a high neck in summer, with white cotton stockings, and in winter a thick purple dress and black woollen stockings. Holland pockets were tied on in front, to serve as workbags, and at night time they all wore night caps. They wore heavy black shoes and coarse straw bonnets, and for Church on Sundays they had white cotton gloves. Their hair had to be pulled back from their faces and kept short, for Mr. Wilson would not allow hair long enough to be braided or curled. It was a waste of time, he said, and encouraged vanity.

Charlotte they reported to be clever, but Maria, the day-dreamer, was always in trouble. She was punished before the whole school and made to wear the 'untidy' badge on her arm. On other occasions she was turned out of her class and made to stand in the middle of the room, in disgrace. She was brilliant at history, but this did her no good, for her teacher said it only proved that she could do good work if she tried.

Apart from the unhealthy site and the bitter cold of this corner of Yorkshire, the chief trouble at Cowan Bridge during these early months was the appalling food, for despite Mr. Wilson's efforts to provide a cheap but nourishing diet, in the hands of a dirty and incompetent cook whom he seemed afraid to dismiss, it was made not only unpalatable but dangerous.

Mrs. Gaskell, in her biography of Charlotte Brontë, says that the breakfast porridge was often sent up 'not merely burnt, but with offensive fragments of other substances discoverable in it. The beef, that should have been carefully salted before it was dressed, had often become tainted from neglect. . . .' The whole house was pervaded, morning, noon and night, by the smell of rancid fat. Rice puddings were boiled in water taken from a rain butt, which was 'strongly impregnated with the dust lodging on the roof when it had trickled down into the old wooden cask, which also added its own flavour to that of the original rain water. The milk, too, was often 'bingy', to use a country expression for a kind of taint that is far worse than sourness, and suggests that it is caused by want of cleanliness about the milk pans. . . . On Saturdays, a kind of pie, or mixture of potatoes and meat, was served up, which was made of all the fragments accumulated during the week . . . this dinner was more loathed than any in the early days of Cowan Bridge School.'

None of the Brontës was strong and though they were often hungry they could not swallow the food. When the teachers complained to Mr. Wilson, he said that the girls 'were to be trained up to regard higher matters than dainty pamperings of the appetite' and lectured them on the sin of caring over much for carnal matters.

Maria was the first to fall ill, although both she and Elizabeth probably had the seeds of consumption in them before they ever went to the school. Maria slept at the end of a long dormitory, next to the door leading into the bedroom of the hated Miss Scatchard. One morning, when the getting-up bell rang, though she was already very ill and her friends begged her not to try to get up, she struggled to dress herself and began pulling on her black worsted stockings without leaving her bed. Miss Scatchard appeared at that moment, pulled her from the bed and whirled her into the middle of the floor, roundly abusing her for her dirty and untidy habits. And when the sick child at last managed to finish dressing herself and went downstairs, she was punished for being late.

In February, 1825, she became so ill that Mr. Wilson sent for Mr. Brontë, who, deeply shocked at the change in her, took her home by the Leeds coach, but a few weeks later she died of tuberculosis.

In the meantime, typhus had broken out at Cowan Bridge and Mr. Wilson sent for a kind and capable soul who had been a laundress at the school, to come and help nurse the girls. 'When she entered the school-room she saw from twelve to fifteen girls lying about; some resting their aching heads on the table, others on the ground; all heavy-eyed, flushed, indifferent, and weary, with pains in every limb. Some peculiar odour, she says, made her recognize that they were sickening for "the fever".'

Mr. Wilson sent for the doctor and also for his own brother, who was a medical man and who tasted and condemned the girls' food. The cook was dismissed and matters improved. None of the girls died at the school although one died later at her home. And none of the Brontës caught the fever, but Elizabeth was already going the way of Maria, while Charlotte and Emily were suffering from undernourishment.

Elizabeth was sent home in the care of one of the servants from Cowan Bridge and died a fortnight later, on June 15, 1825. And the next day Mr. Brontë set out to retrieve Charlotte and Emily.

For the next few years the girls were taught at home, by their aunt, Miss Bramwell, but in 1831 Charlotte's godparents offered to send her away to school again, this time to the Misses Wooler's School at Roe Head, Mirfield Moor. It was about twenty miles from Haworth and Charlotte, by now fifteen, was happy there, being taught by the five Wooler sisters. There were seldom more than ten girls at the school at any one time and there was a relaxed family atmosphere, although manners were formal and the girls always addressed each other as 'Miss' for at least the first few months of their acquaintanceship.

At this time Charlotte had not yet learnt any English grammar or geography, but had read a great deal of literature, and the girls used to have lively and intelligent debates about books and writers, politics and politicians. Miss Wooler had a knack of making the girls interested in whatever they had to learn, said Mrs. Gaskell, and taught them to think for themselves and be selective. There was plenty of freedom and on half holidays they went for long country walks.

Charlotte stayed there for only three terms but in 1835, as two of the Miss Woolers had in the meantime married, she went back there as a salaried teacher, taking Emily with her as a pupil, with a view to her also becoming a teacher.

Charlotte was put in charge of the youngest girls and found it hard going, for the numbers had increased since her own schooldays, but she suffered less than Emily, with whom she had to share a bed, for Emily could not stand the organized routine of work and play and was too intelligent for the soul-destroying learning by heart of endless dates and facts of history, grammar, geography and literature, many of which were culled from Richmal Mangnall's *Questions*. Within less than three months she became so ill and distraught with home-sickness that she went home, and in October of the same year Anne came to Roe Head in her place.

Two years later, Miss Wooler moved her school to Dewsbury Moor, which was neither so pleasant nor so healthy a spot as Roe Head. Emily, by now nineteen and needing to earn some money, went to Halifax as a teacher in the Misses' Patchett's School, but a few weeks later Charlotte was writing to her school friend, Ellen Hussey, 'My sister E. has gone as teacher in a large school of near 40 pupils near H——. I have had one letter from her since her departure. . . . It gives an appalling account of her duties—hard labour from six in the morning until near eleven at night, with only an half-hour of exercise between. This is slavery. I fear she will never stand it.'

When, some years later, Mrs. Gaskell published this letter in Charlotte's biography, Miss Patchett was deeply offended, for she claimed that her seminary was of the highest order, a finishing school 'for the daughters of gentlemen' rather than a 'cram for tradesmen's daughters'. Less than half the pupils were boarders and the school had five large bedrooms on the first floor and five attic rooms, with spacious ground floor rooms. The schoolroom was in a converted warehouse along-side the house. There were playgrounds and a home farm which supplied good, fresh food. The girls were taught horse-riding and Miss Patchett took them to concerts and museums in Halifax.

Nevertheless, it was too much for Emily, and within six

months she was back at home, soon to be joined by both Charlotte and Anne, for after eighteen months of teaching Charlotte had become morbidly depressed, probably through over-work. She resented the fact that she was plain and must have been an uninspiring teacher. 'I remember I felt my incapacity to *impart* pleasure fully as much as my powerlessness to *receive* it,' she wrote in later years to Miss Wooler, but at the time she quarrelled with her, the immediate reason being that Anne had fallen ill and she felt that Miss Wooler was not taking the illness seriously enough.

That was the last taste of English boarding schools for any of the Brontë sisters, though they had varied experiences as governesses in private families, and in February, 1842, Charlotte and Emily went to M. and Mme Heger's School in Brussels to improve their languages, for they now had the idea of opening a school themselves.

They found the Hegers' School far more comfortable than any English school they had yet encountered, and although Emily did not suffer the routine any more gladly than she had at Roe Head, Charlotte was happy in finding at last an intellectual equal in M. Heger, who was only a year or two older than herself.

It was a large school, part-day, part-boarding school and divided into three classes. In the first were fifteen to twenty girls, in the second about sixty and in the third anything from twenty to thirty girls. The first and second classes occupied a long room, divided by a partition, and in each part were four long ranges of desks, with a platform at the end for the teacher.

School was from nine until twelve noon, when the boarders —about twenty to thirty girls—went to the refectory for bread and fruit, while the day girls, who brought their luncheon with them, went into the garden to eat it. From one to two o'clock they did fancy work, while one of the girls read to them. Lessons continued from two till four, when the day girls left and the boarders dined in the refectory, with M. and Mme Heger presiding.

From five to six the time was their own. Six to seven o'clock was the hour for preparation of lessons, followed by the *lecture pieuse*, a very light supper at eight o'clock, prayers and bed.

The principal bedroom, over the long classroom, had six or eight beds along each side, each one surrounded by white curtains to form a small cubicle.

After nine months at the school, their aunt Miss Bramwell died and the girls returned home. Emily never went back to Brussels but Charlotte returned as an English teacher, with a salary of £16 a year, out of which she paid for German lessons.

Yet her last year at Brussels was deeply unhappy. She was very lonely and found little in common with Mme Heger or the rest of the staff and was made desperately miserable by her unexpressed and unreciprocated love for M. Heger. By January of 1844 she was back in Haworth, but their plans to open a school for five or six boarders at the parsonage came to nothing, for although they had dozens of cards printed announcing their intention, which they sent out to every likely person they knew, they had no response at all. There were already a number of similar schools in Yorkshire, and Haworth was too remote, too bleak and too damp to attract any enquiries.

Mrs. Gaskell, six years older than Charlotte, was for two years in the early 1820s at school at Stratford-on-Avon, and this was probably the same school—Avonbank School for Girls, run by the Misses Mary and Harriet Ainsworth—where Effie Gray spent a year in 1841. In 1854, when her marriage to John Ruskin was being annulled, his father wrote angrily to Mr. Gray: 'If she had when young got the Household taste of her Mother and her domestic turn—her character would have been different, but you sent her about visiting and thinking of Dress till she became unsettled and restless, and then to these Boarding Schools where mistresses pilfer parents and teach Daughters the most approved mode of ruining Husbands. . . .'

Thomas Carlyle, whose marriage, like Ruskin's, was unconsummated, sided with Ruskin in the quarrel, for Millais, whom Effie married shortly after she was free, was writing a few weeks later to Mrs. Gray: 'I have heard that Thomas Carlyle is very boisterous in the question of this *asundering, his judgement is that no woman has any right to complain of any treatment whatsoever*, and should patiently undergo all misery.'

About five years before Effie was at school at Stratford-on-Avon, Frances Power Cobbe was taken by her mother from her home near Dublin, where she had been taught by a governess, for two years schooling at one of the most expensive boarding schools in England. The year was 1836 and Frances was fourteen. Three days by post-chaise brought them from Bristol to Brighton. There were more than a hundred small boarding schools for girls in Brighton at this time, but Frances was destined for perhaps the most expensive of them all, a school for some twenty-four girls at 32 Brunswick Terrace, which had been founded by a Miss Poggi and was now run by Miss Runciman and Miss Roberts. The girls were all well-born, some belonging to the peerage, and the fees for the two years amounted to £1,000.

The education of women was probably at its lowest ebb at this time, wrote Frances Power Cobbe in her autobiography, and considerably poorer than in her mother's time at Queen Square, thirty or forty years earlier. In the 1830s, a girl's education was more pretentious than it had ever been before and 'more shallow and senseless than can easily be believed'.

When she and her mother arrived at Brunswick Terrace, Mrs. Cobbe had pleaded for Frances to have a bedroom to herself and they were shown to a room containing one small bed. But when Frances went to bed that night she found that another bed had been put into it, in which a schoolfellow was already fast asleep. She flung herself down on her knees by her own bed and wept bitterly, and the next morning was reprimanded before the whole school for having been seen to cry at her prayers.

The school, said Frances, obtained the minimum of solid results with the maximum of cost and labour. The staff, in addition to the two proprietors and the sister of one of them, comprised an additional English governess and French Italian and German teachers.

'The din of our large double schoolrooms was something frightful. Sitting in either of them, four pianos might be heard going at once in rooms above and around us, while at numerous tables scattered about the rooms there were girls reading aloud to the governesses and reciting lessons in English, French, German and Italian. This hideous clatter continued the entire day till we went to bed at night, there being no time whatever allowed for recreation, unless the dreary hour of walking with our teachers . . . could be so described by a fantastic imagination.' They walked only six at a time, along the esplanade and surrounding terraces, accompanied by a teacher, and were expected to employ the time usefully by repeating to her French, Italian or German verbs, according to her nationality.

Saturday afternoons were 'Judgment Days', when the two schoolmistresses sat at the head of a long table, the governesses behind them and the girls ranged round the room. On the table in front of Miss Runciman and Miss Roberts were the records of the girls' misdemeanours for the past week—faults such as not finishing lessons, not practising enough, 'stooping', impertinence, disorder in the dress, as for example having a shoelace not properly tied, or telling lies.

Anyone who committed three of these faults in one week was punished by being made to sit in a corner for the rest of the evening.

'Anything more ridiculous than the scene which followed can hardly be conceived,' wrote Frances. 'I have seen . . . no less than nine young ladies obliged to sit for hours in the angles of three rooms, like naughty babies, with their faces to the wall; half of them being quite of marriageable age, and all dressed, as was *de rigueur* with us every day, in full evening attire, of silk or muslin, with gloves and kid slippers.'

Saturday evenings were the worst time of the whole week, and although this was when the girls who escaped punishment were allowed to write home to their parents, they could not write freely, for their letters were scrutinized by the teachers before being dispatched.

Music and dancing were considered the most important subjects in the curriculum. The girls had to practise the piano for two hours a day, under the supervision of a German teacher, and had lessons two or three times a week from piano and singing masters. A Frenchman gave harp lessons at a guinea a time and some of the pupils also took lessons in the concertina and accordion. As several of the girls, including Frances, had no ear at all for music, 'the waste of time involved in all this, the piles of useless music, and songs never to be sung, for which our parents had to pay, and the loss of priceless time for ourselves, were', as she rightly says, 'truly deplorable'.

Madame Michaud and her husband taught them dancing, the stout and elderly Madame dressed in a heavy green velvet dress, with a hem of sable a foot deep, to demonstrate not only all the dances popular in England, but almost every national dance in Europe—the minuet, gavotte, cachucha, bolero, mazurka and tarantella, a sight which was not easily forgotten.

They also had calisthenic lessons from a 'Capitaine' each week for their deportment, involving exercises with poles and dumbbells.

Drawing took up a lot of their time, although it was not well taught. And next in importance were modern languages. They learnt no Greek or Latin but until six o'clock in the evening the girls had to speak in either French, Italian or German, with 'bad marks' for speaking the wrong language at the wrong time.

The study of English was secondary to that of modern foreign languages, but they had an English master and also a writing and arithmetic master. As for history and geography, they had one lesson of each in alternate weeks, mostly confined to the learning by heart of endless facts and dates.

The question of religious instruction defeated their school-mistresses, but they marched the girls to church every Sunday, unless it was raining, conducted morning prayers and recom-

9. *Left:* The House in Camden Street where the North London Collegiate School opened in 1850.

Below: The school's science laboratory (1850–90). The gymnasium and the laboratory were the first of their kind in girls' schools.

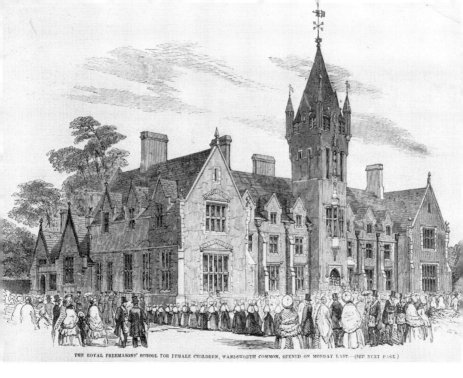

THE ROYAL FREEMASONS' SCHOOL FOR FEMALE CHILDREN, WANDSWORTH COMMON, OPENED ON MONDAY LAST.—(SEE NEXT PAGE)

10. *Above:* The Royal Freemasons' School for Female Children, Wandsworth Common.
Below: A class for girls at the Jews' Free School, Bell Lane, Whitechapel, in 1908.

mended fasting on Ash Wednesday 'as it would be good for the girls' souls as well as their figures'.

Science, for which Miss Runciman and Miss Roberts assured parents that the fullest instruction was given, was covered by a course of nine lectures delivered by a Mr. Walker in a public room in Brighton, comprising one lecture each in electricity, galvanism, optics, hydrostatics, mechanics and pneumatics and three in astronomy.

After two years of this 'mass of ill-arranged and miscellaneous lessons', of the 'shallowest and most imperfect kind', Frances confessed that she had learnt practically nothing but a few facts and figures and a smattering of languages: and it was not until she was home again in Ireland that she began seriously to study and educate herself.

There are countless authenticated stories of girls' boarding schools of the early nineteenth century where the education was as useless as this and conditions of living infinitely worse— schools with insufficient heating, where the food was totally inadequate, the bedrooms dirty and the bed-linen seldom changed, where girls had to sleep two or more in a bed and seldom had any proper exercise or fresh air.

Advertisements for teachers sometimes stressed that they must be able to bear confinement. J. L. Chirol, in his *Enquiry Into the Best System of Female Education* published in 1809, alleged that in some schools bed-linen was 'scarcely changed oftener than every four or five months' and that although the girls washed their hands and faces and combed their hair every morning, their 'other extremities which are more exposed to dirt, are washed only once in six weeks or two months, and the body never, not even in summer'.

The Misses Lawrence, great aunts of the founders of Roedean, kept a school at Gateacre near Liverpool for more than thirty years, and although at the beginning of the century it achieved a high reputation, by the 1830s the standards of both education and living conditions had declined to a point where economy had become 'parsimony which was scarcely honest'. Here the girls slept two in a bed unless parents paid an extra £5 a year for a daughter to have a bed to herself: and even so the beds were pushed so close together 'that they had to be got into from the bottom'.

Yet the niceties of polite society were upheld and during their last meal of the day, which consisted of tea and bread and butter, and followed their 3 o'clock dinner, even though they were hungry again and shivering with cold, they had to maintain the parry and thrust of social conversation while performing the usual balancing act with a cup and saucer in one hand and a plate in the other.

If girls fell seriously ill while away at school and their parents were able to afford a nurse, and if the school were large enough to have a special sick room, they might have been adequately nursed, but for ordinary, mild disorders they were left to recover as best they could. And the almost universal practice of tight-lacing, combined with all the other discomforts, was still wreaking havoc on the health of many a young girl, despite frequent warnings from the doctors. By the 1830s, after the short-lived fashion for the high-waisted Empire dress of flimsy muslin, imported from France during the time of Napoleon and Josephine, which was all right for the young and slender but no good at all for the fat and forties, English women had gone back to waists and petticoats again and corsets were as tight as they had ever been, for a small waist topped by a large bosom was deemed the height of elegance. Girls were again put into their corsets at a very early age and arrived at school in them. Often they slept in them. At one school they were made to wear them continuously, except for a weekly wash. A correspondent to a ladies' magazine of 1830 said she had been fastened into her tight whalebone corset when she was thirteen and made to sleep in it, and another writer that at her fashionable boarding school in the West End of London, where she had arrived when she was thirteen, she had been fastened into her stiff corsets by her governess, and as it laced at the back there was no hope of being able to loosen it surreptitiously.

These corsets were the most formidable and torturing

contraptions. Dr. Willett Cunnington, in his book *The Perfect Lady*, describes the consternation of a tradesman of the late 1820s when his daughter ventured to stoop down in her new corsets. 'Her stays gave way with a tremendous explosion and she fell to the ground,' he said. 'I thought she had snapped in two.'

And James Laver, in his *Concise History of Costume*, quotes the corset-maker who advised a mother 'to make her daughter lie face down on the floor in order that she might then place a foot in the small of her back to obtain the necessary purchase on the laces'.

The tight-lacing often made the girls faint, but this manifestation of fragility and helplessness was considered more attractive than the vulgarity of rude health and more likely to arouse a prospective husband's protective instincts.

Tight lacing also constricted the stomach, so that the languishing young thing had no desire to eat, and the lack of appetite was also thought to be appealing, for no young woman of true breeding would be so ungenteel as to confess to being hungry.

These corsets often caused mortal injuries. There was an extreme case, back in the seventeenth century, of the death of a little girl of two, the doctor declaring that 'her iron bodice was her pain and had hindered her lungs to grow' and the surgeon 'found her breast bone pressed very deeply inwards and he said two of her ribs were broken'.

In 1767, when there was a sharp rise in the cost of food, the *Berrows Worcester Journal* remarked brightly: 'We hear that the Mistresses of several Boarding Schools, having taken into Consideration the present high Price of Provisions, are come to a Resolution to oblige the young Ladies to take in their Stays, in order that their Stomachs may be laced so to accommodate them to the present artificial Dearth'.

Nevertheless, it can have been no laughing matter for many of the poor girls, especially the naturally fat ones.

It was during this period of ridiculous self-consciousness, in the years that Frances Power Cobbe was at school at

Brighton, that Queen Victoria ascended the throne. Although Victoria had many theories about the education of her own family, she was no intellectual and had little interest in the improvement of the education and status of womankind in general. She had not been over-fond of her lessons as a child, though the Duchess of Kent had taken great care of her training.

Victoria complained that during her childhood, despite the devotion of her governess, Baroness Lehzen, she was 'extremely crushed and kept under and hardly dared say a word'. However, she was given a good education, and when she was examined by the Bishops of London and Lincoln they reported favourably of her knowledge of scripture, history, geography, arithmetic and Latin grammar: and she was also taught modern languages, music, dancing, singing and drawing.

Prince Albert had also been carefully trained and educated, first by his tutor, Herr Florschutz, then at the University of Bonn and finally by Baron Stockmar, but like Victoria, he had not been happy in his childhood, mainly, perhaps, because of the estrangement and subsequent divorce of his parents.

He and the Queen took great care with the education of their children and often grieved over the backwardness of Bertie compared with the quick intelligence of the Princess Royal, but they gave their children a happy childhood. 'A good moral, religious but not bigoted or narrow-minded education is what I pray for my children,' said Victoria. Albert said much the same thing, but added that, 'Education must be consistent with the pupil's prospects; nothing is more certain to ensure an unhappy future than disappointed expectations,' and Lord Melbourne, who influenced the young Queen so much during the opening years of her reign, once said: 'Be not over solicitous about education. It may be able to do much but it does not do as much as is expected from it. It may mould and direct the character but it rarely alters it.'

As the Queen matured, she wrote again in her journal about her children's education, prompted this time, perhaps, by the arrival in 1848 of Louis-Philippe, seeking asylum in England.

'I always think and say to myself, let them grow up fit for whatever station they may be placed in, high or low.' Yet on the assumption that the station was going to be high, they were given an education to match, part of the Princesses' training being to walk round a room, addressing pieces of furniture as though they were guests, and changing easily in their conversation from English to French to German.

Yet the Princesses were more liberal-minded than their mother could ever be and both Vicky and Alice shocked their German relatives at times, Vicky in particular when she announced at a dinner party: 'I love mathematics, physics and chemistry', which was regarded as a most remarkable and somewhat indelicate confession. And when she and Alice learned the rudiments of anatomy to help them with their wartime nursing, during the Prussian wars of the nineteenth century, the Queen was appalled, considering such a study 'disgusting'.

She cannot therefore be said to have been of any help to the few English women who by the 1840s and 1850s were trying so valiantly to improve the standard of girls' education in England. She was a great believer in women keeping to their place, and a pretty subordinate one at that, and when, in 1870, there was talk of giving them the vote, she wrote to Mr. Theodore Martin saying:

'The Queen is most anxious to enlist everyone who can speak or write in checking this mad, wicked folly of "Women's Rights", with all its attendant horrors, on which her poor feeble sex is bent, forgetting every sense of womanly feeling and propriety. Lady . . . ought to get a good whipping.'

Chapter Fourteen

THE NINETEENTH CENTURY

IN 1776 THE AMERICAN colonial states had made their
successful bid for freedom from Britain and this was the
year that Adam Smith published his *Wealth of Nations*,
in which he stressed that the wealth of a nation lay in its
labour force. A few years later came the struggle of the people
of France from oppression by the nobility and monarchy, with
the French revolution, which at first had many sympathizers
in England, where industrialism and its attendant evils were
spreading fast. During the Napoleonic wars, the movement
for the abolition of the slave trade grew in strength. The
French Revolutionary Committee made slavery illegal in 1794,
the British in 1807. Yet when the factory and agricultural
workers in Britain voiced their grievances, which were increasing every year, the English government and the employ-
ers, justifiably nervous that there might be a revolution of the
working classes in England, turned a deaf ear. There were
several minor rebellions, the most famous being the machine-
breaking riots of the Luddites, but they were all repressed,
along with the small trade unions which were coming into
existence all over the country.

With the end of the Napoleonic wars, in 1815, the condition
of the agricultural workers, the miners and the industrial
workers of England was little better than slavery, yet the
country was now set to become, for a time, the richest in the
world, with a mighty empire which, after the defeat of
Napoleon, now included the Cape Colony of South Africa.

For the middle and upper classes of England, the increasing

wealth of their industries, estates and farms had offset the trials of the war and they had been affected by it very little. They lived comfortably in their town and country houses, well apart from the scenes of poverty in the industrial and mining districts of the midlands and the north, and turned a blind eye on the misery of the agricultural labourers.

At the time of Queen Victoria's accession, England was extremely wealthy, though the wealth was in the hands of a comparative few. Never had the contrast between rich and poor been more marked and never had the country been more class conscious. Social classes have never been inflexible. With sufficient money and wits and the right personality it has never been particularly difficult to rise in the social scale, provided one is willing to ape and assimilate the manners and customs of one's betters, and this has never been truer than during the nineteenth century, when large fortunes were being made very quickly. One could always lose one's money and sink again, of course, but though the movement from class to class was possible, the classes themselves remained as clearly recognizable strata.

At the top were the nobility and landowners, for ownership of land remained the highest social distinction. These were the families who during the eighteenth century ruled Britain through Parliament. As late as 1900 one in ten of the population were domestic servants, so this upper crust had no problems in the running of their large town and country houses and they often employed forty or more indoor servants.

Below them were the rich upper classes—lesser landowners and country squires and members of some of the professions. The sons of these two top levels of society were sent to the public schools and universities, for they usually entered one of the accepted professions, and the daughters were taught at home by a governess or sent to one of the fashionable boarding schools, learning the usual accomplishments and little else, though some were trained to administer to the poor, as part of their social duty, so that when they left the schoolroom they were ready to become the wives of neighbouring squires, of officers in the army or navy, of Indian or Colonial civil servants, of university professors or teachers in public schools, of clergymen, barristers or doctors.

The middle classes had their own subdivisions. The upper strata were usually wealthier but less well educated than those above them, having made their money in the mills and mines and by industrial speculation. Their children developed according to their mental abilities and personalities. Some moved easily into the upper classes, either by marriage, by entering one of the professions or merely by living on first-generation, inherited wealth. Others followed their fathers into the family business and created their own middle-class social world.

The women of all these social classes, with a good supply of servants and a nursery staff for their children, had no household duties which could not be delegated and were able to fill their time as they pleased.

The core of the middle classes—merchants, owners of small businesses and shops, members of some of the less socially acceptable professions and lower-grade civil servants, living on perhaps a tenth or less of the incomes of the upper ranks of their own class, strove to achieve the same pattern of security, formality and comfort, maintaining a semblance of prosperity and decorum, with the help of two or three servants, or perhaps only one unfortunate maid-of-all-work.

All these sections of the community, from the lowest of the middle classes upwards, strove to copy to the best of their ability the manners and customs of the class immediately above them.

At the bottom of this social structure, however, well below any real human contact and understanding, existed the bulk of the country's population, the unconsidered poor whose numbers were so vast that some foretold that, if they were not kept in their place, they might one day threaten the financial security of the entire country. These were the artisans, the factory workers, the miners and industrial workers, the fishermen, farm hands, dockers, seamstresses and domestic servants, the shop assistants, and, even lower, the residue of casual labourers and vagrants. They worked incredibly long hours for starvation wages, had no education and were appallingly badly housed.

The population was rising at an unprecedented rate and in 1851, when it was around seventeen million, having doubled itself since 1800, fifteen and a half million men and women were wage-earners. This was the working class, a large majority of whom were employed in industry, and the figure did not include children under ten, many of whom were already earning their own living.

Only about one tenth of the population had any schooling and half of London's one and a half million people could not read or write.

The Children's Employment Commission of 1842 reported on women mine workers who laboured in the pits for twelve hours a day and spent half the night washing, cleaning and cooking. Children were taken down the mines, usually at the age of eight or nine, but sometimes when they were only four or five years old. Both women and children were employed to carry baskets of coal on their backs along pit passages and up steep ladders to the surface, and girls of six were found carrying half-hundredweight loads of coal. The mining children usually worked twelve to sixteen hours a day below ground, but there were exceptional cases where they had been in the pits for thirty-six hours at a stretch. The Mines Bill, passed that same year, 1842, made it illegal for boys under ten years of age to work in the pits or for women and girls to be employed underground at all, but the lot of the miners as a whole remained soul-destroying. They worked below ground for twelve to fourteen hours a day and large numbers contracted silicosis or tuberculosis and died before they were forty-five.

Factory conditions were no better. At the stocking-weaving factory at Hinckley, for example, where both parents and their children were employed, the average earnings of the entire family were 11s. 4d. a week. They lived on bread and porridge and had to work for seven days a week to avoid starvation; and in the sheds and cellars where they slept they could not afford beds. The nail workers of Sedgeley were found to be living on the meat of diseased animals, which had been discarded for normal human consumption. The knife grinders of Sheffield were dying in their late twenties or early thirties through working continuously in a bent position and inhaling metal dust particles. Men, women and children in the potteries spent long hours dipping finished pots into fluids containing lead and arsenic. Their hands were always wet and the poison penetrated the softened skin, all too often producing paralysis, epilepsy and fatal poisoning. The lace-makers of Nottingham employed children of seven or even younger as runners, who had to follow the threads of the elaborate patterns and withdraw them with a needle; and the work was so detailed and fine that after a few years many of the children became incurably blind. The bobbin lacemakers were usually very young girls who had to sit for hours bent over their cushions, and as they wore stays with wooden busks, their ribs became displaced and they often died of consumption.

The makers of neckties contracted to work sixteen hours a day for 4s. 6d. a week and shirtmakers, working from four or five in the morning till midnight, received 2s. 6d. to 3s. a week. Dressmakers worked in similar intolerable conditions, in workrooms which were ill-lit and cold, for all the daylight hours, which in summer time often extended to midnight. The girls never stood the strain for long. Those who did not marry or find other work, broke down in health, usually dying of tuberculosis, and the system was maintained only by a constant supply of fresh girls from the country.

The first Reform Bill of 1832 had given 143 more seats in Parliament, to represent the new towns of the industrial areas, so that there was at last the beginning of a fairer representation in Parliament, but the numbers of the electorate remained very low, for to the existing 440,000 out of a population of some fourteen million people, only another 22,000 voters were added: and it was not until the Second Reform Bill of 1867 that working men in the towns were given the right to vote, and agricultural working men were not to receive it until 1884. In 1832 the problems to be discussed were child labour; housing; conditions in the factories; the right to form trade unions, now that the apprenticeship system had inevitably broken down, with the spread of industrialization, and wages were no longer fixed by law; and the vexed question of education.

The first trade unions were formed but women were not welcomed in them, for it was feared that they would tend to keep wages too low. In regard to education, for the children of the poor there were still a few charity schools, although where endowments had been reinvested and schools re-organized, the money had nearly always gone to the foundation of schools for boys, and the girls were ignored. There was also a slowly increasing number of schools provided by the British and Foreign School Society and the National Society for Promoting the Education of the Poor in the Principles of the Church of England, known more familiarly as the British and Foreign Schools and the National Schools. But the population went on growing, spreading over the countryside, turning villages into towns and towns into industrial cities, and the numbers of schools available were soon hopelessly inadequate, nor were there enough teachers available, nor enough means of training them.

In 1833, the year that Great Britain abolished slavery throughout the Empire and appointed the first factory inspectors, to check the hours and conditions of work of children in industry, the government made a grant of £20,000 to the British and Foreign Schools and the National Schools, for the extension of their work, but the sum was far too small to make any impression on the growing problem.

In 1839 a committee of the Privy Council was set up to consider 'all matters affecting the education of the People'. The question of compulsory education was discussed and many urged that it was now necessary, as the country could no longer afford to employ such a large body of unskilled and uneducated labour. The members in one of the earliest unions, the Amalgamated Society of Engineers, were all skilled men who had served an apprenticeship, for with the increasing skills demanded by the new technologies of industry, the apprenticeship system was revived for a time, in this and other specialized crafts and trades; and only in 1919, when the engineers amalgamated with six other unions and became the Amalgamated Engineering Union was membership no longer restricted to skilled craftsmen.

However, in 1839 the majority of the Privy Council committee disliked the new trade unions as much as the thought of an educated working class. On March 29, 1834, the Liberal *Morning Post* had declared that 'the Trades' Unions are, we have no doubt, the most dangerous institutions that were ever permitted to take root, under the shelter of the law of any country'. Two days later, *The Times* wrote that 'the real gravamen of their guilt was the forming a dangerous Union to force up, by various means of intimidation and restraint, the rates of labourers' wages. . . .'; and the following day the *Morning Herald* announced that 'Trade Unions are bad things. They are bad in Principle, and they lead to consequences in unison with that badness of principle.'

In regard to education, all the old arguments and doubts were raised in Parliament and the Press about the need, or even the advisability, of educating the poor, while a new cry was now heard, suggesting that compulsion was an 'infringement of liberty'. And if it were to be compulsory, should it be free? And should it be denominational? The argument was to go on for the next thirty years and there was little pity in their hearts for the plight of the hundreds of children growing up in abysmal ignorance during the prosperous years of the forties and fifties, although additional grants were made, from time to time, to the British and National Schools, who did their best and developed a system whereby their own pupils, who wished to become teachers, were able to practise as pupil teachers—a development of the monitor system.

They were not the only ones concerned about the teaching of

poor children. Early in the century Robert Owen, a factory owner of Clydeside, found amongst his two thousand employees that a quarter were children between five and six years old who came from the workhouses of Edinburgh and Glasgow, and none of the other three quarters had had any education at all and came from families whose home was a single, squalid room. For the children he provided, in 1816, schools where they learned, in addition to the three R's, geography, history, nature study, singing and dancing. They received this education from the age of five, and not until they were over ten years old were they admitted to the factory to work.

Inspired by the work of the Swiss Italian Pestalozzi, Owen believed that rich and poor should have the same educational opportunities and needed a proper environment in which to develop intellectually, morally and spiritually. In addition to providing the schools, he improved the housing conditions of his employees and opened a store where they could buy good-quality food at a little more than cost price—a beginning of the co-operative movement. Life in Owen's mills became a blessing instead of a burden.

For the pauperized unemployed Owen advocated communities of about 1,200 people, settled in areas of about a thousand acres, living in one large building with communal kitchens and dining rooms, but separate family accommodation, working communally and sharing the profits of their labours. Each family was to have the care of its children until they were three and after that, he said, they should be brought up by the community.

His plan aroused a good deal of interest at the time, when the unemployment after the Napoleonic wars was so widespread, but it was later argued that, with the rising tide of industrialism and its world-wide ramifications and competition, isolated communities which stepped aside from the main stream, to work out their own salvation, had no chance: and when Robert Owen died, in 1857, the prosperity of New Lanark came to an end.

In 1824 a London Infant School Society was founded by Samuel Wilderspin, its object being 'to care for children from the age of two to six, while their mothers were at work'. This first nursery school declared for its aim 'the acquisition of habits of cleanliness and decorum, of cheerful and ready subordination, of courtesy, kindness and forbearance, and of abstinence from every thing impure and profane, a scene, in short, at once of activity and amusement, of intellectual improvement and moral discipline'.

Understandably there was a shortage, if not an entire absence, of teachers who could face such a daunting challenge, but it was not until twelve years later, in 1836, that the first college for training them was established. This was the Home and Colonial Infant School Society, opened in the Gray's Inn Road for the training of infant school teachers. They were given a few weeks of special training in the teaching of very young children, based on the theories of Pestalozzi, as well as a little general education, and later a short course in the training of older children was given here.

Sir James Kay-Shuttleworth, the secretary of the 1839 committee of the Privy Council on education, had studied the problem widely throughout England and Scotland, and also in Europe, and he introduced a system of inspection of all the government-aided schools. He arranged for better education in some of the workhouse schools and in 1840 opened a training school for teachers in Battersea. Two years later, the National Society founded Whitelands College for Women in Chelsea, its plan of education and teacher-training based on Kay-Shuttleworth's ideas. By 1846 there were nine colleges in which women could train to be elementary school teachers, most of them under the charge of an Anglican clergyman who was also the college chaplain. In the early days, most of the students had come from the elementary schools themselves, having become pupil teachers, and at the colleges they were given a secondary education as well as training in teaching, the length of the course varying in each college, from a few months to two or three years.

In the National and British Schools conditions were slowly improving, but the same could not be said for many of the Charity schools. At the Grey Coat School, for example, changes were gradually made in the children's dress. The boys' leather breeches were replaced by corduroys and by 1834 the girls were in straw bonnets instead of the old coifs. They were wearing petticoats of blue baize and had discarded their leather bodices for home-made stays, which were made of a material described mysteriously in the accounts as 'foul weather'. The laundress no longer slept in the ironing room and iron bedsteads, hair mattresses and bolsters had replaced the old wooden bedsteads and flock mattresses. Lavatories were installed and the boys no longer had to wash in the trough in front of the school house. A gift of £200 had been received, the interest of which was to be spent on prizes for the children, but for many years the money invariably went to the boys and not the girls.

The governors were all distinguished men, including Archbishops of Canterbury and Deans of Westminster, but in 1834 the Royal Grant of £15 a year was withdrawn, for no apparent reason, and in the teaching and conduct of the school matters were as bad as during the reign of George III. In 1822 the treasurer reported that he had received a letter complaining that the conduct of the mathematical master was 'very depraved, particularly for one having the care and instruction of Youth', that he was frequently absent from duty and had been in prison for some long time for debt.

He was dismissed, but the governors do not seem to have asked the headmaster why he had not reported his absence before. Instead, the headmaster, James Lancaster, appointed his son John as mathematical master, and when James died, in 1824, John took his place, at the age of twenty-four, with his mother still acting as matron.

The boys were mercilessly flogged and many ran away, while no less than seven summons in one day were applied for against Mrs. Lancaster, accusing her of gross cruelty to the girls. The magistrate referred her back to the governors, who inexplicably overlooked the complaints, and for the next eleven years the Lancaster family remained in office. Then an assistant master lodged another protest to the governors, complaining of John Lancaster's brow-beating insolence and ignorance and mentioning, incidentally, that the girls had had no lessons in writing or arithmetic for the previous five weeks.

The Lancasters went at last and the school, with now about a hundred children, battled on, its surroundings vastly improved when, during the 1840s, the Westminster Improvement Commissioners cut the New Street from Chelsea Road to the Abbey, later to be called Victoria Street, through the terrible Westminster slums, and many of the murky alleys and crumbling courtyards of that Devil's acre were cleared away.

At the Bridewell, the number of apprentices was still declining. In 1806, 358 vagrants had been admitted and 970 poor persons were temporarily detained there. By 1792 there had been no apprentices left at all at the Bridewell, but on the urgent insistence of the Chaplain, Thomas Bowen, that the original purpose of the foundation had been to provide for the homeless London apprentice, who after the completion of his education and training should be made a freeman of the City of London, a few were again admitted, mainly from Christ's Hospital: but after Bowen's death, little interest was taken in them or their education.

In 1807 there was an enquiry into the question of the Bridewell children and a Parliamentary report declared that the revenues of the hospital amounted to £7,000 a year but were not well applied. 'Apprentices are admitted and taught by art-masters, but they might better gain a knowledge of their trades elsewhere, at far less expense.'

Within a few years the apprentices had been moved, and in 1830 the Bridewell governors had opened the House of Occupation at St. George's Fields, to provide a general and industrial education for boys and girls between the ages of eight and eighteen. About the same time, the Philanthropic Society founded a small industrial school in the grounds of their sister foundation, the Bethlem Hospital—and this at a

11. *Above:* Roedean, the famous girls' Public School, situated between Rottingdean and Brighton.
Below: Old Hall, Newnham College, Cambridge, as it was in 1875.

12. *Above:* Girls in modern uniform going to afternoon lessons at Christ's Hospital School.
Below: Woodberry Down Comprehensive School in the London Borough of Hackney.

time when more than two million English children were receiving no education at all.

By 1840 the school at St. George's Fields was successfully established and expanding. There were two hundred and twenty boys and girls by now, their careers largely directed by the superintendent, Joseph Myall. As at the Grey Coat school, many boys went into the navy, while the girls were trained for posts in hospitals or private families.

When the dreadful old Bridewell was at last closed down, in 1855, the revenue from the property was used for its original intention—the education of the children, and in 1860 the name of Bridewell, with all its grim associations, was dropped and the new organization became known as King Edward's School. By 1867 a new school for a hundred boys had been built at Witley in Surrey, to which the boys were moved from London, while the girls remained at St. George's Fields.

Things did not go so happily for the Grey Coat children, for this was the year of the 'Great Rebellion' when the boys staged a full-scale uprising against their brutal and bullying headmaster. Some were expelled but the master resigned and the governors made tentative efforts to improve matters by extending the holidays, slightly improving the food and introducing new subjects into the curriculum: but it was to be several years before anything constructive was done about the school and its unhappy children.

There was the most appalling poverty in London at this time and in 1844 the Ragged School Union was established, a charity which aimed to give a rudimentary education to the destitute and neglected children of the city and its suburbs. The education was described as 'secular, moral and religious' and was intended 'to induce habits of industry, and to provide a refuge for the friendless and the fallen'.

A few years later the Ragged Church and Chapel Union provided places of worship for them, and by 1862 there were 146 Ragged Schools in London, attended each day by more than 17,000 children, as well as forty churches and 'preaching stations', where the average attendance was 2,500 each week.

Nearly three thousand of the teachers at the Ragged Schools were voluntary, but there were four hundred paid teachers and four hundred monitors. Many of the children were placed in work and the Union gave a reward to those who held their jobs, with good characters, for twelve months.

For boys an off-shoot of this was the Ragged School Shoe-black Society in Ship Yard, Temple Bar, which gave accommodation and employment for seventy-five boys between the ages of twelve and sixteen, who had been recommended by the Ragged School Union. For the girls, there were scores of small refuges in London, run by various charities, but in connection with the Ragged Schools was the King Edward Ragged and Industrial School and Refuge for Destitute Girls, founded in Spitalfields in 1846. They had accommodation for seventy girls between the ages of ten and sixteen who were entirely destitute—either orphaned, abandoned or the children of criminals—many of them being sent there from the Ragged Schools or Nightly Refuges, and during the 1860s the Spital-fields School had forty residents and four hundred day girls, for most of whom work was ultimately found, mostly in domestic service.

In the early years of the nineteenth century, the education of the middle and upper classes was also beset with problems. As industry and commerce grew increasingly technical, it became apparent that the education of boys must be adapted to the changing times. The old, endowed grammar schools, apart from a few notable exceptions, such as the Manchester Grammar School, had been in decline since the end of the seventeenth century, and the Dissenting Academies, which had done such valuable service during the eighteenth century, gradually, one after another, closed down. The fashion was for more public schools, and of the existing eighty-nine independent public schools in England and Wales, fifty-four were founded during the nineteenth century, including Cheltenham, Marlborough, Wellington, Haileybury, Clifton and the City of London.

Dr. Arnold, who was headmaster of Rugby from 1828 to

1842, made many reforms which were soon to be adopted by other public schools. He was a disciplinarian and suppressed the bullying, drinking and rowdyism which had been rife in the earlier days. He introduced the prefect system, developed the House system and encouraged organized games, as a useful aid to character building. Thus, well grounded in the Classics, cricket and Christianity, the English public schools turned out young men who, if they had no outstanding intellectual attainments, nevertheless bore the stamp of assurance which was often the envy and despair of many other European countries. These were the men who became the Empire builders, the governors, magistrates, district commissioners and army officers.

In 1864 a commission investigating the teaching in the public schools reported that not only was too much emphasis given to the teaching of the Classics, but the teaching itself was inadequate. Character was being developed at the expense of scholarship. The syllabus was extended and by the end of the century public schools were giving a liberal education which included mathematics and the sciences, with modern languages as well as the Classics.

The long overdue reforms at Oxford and Cambridge took place gradually, throughout the century. Obsolete laws in regard to the holding of professorships and fellowships were set aside and in 1877 the religious tests were abolished, making the universities open to Nonconformists and Roman Catholics. Fellows were no longer expected to take holy orders or to be celibate. The whole standard of examinations was revised, curricula widened and the level of scholarship raised, so that, during the second half of the century, the number of students rose considerably.

At the same time several new universities were founded. The London University received its charter in 1836. The following year Durham University was founded, and between 1851 and 1892 colleges were established at Manchester, Leeds, Bristol, Sheffield, Birmingham, Liverpool and Reading, all of which ultimately became universities.

Provision for the education of girls was an altogether different and thornier problem, for there was still a very strong feeling to be found in every rank of society that they got on better without it. The old contention that they had not the same mental capacity as men was still firmly held by most men, and many women as well.

The standard of education in the middle-class girls' boarding schools was actually declining and many of the teachers were themselves uneducated. Even in the schools which claimed French, Italian and German in the curriculum, girls were not able to speak or write them correctly, while the endless lists of facts which they were obliged to learn by heart from Mangnall's *Questions* and Mrs. Markham's *History of England* were unrelated, meaningless and quickly forgotten.

The private governesses were, for the most part, as poorly equipped for their work as the teachers in the boarding schools, and for those who were residential, their lives were divided between a bleak, back bedroom and the schoolroom. Here the governess's meals were brought to her by one of the servants, who usually despised her for being neither one of them nor one of the family. The highest wage was £30 a year and it was not unknown for a governess to be asked for an advance to her employer of £50 in exchange for a comfortable home, which was repaid in instalments as a salary.

The expensive finishing schools to which the daughters of the wealthy were sent were more concerned with etiquette, stylish behaviour and accomplishments than learning.

Although the system of the marriage dowry was disappearing, throughout the nineteenth century it was still assumed that girls of the middle and upper classes would be kept by their fathers until they married and then by their husbands. The daughters of the poor were a remote and alien breed who had to fend for themselves at a very early age and usually worked after marriage as well, but such work as was available to them did not need an education. In the census of 1851 well over a million girls and women of the nine million of them throughout England and Wales were domestic servants or agricultural workers and thousands more were working in the factories, particularly the textile industries.

This census also revealed the fact that there were more women in the country than men. For every 1,042 women there were only 1,000 men. And the disparity in numbers was rising. By 1881 the surplus of women had risen to 1,055 women to every 1,000 men and this trend continued until well past the middle of the twentieth century, brought about in the first place by large-scale emigration of men to the Colonies and the United States and later by the losses of life during the two World Wars.

For mid-Victorian girls, brought up to the one aim of marriage, as the only alternative to lonely spinsterhood, the gradual realization that there were just not enough young men to go round offered a grim prospect.

'Whenever I have seen, not merely in humble, but affluent homes, families of daughters waiting to be married,' said Charlotte Brontë, 'I have pitied them from my heart.'

For the daughters of the wealthy, the economic prospect at least was bearable, but while Victorian fortunes were being made, others were being lost. The halcyon days of England's supremacy in the world's markets were not very long, and as the century progressed, although in every field of industry the country appeared to be expanding its economy, using more wool and cotton, producing more coal and pig iron, gradually her commercial position began to decline relatively through competition from other countries, many of which had become industrialized with British capital. It was no sudden collapse but a slow, inexorable erosion which was barely discernible until the 1870s.

But well before this time the question arose that if a girl could not find a husband and her father were unable to leave her enough money for a private income, what was she to do? She could become a paid companion or she could enter the only profession open to her, which was teaching, and for this she had no solid learning or training to offer, even if she had possessed the aptitude. Work in a factory or shop was unthinkable, for she must, come what may, maintain her social status.

It was no use telling her, when she was faced with the economic necessity of earning her living or starving, that woman's place was in the home, safe from the wiles and snares of the outside world and protected by her menfolk, yet the mid-Victorian male clung tenaciously to the principle that his women folk must be pure and unsullied, living a secluded life, subservient to his wishes. Any independent action would be an infringement of his rights.

They were brought up in abysmal ignorance about sex and as their wedding day approached were conditioned by their mothers to believe that they must tolerate love-making as best they could and regard it as an unpleasant fact of life which must be endured.

In this age of repression, prostitution inevitably flourished, but since the prostitutes were mainly from the lower classes, they were socially unacceptable anyway, and undeserving of the chivalry which must be extended to women of the middle and upper classes.

There were, of course, exceptional women who did not conform, as George Eliot, who lived openly with the un-happily married George Lewes, yet most of the women novelists reflected in their works the beliefs and attitudes to men and marriage in which they had been indoctrinated. The Brontës revealed a passion which was seldom expressed elsewhere with such anguish and drama, but Jane Austen, though she never married, gave a faithful picture of the society in which she lived, and so did Mrs. Gaskell and Mrs. Craik.

When Charlotte M. Yonge began to write, in the 1840s and 50s, her family regarded authorship as unladylike and they would consent to the publication of her first book only on condition that she would accept no money from it for her own use: and this provision she willingly accepted.

Frances Power Cobbe's father turned her out of the house when she confessed to him that she had lost her faith in the

Trinity, though he allowed her to return to nurse him during his last illness.

Although both men and women writers were still maintaining that women were mentally inferior to men, or alternatively that men did not like clever women and that for a girl to betray any flicker of intellectual activity reduced her chances in the marriage market, a growing body of both sexes began to express concern and indignation at the plight of the governesses. In 1843 the Governesses' Benevolent Institution was formed, by a group of Anglican clergymen and others, to help the hundreds of decayed gentlewomen who had grown too old to teach and were faced with an old age of destitution. It was a step in the right direction, although as late as 1869 an advertisement in the *Daily Telegraph* shows that their status in the labour market was still abysmal. 'Wanted Daily Governess. Hours ten to six. For three children aged eight, ten and eleven. Requirements English, French, Music and Needlework (and perhaps Drawing). Salary to commence at seven shillings a week.'

The honorary secretary of the Governesses' Institution, the Reverend David Laing, also opened an employment registry for girls and young women who wished to become governesses, and very soon realized how hopelessly inadequate their education had been. A college for the education of prospective governesses was not only necessary, if the standard of girls' education generally were to be raised, but it was realized that a proper training would give the governesses the right to command higher salaries.

By October of 1847 the institution had enlisted the help of some of the professors from the Anglican King's College in the Strand, all of them clergymen of the Church of England, who without fee gave free lectures to some of the young women enrolled on Dr. Laing's registry. These were so successful that day lectures were also given to young women who were free to attend them.

The Honourable Miss Murray, one of Queen Victoria's ladies-in-waiting, had been collecting money for the

establishment of a women's college and this she now handed
over to David Laing. A house was acquired in Harley Street,
the Queen allowed it to be called Queen's College and
established some scholarships, and it opened its doors in the
spring of 1848.

Queen's was soon offering an education to girls over twelve
years old, whether they intended to teach or not, and amongst
its early pupils were Sophia Jex-Blake, who was destined to
win the battle for the entry of women into the medical
profession and found the London School of Medicine, and
Dorothea Beale, while Frances Mary Buss, already teaching
during the daytime, enrolled as an evening student.

The board of governors of Queen's College were all men
and so was the principal. Professor Maurice, professor of
English literature at King's College, was Principal from 1851
to 1853, and he defined the difference between school and
college teaching. 'The teachers of a school may aim to impart
information; the teachers of a college must lead to the ap-
prehension of principles,' he said, though many school teachers
today would say that the main purpose of teaching is to inspire
interest, so that the pupil is moved to find out more about the
subject for himself.

Queen's was described as a college, although it never
acquired university status, and was really an exceptionally
good school, giving courses, in the manner of a university, in
English, theology, history, geography, Latin, mathematics,
modern languages, natural philosophy, music, fine arts and
pedagogy. Students could take whichever courses they wished
and the college set its own examinations, issuing certificates
to the successful students.

The college was a success. In the first term two hundred
students enrolled, of whom 132 were evening students. The
association with the Queen and Miss Murray gave it social
distinction, while the connection with the Governesses'
Benevolent Institution and King's College gave it the blessing
of the Church. All the professors, with the exception of those
for fine art and music, and two foreigners, were Anglican

clergymen, for as headships of the public schools were not yet free to the laity, it was still usual for men entering the teaching profession to take Holy Orders.

It was considered improper for young women to be alone with a professor so, in order to maintain the proprieties, a lady resident was appointed to watch over them and 'lady visitors of rank and talent' were recruited, who volunteered a number of hours each week for the express purpose of sitting with the girls while they attended the lectures.

Very soon after Queen's College was launched, Mrs. Elizabeth Reid, a rich widow, friend of Harriet Martineau and Henry Crabb Robinson, revealed the plans she had been cherishing for years for a somewhat different women's college. At a time when Oxford and Cambridge were still barred to any but Anglicans, but university colleges free of any religious tests were being founded throughout the country, she wanted to establish for young women not another school but an institution 'to provide for ladies, at a moderate expense, a curriculum of liberal education'. The instruction was to be given 'on the same plan as in the public Universities, of combined lectures, examinations, and exercises'.

In contrast to Queen's, Mrs. Reid wished her college to be undenominational and to include women in its government. The aims of the college were therefore not so utilitarian as Queen's, which was founded in the first place for the teaching of governesses. It aimed at giving girls a higher education for the sake of the education itself and the enjoyment of widening horizons which it would afford.

As had happened when Queen's was first planned, Mrs. Reid's scheme was ridiculed in the Press. Moreover it was associated with the unorthodox Unitarians and many regarded it as a dangerously radical undertaking, particularly when Francis Newman, a younger brother of the Cardinal, who, in contrast to his brother, had moved towards Dissent, was appointed secretary of the Board and also to the council of the new college. He was professor of Latin at the godless University College in Gower Street and so rationalist in his views and eccentric in his appearance that parents hesitated to allow their daughters to come under his influence, despite the army of Lady Visitors appointed to observe decorum.

However, in October, 1849, Mrs. Reid's Ladies' College was opened at 47 Bedford Square, with a staff of thirteen professors, of whom only five were clergymen. Three of these were Anglicans from King's College, who gave their services free, and the other two were Dissenters. Most of the professors held university chairs and the others were given the courtesy title of professor.

During the early years of Bedford College it attracted so few students, and the internal dissention between the various committees, the teaching staff and the lady visitors was so bitter, that the project very nearly floundered.

In December, 1849, the Council reported to the Board that 'the total number of attendants on the College lectures, we find to be 68. Of these, as many as 42 attend only one set of lectures each, a considerable fraction of the 42 being ladies of mature age, who have chosen to avail themselves of the services of your professors. Of the rest, 15 attend two sets of lectures each, 8 attend three sets each, and only 3 four sets.'

To keep things going, they were soon admitting any girls over the age of twelve, and this, diverging from the original aim of the college, created further dissension in the governing council. The professors from King's had to resign when Dr. Jelf, their principal, declared that they must not hold office in an institution to which so many Dissenters were attached, in particular the professors from University College, including Francis Newman.

Several other resignations followed, probably because there was little or no fee offered—the maximum being 10s. 6d. an hour—or because the quality of the students was too low. Seven subjects had to be dropped from the curriculum because there was no staff to teach them and the number of students continued to decline. Then Newman resigned.

'Can anyone explain the failure of this College?' wrote Mrs. Reid at the end of 1851, 'or tell how it is that, where one might reasonably expect several hundreds, the number who seem to look for Education here is somewhere under nineteen?'

Yet they struggled on. New teaching appointments were made which proved successful and popular with the students, and more enrolled, bringing in badly needed fees. The library was founded and Mrs. Reid offered scholarships 'to be devoted to the encouragement of persevering attendance in the studies of the College'. The Council demurred at first in regard to the scholarships, thinking that 'competition was dangerous to the health of girls', but Mrs. Reid prevailed and the scholarships were accepted.

Early in 1853 a junior school was opened for girls from the age of nine, some of whom arrived with their governesses or nurses, who sat through the classes or waited outside till their charges were ready to be taken home again. Their lessons were directed to prepare them for the senior school and their fees helped to steady the shaky finances of the college.

Slowly it began to make headway and more organized courses of study were planned, with more scholarships as well as prizes and terminal examinations, yet for the ageing Mrs. Reid these were years of disappointing struggle and dis-illusionment. Writing to Crabb Robinson in 1856 she lamented that it was difficult to find a single man 'who is deliberately of opinion that Female Education, the improvement of the Moral and Mental education of Women, is of any importance to society;—while all the time the good man may be teased with a very silly and tiresome wife himself who is spoiling the minds of his children'.

In 1861, when the house next door fell vacant, the college was able to extend its premises to 48 Bedford Square, part of the house being devoted to the work of the college and the rest to a new venture—a boarding house for the college students.

Chapter Fifteen

MISS BUSS AND MISS BEALE

FRANCES MARY BUSS was born in 1827 in Mornington Crescent, off the Hampstead Road in north-west London, the daughter of gifted and highly intelligent parents, her father being an artist. Frances was sent to a small day school for girls near her home, run by a Mrs. Wyand, where she received a conventional but rather better than average schooling, but her father encouraged and directed her reading and it was from him and her mother that she gained her real education. At fourteen she had begun to teach in Mrs. Wyand's School and a few years later her mother took a short course of training at the Home and Colonial School Society and opened a little school for small boys and girls in Kentish Town. Frances, by now eighteen, left Mrs. Wyand's and opened a school for 'a select number of Young Ladies as Morning Pupils' in the same house as her mother's school.

Frances was always very conscious of her own shortcomings and when Queen's College opened, in 1848, she gladly seized the opportunities it offered and enrolled as an evening student. Amongst her new teachers were Charles Kingsley, Dean Trench and the Rev. E. H. Plumptre. 'Queen's College opened a new life to me intellectually,' she wrote later. 'To come into contact with the minds of such men was a new experience to me and most women. I was a member of the evening lectures at the outset.'

While she was attending Queen's College, she and her mother moved their schools to a larger house nearby and here both her father and the brothers helped with the teaching: and when she left Queen's, at the age of twenty-two, she and her mother gave up this establishment and Frances opened the North London Collegiate School for Ladies in Camden Street, her family joining her as part of the staff.

While Frances had been an evening student at Queen's, Dorothea Beale, four years her junior, had been a day student, so although they were to become lifelong friends they did not meet until some years later.

Dorothea's family was comparatively wealthy. Like Frances she had the same help from her parents with her studies, particularly from her father, who was a doctor. After a sketchy education from a succession of visiting governesses, she had been sent to a boarding school where, though it was regarded as one of the best, the teaching was poor and mechanical, and by the time she was thirteen she was home again. And here she remained for the next three years, educating herself to a large extent, but sharing the Classics coach who had been engaged by her father for her two brothers at the Merchant Taylors' school. She read widely and deeply and attended the lectures at Gresham College and the Crosby Hall Literary Institute.

When she was sixteen, she and her two elder sisters were sent to a fashionable finishing-school in Paris, but the stay was cut short by the Bonapartist revolution of 1848, the deposition of Louis Philippe and the triumph of Louis Napoleon. One of her brothers was sent over to bring the girls home again. But this was also the year of the opening of Queen's College. Dorothea enrolled as a day student and did brilliantly, being awarded certificates in mathematics, English, Latin, French, German and geography, and at the end of the course was offered a post on the staff, the first woman to be appointed.

After seven years at Queen's, first as mathematical tutor, then as Latin tutor and finally as headmistress of the school attached to the College, she resigned, her reasons being that she felt that the principal vested too much authority in himself, and the powers of the women tutors were too restricted: and that by lowering the entrance standard to the College of the girls coming in from the school, the prestige of the College would be damaged.

She took the post of headmistress of the Clergy Daughters' School which the Brontë sisters had attended and which in 1833 had moved from Cowan Bridge to Casterton, near Carnforth. Though it had improved since the days when the Brontës had suffered so sorely it was still a grim place, and although the Rev. Carus Wilson had retired, he was still a constant visitor, casting his gloomy shadow over the place. The girls wore a hideous uniform, discipline was rigid, punishment frequent. There were no rewards for good work and the school was so understaffed that Dorothea, in addition to her work as head-mistress, was expected to teach Scripture, ancient, modern and Church history, physical and political geography, English literature, grammar and composition, Latin, French, German and Italian.

The school, she said later, she found to be 'in an unhealthy state. There was a spirit of open irreligion and a spirit of defiance very sad to witness, but the constant restraints, the monotonous life, the want of healthy amusements were in a great measure answerable for this.'

She took endless pains with the preparation of her lessons and treated the girls with a friendliness and charm that they had never before known. At the same time, sincerely convinced that she was an instrument of God to improve conditions in the school, she appealed to the governors for various reforms and a less inhuman attitude to the girls. They were not prepared to listen to her and in December, 1857, less than a year after her appointment, she was summarily dismissed by the chairman of the committee.

This was the year that the Social Science Congress was established, under the presidency of Lord Brougham, to discuss the social problems of the day. Two years later the Register of Women's Work was compiled, which soon developed into the Society for Promoting the Employment of Women. Yet what employment was open to them? The root of the trouble was still untouched, for in 1860 the majority of women were no better educated than they had been in 1660 and parents still did not trouble a great deal about their daughters' education.

The North London Collegiate School for Ladies had opened in April, 1850, with thirty-five pupils, who were children not only of professional people but also clerks and the more 'respectable' tradesmen. The Buss family lived in the attics and basement and the rest of the large house and garden in Camden Street was given over to the school. It was under the patronage of the Vicar of St. Pancras and the Rev. David Laing was school superintendent, teacher of Scripture and friend and adviser to Frances Buss.

By the end of the year the numbers had grown to one hundred and fifteen, for the school filled a growing need. While provision for the education of children of the working classes was increasing, with the establishment of more British and National schools, staffed by now with properly trained teachers, for girls of the middle classes there were still hardly any schools offering an education worth having.

At the North London the curriculum comprised Scripture, English, history and geography; arithmetic, French, elementary Latin; drawing, class singing and callisthenics, with Italian, German, music, painting and dancing as extras. Some of these subjects were taught by members of the Buss family but there were also, as well as David Laing, visiting staff from among the professors at Queen's College, and when additional teachers were needed Miss Buss insisted that they had received a teacher training at the Home and Colonial College, where she had recently helped to inaugurate a three-months course for secondary teachers.

Within a few years, Frances Buss declared that her school was open to children of all classes and all creeds. In an age of rigid class distinction this was an innovation which caused some dismay, but Frances Buss did not swerve from her intention. Anyone whose parents could pay the modest fees was admitted: and as there was no compulsion for girls to receive any religious teaching to which their parents objected, it was open to Jewesses, Roman Catholics, Nonconformists and members of the Church of England alike.

In 1854, four years after the opening of the North London, the Ladies College, Cheltenham opened—the earliest proprietary girls' school in England, the founders having issued £10 shares to the value of £2,000. Unlike the North London, this was a very exclusive school 'for the daughters and young children of Nobelmen and Gentlemen', where the background of each prospective pupil was carefully examined and no tradesman's daughter was admitted.

In outlining the aims of the college, the governing body informed shareholders that 'Female education in England is either excessively expensive or imperfect. There is in many quarters a strong prejudice against the development of girls' intellectual powers, from the impression that all well-educated women are blue-stockings, and that learning unfits them for their domestic mission. . . . In founding this Institution, your Council . . . felt that a due cultivation of women's minds is not only desirable in itself but that the general welfare of society at large depends greatly on it. . . .'

There were two departments—a junior school for boys and girls under eight, and the school proper, where the curriculum was similar to that of the North London. But the parents of Cheltenham were not yet ready for such advanced ideas. They criticized the 'advanced' education given to the older girls at the expense of the traditional accomplishments and needlework. Numbers began to fall. In 1858, only four years after the school had opened, Dorothea Beale was appointed Principal. Parents were still suspicious and for the next two years the decline in numbers persisted. Even the teaching of arithmetic came under criticism. One father thought it so unsuitable that he took his daughters away, and the end of that story was a cautionary tale reminiscent of Mrs. Drake's warning of a hundred and fifty years earlier. The father died, leaving his daughters a large fortune, but as there was no one to manage it, and they were incapable of looking after it themselves, they became 'involved in pecuniary difficulties'.

However, as Dorothea Beale's brilliant intellect and almost mystical dedication to her school enhanced its prestige, numbers began to rise. By 1863 there were 126 pupils and very cautiously the curriculum was widened to include mathematics, science, Latin and Greek. At first it had been a day school but the following year the first official boarding house was opened.

The founders of the Society for Promoting the Employment of Women discovered that one of the obstacles to employing women as shop assistants was the old bugbear, poor arithmetic, and they therefore started a book-keeping class at their headquarters in Langham Place, which soon developed into a regular day school. It was known as the Ladies Institute and its members were united in a desire to advance women's opportunities for education and employment. Two of its members were Emily Davies and her friend Elizabeth Garrett, who had already announced her bold and, to some minds, shockingly revolutionary intention of becoming a doctor, although in 1862 the London University blocked the way by refusing to allow her, as a woman, to sit for the matriculation examination.

Emily Davies responded to this piece of intolerable discrimination by forming a committee whose object was to gain the admission of women to these university examinations. At the annual conference of the Social Science Association that year, Frances Power Cobbe took the idea to its logical conclusion by reading a paper in which she advocated the granting of degrees to women. The Press poured scorn on the idea. 'Every daily paper in London laughed at my demand,' she said, 'and for a week or two I was the butt of universal ridicule.'

Notwithstanding, Emily Davies, with dogged determination, pursued the campaign. First girls should be allowed to sit for the university local examinations and ultimately for the degree examinations. London rejected the idea. So did Oxford. They were prepared to consider the idea of a separate examination for girls but could not allow them to sit in competition with boys. This was not what Emily Davies and her committee wanted. They wished for an absolute assessment of girls' scholastic attainments in competition with boys. Undaunted, an application was made to Cambridge, who at last agreed that at the Cambridge local examinations, which were to be held on December 14, 1863, only a few weeks after the application was made, a batch of identical papers would be delivered to a centre in London where girls might sit the examination.

Miss Davies hurriedly collected eighty-three girls to sit for the senior and junior examinations, twenty-five of them from the North London Collegiate school, others from Queen's and Bedford, a few from other newly-established schools, including Octavia Hill's School in Nottingham Place, but none from Cheltenham. The perfectionist Miss Beale said she disliked the idea of the competitive spirit in scholarship, although in later years she was to express her gratitude for the opportunity Miss Davies's zeal had given to girls. Dorothea Beale at this time was less concerned with the pressing economic needs of so many women as with a desire to see her girls properly educated and trained for the spiritual, mental and moral benefits it would bestow on them. Girls' education she regarded as 'the cultivation and improvement of the mental and moral capacities with which they had been endowed for the glory of the Creator and the relief of man's estate'.

She had declared: 'I desire to institute no comparison between the mental abilities of boys and girls, but simply to say what seems to be the right means of training girls so that they may best perform the subordinate part in the world, to which I believe they have been called': and in regard to marriage, she told her girls that it should be considered 'not as an object to be striven for, but to be received as the supreme grace of fate when the right time and the right person came'.

Despite many gloomy prognostications that they would all collapse with nervous hysteria and ultimately die of brain-fever, in London on that important December day of 1863 girls sat for their first Cambridge Local examination. Apart from a high percentage of failures in arithmetic, amongst both the boys and girls alike, which in both cases was attributed to faulty teaching, the results were so satisfactory that Emily Davies and her committee scored a victory. From 1865 girls were freely admitted to the examinations.

Again there was a storm of protest against the whole concept of higher education for women, a writer in the *Saturday Review*, always one of the most vitriolic critics, saying: 'There is a strong and ineradicable male instinct, that a learned, or even an over-accomplished woman is one of the most intolerable monsters in creation', while Dr. W. B. Hodgson, the educational reformer who was sympathetic to the movement and had been co-opted on to Emily Davies's committee, nevertheless, raised a warning voice, saying that it was not necessary 'to maintain that in the highest departments of original or creative power the mind of woman is, or ever can be, equal to that of man—at least, of certain men', the question being 'whether any of the differences commonly affirmed or admitted to exist between them ought in any way to prevent similarity and equality in the mental training of both'.

Emily Davies and her committee now urged that the survey of the Schools Inquiry Commission, undertaken between 1864 and 1867, should include an investigation into girls' schools as well as boys, pointing out that, at the earlier commission on charities, it had been revealed that, in many cases, endowments which had been intended for the education of both girls and boys had been diverted mainly to the benefit of the boys and the girls had been shamefully neglected.

Miss Buss and Miss Beale were invited to give evidence on the Schools Inquiry Commission, as well as Emily Davies, and this in itself was a triumph, for it was one of the first occasions when women had given evidence before a Royal Commission. Both Emily Davies and Frances Buss were nervous, but all three gave their evidence calmly and factually, and the Committee applauded them on their 'perfect womanliness'.

Miss Davies pleaded for the ancient endowments to be properly divided, so that girls' schools and colleges should have their proper share, and that public examinations should be freely open to girls, so that their work could be properly assessed.

Frances Buss described the ignorance of the girls who first came to her and stressed that she was giving particular attention to the teaching of arithmetic since the result of the first Cambridge Local examination. She echoed Emily Davies's plea for the re-allotment of endowments and said the root of the trouble was that there were so few schools offering an adequate education and so few competently trained teachers. 'Mostly,' she said, 'a schoolmistress opens a school simply because she must make a living . . . she has no knowledge of teaching,' and added 'that she would like to see every teacher trained in the art of teaching, after having received a certificate of attainment.' Students from the existing training colleges at Battersea and Whitelands, and the newly founded St. Mark's, in Chelsea, for men teachers, were sent automatically to the elementary schools.

She also firmly asserted, in answer to questioning, that examinations put no undue strain on the girls, whether they were the routine private school examinations or those held in public, such as the Cambridge Local: and she made her first tentative suggestion that there was no reason why they should not in time sit for a higher standard of examination, having in mind, of course, the university degree examination.

Dorothea Beale also stressed the ignorance of the girls who came to her school, giving her evidence from the results of the entrance examinations and her own observations. The standard of arithmetic was appallingly low and spelling not much better. In fact the standard of education of girls on admittance was lower than that of many of the children in the National schools. She agreed that teachers should be adequately trained and also that study in no way injured a girl's health but actually improved it, diverting her attention from 'sensational novels and things much more injurious to her health. . . .'

In regard to the maintaining of discipline, she relied mainly on the personal influence of herself and her teachers, while the reading aloud of a girl's marks each week, in the presence of her teacher and the class, was an important check on those inclined to be lazy. For a case of real insubordination she would enlist the help of the parents, with whom she was in close touch.

She also established, quite clearly, that Cheltenham was intended only for the 'daughters of independent or professional men' and that girls from a lower class would not be admitted.

The Assistant Commissioners forthwith set out to inspect girls' schools throughout the country. At Bath and Clifton the headmistresses of several schools united in refusing them admission, on the grounds that no one had the right to interfere between the school authorities and the parents, 'who were, and ought to be, the sole judges of what was the proper course of education for their children'. Others admitted them under protest, saying that mothers did not wish their daughters to receive an education which might turn them into blue-stockings.

The Commissioners heard a complaint from many teachers, which was to be repeated well into the present century, that parents often lavished all they could afford on the sons' education but spent hardly anything on that of their daughters. Quentin Bell, in his life of Virginia Woolf, describes just this attitude. 'It was the boys on whom money was spent for education. . . . Cambridge was then a place reserved for men and one in which their sisters could hardly enter, save as rare and shy intruders. . . . She and her sister might spend the mornings studying Greek or drawing from the cast; but their afternoons and their evenings were given up to those occu-pations which the men of the family thought suitable, looking after the house . . . presiding at the tea table. . . .' The 'grand intellectual adventures and liberties' were kept for the brothers, 'and if this cost money, as it did, then they, the daughters, would be sacrificed for the benefit of the sons. Clearly it was the sons who were to have the lion's share of life.'

In many of the schools inspected by the Commission there were only fifteen or twenty girls, which they considered to be 'a waste of money and of educational resources'. The low standard of arithmetic was almost universal, fostered by the myth that 'girls had an innate incapacity for numbers'. The teaching of French showed an abysmal ignorance of elementary grammar and Mangnall's *Questions* supplied their education in history, English and general knowledge, which must have given many a girl a most tortuous view of things, particularly if she were unfortunate enough to learn the answers in the wrong order.

All the old arguments against girls' education came into full play, with the added suggestion that it was both unrefined and immodest, so that Mr. Fitch, one of the Commissioners, felt impelled to state that it was not true that 'the schools in which the intellectual aim is highest, show any deficiency of good breeding'. Nevertheless, they were opposed to the vulgar and immodest suggestion of actually publishing the names of young ladies who had acquitted themselves well and passed their examinations successfully.

In their report, the Commissioners asserted 'the general deficiency in girls' education. . . . Want of thoroughness and foundation; want of system; slovenliness and showy superficiality; inattention to rudiments; undue time given to accomplishments and these not taught intelligently or in a scientific manner; want of organization. . . .'

E. Nesbitt described more poignantly than any Commission the agonies of one small girl trying to understand arithmetic as it was taught in the average boarding school at this time. She was at school at Stamford during the eighteen seventies and declared that she would have preferred a penal settlement. Her chief trial was arithmetic but she had an indignant sense that she could do the sums, if anyone would tell her what they meant. But no one did, and day after day the long division sums, hopelessly wrong, disfigured her slate, and were washed off with her tears.

'Day after day, I was sent to bed, my dinner was knocked off, or my breakfast, or my tea. I should literally have starved, I do believe, but for dear Miss Fairfield,' she said. 'She kept my little body going with illicit cakes and plums and the like, and fed my starving little heart with surreptitious kisses and kind words.'

The mistress who was responsible for all this suffering was away for a week or two, but when she returned 'long division set in again. Again, day after day, I sat lonely in the school-room . . . and ate my bread and milk and water, in the depths of disgrace—and those revolting sums staring at me from my tear-blotted slate. Night after night I cried myself to sleep in my bed—because I could not get the answers right.'

The report of the Schools Commission proved of vital importance to the cause of girls' education. Defying all the old prejudices, still tenaciously held by the die-hards, it was the turning point, leading to the acceptance of a girl's right to the same education as her brothers.

Dorothea Beale's school at Cheltenham had convinced the Commissioners that 'the essential capacity for learning is the same, or nearly the same, in the two sexes'. They agreed that the remedy for bad work was to bring it to light by means of regular school inspection. And the appropriation of almost all the existing endowments to the education of boys they admitted to be a cruel injustice. They went even further by saying that 'the education of girls is as much a matter of public concern as that of boys, and one to which charitable funds may properly be applied even when girls are not expressly mentioned in the instrument of foundation'.

The Commission, feeling that for girls coming from good, middle-class homes, day schools were probably preferable to boarding schools, proposed the establishment of schools for girls under public authority and supervision, changes in the course of instruction now received by girls of all classes, and institutions which would give women the same opportunity of obtaining the higher education which the universities gave the boys.

And Dorothea Beale, who edited the volume of the report dealing with girls' Education, said in her preface that 'a good education is a sort of insurance' and now advised parents to take advantage of the university examinations open to girls as it was clear that it would 'soon be impossible in England, as it is now on the Continent, for any one to obtain employment as a teacher without some attestation'.

'And lastly,' she said, 'why should it be thought dishonourable for a woman to earn money?'

The immediate result of the Commission was the Endowed Schools Act of 1869, in which the distribution of existing educational endowments was revised, to give girls a fairer share. This led to the establishment of a few new girls' schools and the expansion of the existing twelve: and where only comparatively small sums of money became available, scholarships and exhibitions were established.

Among the girls' schools to benefit from this were Christ's Hospital at Hertford where, by 1865, the school had run down to only eighteen girls, receiving a bare minimum of education from a single mistress, while the boys in London numbered 1,192 and had twenty-seven masters. Today the school has nearly three hundred boarders, receiving a grammar school education. The Red Maids school at Bristol was similarly transformed and today, established in a suburb of Bristol, with some 130 boarders and 237 day girls, offers a grammar school education. At the Grey Coat Hospital, the boys were transferred to other endowed schools, and by 1874 the Grey Coat Girls' School had become one of the pioneer day schools providing higher education for girls, while in 1894 the Governors founded Queen Anne's School, Caversham, as an independent boarding school. In 1904 St. Paul's Girls' Day School was established with an endowment from the Governors of the boys' school.

This revision of the charities was a useful beginning, though it hardly touched the main problem of establishing efficient schools for the middle classes and the training of teachers, but from this point in the story, the pace quickened.

Chapter Sixteen

EDUCATION FOR ALL

THE COMMISSION HAD recommended that a school on the lines of the North London Collegiate should be established in every town throughout the country which had four thousand or more inhabitants, and suggested that the education should include more arithmetic and, where possible, mathematics and Latin. They also recommended that women should be given the same opportunities for higher education as men.

But we have reached the important year 1870, which saw the Elementary Education Act, ensuring elementary education for every child in the country, with possibilities of secondary education for those with sufficient ability to profit by it. There was still a great deal of controversy as to whether education should be compulsory and also free, and whether or not it should be denominational, and in the end it was made both compulsory and free, although for the first few years many parents had to pay a few coppers a week. In regard to the problem of denominationalism, there was a compromise. School Boards were set up and two types of elementary schools came into existence, one provided by the churches, with financial help from the government, and the other by the School Boards.

Hundreds of schools were now built all over the country and many more colleges for the training of men and women teachers were established. The first elementary school was opened in Whitechapel in 1873, and by 1900 London alone had 481.

In 1899 a Board of Education was created and the Education Act of 1902 abolished the School Boards and handed the responsibility of education and the control of schools to county councils, county borough councils and certain borough and urban district councils, who became local education authorities, responsible for the children in their areas all receiving an education between the ages of five and fourteen, although in the early days babies of three were often brought along to the schools and many children left when they were eleven or twelve, or even younger, because their parents needed them to earn money.

Although a level standard was assured by a system of regular inspections, the early elementary schools have been accused of giving an education which was an 'irreducible minimum', but most of the teachers did valiant work, grappling with classes of fifty, sixty and sometimes seventy children. Many of them were hungry and they were all poorly clad, the boys in cheap, shoddy jerseys and knickerbockers, the girls in rough serge dresses: and their boots were seldom waterproof. They suffered from tonsils and adenoids, bad teeth, squints and other eye troubles. They sat on wooden forms and wrote on slates. And when school was over, they had nowhere to play but the slum streets. In 1889 some 50,000 London schoolchildren were found to be underfed and Booth reported that 'puny, pale-faced, scantily clad and badly shod, these small and feeble folk may be found sitting limp and chill on the school benches in all the poorer parts of London'. And the same was true in the industrial slums throughout the country.

Their parents took some time to get used to the idea of this education for their children. 'Here's John-Henry nine years old and never earned a farthing yet,' complained one woman, and another remarked apprehensively: 'I don't mind their learning Emma jography—but history, I don't call it according to her station.' Yet they became immensely proud of their children's schooling and for the children themselves it doubled the years of their all too brief childhood.

By 1872 it was felt that room should be made in the existing training colleges for 'Christian gentlewomen', in addition to those who had come from the elementary schools by way of pupil teachership. Not only would they be a better influence on the children but, low as the pay was—well under £100 a year—teaching in an elementary school would give them a higher salary than they were likely to have received as governesses in private families.

In 1873, therefore, the Bishop Otter Memorial College at Chichester, a college which has been founded some years earlier for the training of schoolmasters and later closed, was re-opened 'for the purpose of training ladies as elementary teachers in the principles of the Church of England', though pupil teachers from the elementary schools, not yet technically regarded as ladies, were also admitted. It was found that the 'ladies' were far better pupils, however, and in time the pupil teacher system was dropped and more training colleges opened.

During the eighties and nineties, as the standard of education in the teachers' training colleges steadily improved, and with it the quality of the teachers, higher grade elementary schools and secondary schools were also established, very much on the lines of the grammar schools. To these schools children who passed a scholastic test could go at the age of eleven and stay until they were fourteen or fifteen. Alternatively, places were provided for them by their education authorities in local grammar schools or similarly endowed schools, over some of which they had taken control, and here they were taught history, grammar, French, mathematics and some elementary science subjects. But although these opportunities existed, there were very few of them, so that for many years not many elementary schoolchildren were able to benefit from them, and by 1904, among the 5,000,000 school children in the whole of England and Wales, there were only 86,000 who were receiving secondary education.

During the second half of the nineteenth century the pace of life quickened and the population increased at an unprecedented rate, and with it the reading public. Between 1800 and

1850 it had risen to 17,000,000. By 1875 it was 23,000,000 and by 1901 32,000,000. Popular education became fashionable and between 1859 and 1868 W. and R. Chambers published the ten volumes of their Encyclopaedia, a 'dictionary of useful knowledge'. The magic lantern was the great Victorian standby for informative and educational lectures and continued to be used long after 1897, the year of the first public showing of a moving picture by means of Friese-Green's Magic Box.

The writings of Darwin, Wallace, Herbert Spencer and Huxley were bringing about profound changes in the thinking of many educated men and women and their attitude to the Church: and the new scientific rationalism resulted in a decline in church attendance, but the Church was fighting back, developing its educational work and maintaining its prestige, and it was a long time before the dramas of social realism of Ibsen and George Bernard Shaw could find a producer.

Until the middle of the century books had been expensive but by the 1850s the demand for good, inexpensive literature was just beginning. There were plenty of magazines, journals and newspapers for men, which women also read, but Sam Beeton, after his success with the first English edition of *Uncle Tom's Cabin*, was the first to issue a popular magazine catering especially for women's interests. He planned and launched the *Englishwoman's Domestic Magazine* in 1852, offering for twopence articles on household management, cooking recipes, dressmaking, gardening, household pets, literary criticism and fiction—both short stories and serials— and introduced Cupid's Postbag, answering the letters of young women entrusting to him their love and matrimonial problems. His *Boy's Own Journal* was the first in the field of the boys' monthlies and when he and Isabella were preparing for their marriage in 1856 and Isabella was immersed in all the problems of preparing their new home and engaging the servants, she exclaimed to her sister Lucy, 'Why hasn't anyone written a book—a good book for brides—to help them learn these things?': and within a few years had written it herself.

For the next few years Sam Beeton's publishing firm, in addition to its magazines, specialized in handbooks of popular knowledge, which were widely read and filled a great need. Isabella helped him from the outset, particularly with the *Englishwoman's Domestic Magazine*, for she had been well educated, first at Miss Richardson's Academy at Islington, Miss Richardson being 'a very genteel lady indeed', and then at a finishing school at Heidelberg, where she had learned both French and German and shown her first interest and skill in cookery. Her *Book of Household Management*, in which she and her cook had tested every recipe, appeared at first in monthly instalments, the complete book being published in 1861, only four years before her tragic death in childbirth, at the age of twenty-eight.

It was in 1866 that Anne Clough, sister of the poet Arthur Clough, and Josephine Butler founded the Liverpool Ladies' Educational Society, arranging a course of lectures which called for serious and sustained study on the part of the ladies. The course was so popular that University lecturers were enlisted to help with more lectures and before long other towns in the north of England joined the society, which became known as the North of England Council for the Higher Education of Women, with Mrs. Butler as President and Anne Clough as secretary.

As educationists, they were naturally extremely interested in the Schools Inquiry Commission's recommendations, but the first move for the provision of schools for girls of the middle classes came from London. Mrs. Maria Grey and her sister, Emily Sheriff, were two brilliant and naturally scholarly women, born during the Regency, who had largely educated themselves, encouraged by their father, Admiral Sheriff, despite their mother's view that learning in a woman was 'not only unnecessary but undesirable'. Maria had published one or two novels: jointly the sisters had written *Thoughts on Self-Culture:* and a few years later Emily had written *The Intellectual Education of Women*. The Dowager Lady Stanley of Alderley, a few years older than Maria and Emily, had an equally lively mind and had done her best, in defiance of the criticism of her mother-in-law, to provide governesses for her daughters who could give them a far wider education than most girls in their position were receiving. Mary Gurney was much younger than the other three women, a natural student who lived with her father and step-mother in a southern suburb of London and delighted in teaching her young step-sisters.

Maria Grey and her sister were already becoming known for their interest in women's education as well as women's suffrage, but when they were asked to stand for the Borough of Chelsea's approaching election for the first School Board of London they were dumb-founded. 'The position was such an entirely novel and unheard-of one for a woman to assume that the proposal revolutionized all one's ideas,' wrote Maria. 'Emily refused at once. I took a few days to consider, and then refused also.'

But then Maria, far stronger physically than Emily, had second thoughts and plunged more boldly into the fray. She stood for election but lost by a small margin. Nothing daunted, she went into battle again. Now that the Education Act of 1870 had given the girls of the poor an equal chance of education with the boys, the cause of the middle-class girls was even more urgent. She first outlined a scheme to Anne Clough's North of England Council for the Higher Education of Women and here she met Dorothea Beale. In October, 1871, the Social Science Association met at Leeds. Maria read a paper *On the Special Requirements for Improving the Education of Girls* and met for the first time Mary Gurney, who had prepared a paper on *Middle-Class Schools for Girls*, based largely on the work of Frances Buss at the North London Collegiate.

This was the year that the school had been reorganized. Miss Buss had relinquished her private interest and it had become a public school with Trustees and a governing body, Miss Buss remaining as headmistress, but on a fixed salary, and responsible to the Board. The school had moved to a new and larger building in the Camden Road and been renamed the

North London Collegiate School for Girls, and in the old building in Camden Street she established a new school, the Camden, under its own headmistress, which offered a simpler form of education for only £4 4s. a year, for girls up to sixteen years of age, with a few scholarships which might take them on to the North London.

At the 1871 Social Science Congress Maria Grey was able to form, with a provisional committee, her *National Union for the Education of Girls of all Classes above the Elementary* and Lady Stanley willingly agreed to become one of the Vice-Presidents. Among others who were invited there were many refusals, on the old grounds that woman's place was in the home and she had no need of education, but when Princess Louise became President a long list of important Vice-Presidents was not difficult to achieve, and it included Sir James Kay-Shuttleworth. Maria Grey, Emily Shirreff, Lady Stanley and Mary Gurney were the driving force of the National Union, which now set about its business of founding schools for girls whose educational needs were not covered by the Education Act of 1870. It was decided that the schools must be self-supporting and they created a Limited Liability Company, issuing £5 shares. In June, 1872, the Girls' Public Day School Company was launched. Based on the North London Collegiate principle, the new schools were to have no denominational teaching and no class distinctions. This in itself raised criticism in many quarters, but plans went ahead, and with a capital sum of £12,000 they opened their first school on January 20, 1873, in an interesting if rather decrepit old house in Chelsea, with twenty pupils; and later that year the Union offered its first scholarship to a girl from an elementary school to finish her education either at Chelsea or the North London. In September, 1873, the second school was opened in Notting Hill and by 1890 there were thirty-four throughout the country. By 1901 there were four more, with a total of 7,209 pupils, although four had been closed, partly because of competition from other new schools, but mainly because they were in districts from which the middle-class population was moving away and poorer people moving in. Fees were reasonable and they were known as High Schools, apart from a few somewhat cheaper schools, with a modified curriculum, established in the less prosperous neighbourhoods, which were known as Middle Schools. A few had boarding houses attached but mainly they were day schools, the school hours being from 9.15 to 1.30, with a voluntary study and preparation period in the afternoon for girls who preferred to stay at school, take a school dinner which was provided at low cost, and go home later.

Girls were prepared for the university local examinations, the curriculum including religious instruction, reading, writing, arithmetic, book-keeping, English grammar and literature, history, geography, French and German, physical science, drawing, class-singing and gymnastics, and for the older girls there was also Latin, sometimes Greek, literature, history, mathematics, physical science, social and domestic economy.

To train teachers for these schools the *Training College for Teachers in Middle and Higher Schools for Girls* was established in 1878, first in Bishopsgate and then in Fitzroy Square, when it was named the Maria Grey Training College.

Even before the formation of the Girls' Public Day School Company, Emily Davis was tackling the even more controversial question of the provision of opportunities for the higher education of women, which the commission had recommended. She and a group of sympathizers formed a committee, established their aims and by the beginning of 1868 had collected £2,000 to found a college. In 1869 it was opened in a small house in Hitchin with five students. After months of argument, during which Cambridge University suggested that a special examination should be set for the girls, they at last agreed that the students should be allowed to sit for the 'Little Go' entrance examination and ultimately for the Tripos examination. The girls had visiting professors from Cambridge. They worked hard—and by 1873 two had passed the Tripos in Classics and one in mathematics.

The next year the Hitchin College had moved to Girton and was incorporated as Girton College. It was a great step forward, though it was not the ultimate victory for which Emily Davies was striving, for the girls were not yet granted degrees, and although they continued to sit for the Tripos examination on the same terms as the men students, this ban lasted for many years.

With the creation of the higher Cambridge local examination, a course of preparatory lectures for women students was established at Cambridge, which developed into the Association for Promoting the Higher Education of Women. Emily Davies, with her eye on full membership of the University, felt that this was side-stepping the issue and would have nothing to do with it, but Anne Clough was invited to take charge of Merton Hall, at Cambridge, where the girls for these courses were to live. She accepted and the new college was so successful that in 1873 it was moved to Newnham and in 1880 incorporated as Newnham College. Here, in 1890, Philippa Fawcett ended for all time the illusion that women were constitutionally incapable of equalling men at mathematics by being placed above the Senior Wrangler. 'Thank God, we have abolished sex in education!' wrote Miss Buss when she heard the news. And yet it was not until 1948 that women at Cambridge were granted degrees on the same terms as men.

At Oxford the story was much the same, beginning in 1865 with classes held in Oxford for girls who had left school and wished to continue their studies. Within a few years the lectures were linked with the university. The Anglican Lady Margaret Hall and the undenominational Somerville College were both established in 1879, followed by St. Hugh's in 1886 and St. Hilda's, founded by Dorothea Beale in 1893, and women were admitted to many of the examinations, but they were not granted degrees and full membership of the university until 1920.

Bedford College had continued to prosper and expand and soon the school for younger girls attached to it was crowded out. In 1868, eight years after Mrs. Reid's death, the school was closed and in 1874 the college moved to York Place, the following year receiving its charter as the Bedford College for Women. In 1878, the University of London, more accommodating than Oxford or Cambridge, admitted women to its degrees, and in 1898 Bedford College became part of the London University. In 1913 the buildings of its present home in Regent's Park were opened, the end of the story being that within the last few years it has opened its doors to men students and the college has become co-educational.

Queen's College, Harley Street has remained part school, part college, but in 1882 Westfield College was founded as part of the London University, in the first place only for women but now co-educational, and in 1886 the Royal Holloway College. King's College became part of the University in 1900 and the women's department in Kensington moved into the Strand building with the men. The London School of Medicine, founded in 1874 by Sophie Jex-Blake, and now the Royal Free Hospital, also became part of the London University: and during these years women were being freely admitted to the new provincial universities.

Soon there was a good supply of university trained women, many of whom were to become teachers. Following the success of the Girls' Public Day schools, many more similar day schools were opened throughout the country and also the first expensive residential public schools for girls, St. Leonards, at St. Andrews, in 1877, Roedean in 1885, moving to its present site on the cliff-tops between Brighton and Rottingdean in 1898, Wycombe Abbey in 1898, closely followed by St. Felix at Southwold and Sherborne in Dorset. Benenden was founded in 1923 and Westonbirt, in Gloucestershire in 1928.

Many of these schools were modelled on Dr. Arnold's tradition of the nineteenth-century boys' public schools, with prefects and school uniforms, and, after the introduction of organized games in the eighties and nineties, house matches: and they successfully withstood the early criticisms that, with the acquisition of the Classics, mathematics and the sciences, these hockey-playing, mannish girls were becoming sexless and tending to despise the gentler domestic arts. Many of them had neither the economic need nor the inclination to make careers for themselves after leaving school, but their school-days were an invaluable break from the sometimes oppressive and restrictive atmosphere of Victorian family life.

Although the Church of England had done so much for the education of poor children, they had as yet provided no schools for girls of the middle classes. The Reverend Francis Holland, minister of the Quebec Chapel near the Marble Arch, and his wife were both keenly interested in education. With the establishment of the G.P.D.S. company's schools at Chelsea and Notting Hill, Mrs. Holland visited them both and compared them with the crop of small Ladies' Academies around her husband's parish. She and her husband were deeply impressed, regretting only that the new schools were undenominational. They made their plans and by 1877 Francis Holland had formed the *Church of England High Schools For Girls Company, Ltd.*, which in later years was to be known as the Francis Holland Church of England Schools Company. A site was chosen at 6 Upper Baker Street and a new school built, which opened on October 1, 1878, with fifteen pupils, a head-mistress who had come from the Notting Hill High School and two assistant mistresses. The girls were given a preliminary examination and divided into three forms. Fees were not high, for the school was intended mainly for the daughters of clergy-men and young professional men, but from the outset it was a happy place. Discipline was fairly strict and as at Cheltenham there was a silence rule for many of the school hours. The curriculum was similar to that of the High Schools and the hours of work the same. Francis Holland was responsible for the religious instruction and lessons. The school was regularly inspected by the Board of Education and scholastically did well, the girls taking the Cambridge Higher and Senior Local examinations, as well as the London Matriculation, and several won scholarships to Oxford and Cambridge.

Numbers increased with the growing prestige of the school

and the company set about opening a second school in Belgravia. A private house was taken in what is now Eaton Terrace and the school opened in March, 1881, with eighteen pupils, whose ages ranged from nine to sixteen, with a headmistress and two assistants. By the end of 1881 there were sixty-eight pupils, a year later one hundred and eight, and before long numbers had grown so much that a new school was built for them in Graham Street, near Sloane Square, which was opened in 1884.

In 1882 Francis Holland became a Canon of Canterbury Cathedral but he kept in close touch with his schools and came to London once a week to visit them. They were run on similar lines. Both established kindergartens to which small boys were admitted and both had boarding houses, for girls from the country districts where there were as yet no schools which could offer the kind of education to be found at the Francis Holland Schools. The Council, while taking no financial responsibility for them, recommended various suitable boarding houses such as the one in Gloucester Place for the Baker Street girls, where Miss Price and Miss Woods looked after girls not only from the Francis Holland School but also girls from Queen's College, the Royal Academy of Music and the Slade School. For girls from some remote country vicarage, these were exciting days, opening out new contacts, new scenes, new education and new prospects. The girls from Graham Street boarded first in St. George's Square, Pimlico and later at a house conveniently next door to the school.

Such girls as were allowed by their parents to 'do' gymnastics were taught at both schools by Sergeant McPherson and everyone was taught callisthenics by Miss Snell, who, wearing a long and voluminous skirt and, since she was a visiting mistress, a hat, which was firmly skewered to her head with hatpins, taught the girls the art of deportment.

There was no room for outdoor games at these schools but arrangements were made for their use of a tennis court and later a hockey field. In the Baker Street School Magazine girls were advised, when playing tennis, not to handicap themselves with tight, heavy clothing and not to let their skirts sweep the ground. It was also suggested that a low, underhand service was best for girls. 'Their height is usually insufficient to make overhand service effective, not to mention that it is extremely inelegant.'

In the delightful book of reminiscences *Graham Street Memories*, edited by Beatrix Dunning, two customs of the school are often recalled, the silence rule during school hours and the weekly reading of marks before the whole form, both of which had been introduced by Dorothea Beale at Cheltenham. There is the report of a complaint, in 1897, that hockey players 'keep the ball too much under their petticoats'. Five years later, when the girls from a country school had taken to shorter skirts, they are reported to have put on their long skirts again when playing matches against less emancipated girls, so that they should not have an unfair advantage. Today such courtesy and stylish sportsmanship sounds like a fairy tale from the days when all the world was young and fresh and innocent.

In 1913 problems arose over the lease of the Baker Street school site and in December, 1915, the school moved to its new building close by in Clarence Gate. Since those days both schools, both still independent, have maintained their traditions and standards of education and training and are as sound as they ever were.

During the 1880s and 90s the Roman Catholics also established good day and boarding schools for girls. Then came the controversial co-educational schools. J. H. Badley had been head boy at Rugby and realized that by the end of the nineteenth century the world was changing so quickly that Dr. Arnold's ideals were no longer enough. In 1893 he opened Bedales and six years later, encouraged by his wife, who was a feminist, introduced the startling innovation of admitting girls. In 1900, when the school moved to Steep, in Hampshire, there were seventy boys and seven girls, though the girls were by no means welcomed by the boys at first.

In this new type of public school fagging was abolished and

there was no school chapel, simple non-denominational services being taken either by Badley or a member of the staff. And in addition to the usual academic work the boys and girls were given every facility for manual work and such crafts as wood and metal work and were taught to be practical. It was a foretaste of the Do-It-Yourself days and thousands of men and women today have lived to regret that they never had such opportunities during their schooldays. King Alfred's, the co-educational day-school, opened in 1898.

With all these facilities for education, a far wider scope of employment was opening for women. A report read in 1886, at the Oxford Conference of the Headmistresses Association, on 'Occupations of Women, Other than Teaching', gives an idea of the ways in which women were by now beginning to find a livelihood.

Three hundred and eighteen women were employed as prison officers and there were three lady superintendents, though the headmistress added that gentlewomen did not often apply for these posts. About forty women medical practitioners were already registered, a tribute to the courage and patience of Elizabeth Garrett Anderson, and one hundred and seventy dispensers. Masseuses earned 3s. or more an hour and there was an opening for women as attendants in county lunatic asylums.

In literary work there was little scope. There were a few women editors, copyists at the British Museum were paid $3\frac{1}{2}$d. a folio of seventy-two words and research workers one shilling an hour.

The report dealt with a wide variety of arts and crafts, under the general heading 'Artistic', and said that, though hitherto only a few women had been distinguished as painters or sculptors, there was now a society exhibiting ladies' work at the Egyptian Hall, to which each member sent three pictures for exhibition. For china painting, the market was already overstocked, but there were possibilities for painting on glass, and the making, repairing and painting of fans. The art of wood engraving took some years to learn and the pay was only 4d. to

6d. an hour. It was difficult to get employment as a wood carver, but lithography was fairly remunerative and retouching negatives for photographers commanded a salary of about £3 a week. Draughtswomen were now at work on the Clyde and at Gateshead, tracing plans of steam winches, boilers, etc., and women were beginning to be used as decoration designers in the gold and silver trade.

In regard to clerical work, 1,677 women were employed in the post offices of London, Edinburgh and Dublin. Clerks received £65 to £300 a year, returners 14s. to £2 a week, telegraphists 10s. a week to £250 a year and sorters 12s. to £1 a week. Women book-keepers were being employed in houses of business and there was an increasing demand for cashiers and clerks, while there was already a disposition on the part of bankers, accountants and stockbrokers to give preference to women clerks, many being already employed by the Prudential Assurance Company.

The demand for trained hospital nurses, for which the pay was £20 to £100 a year, with board, lodging and laundry, was greater than the supply, and private nursing, surgical, medical, monthly or mental, was remunerative, the pay being £1 1s. to £4 4s. a week. Matrons were needed in large institutions, wardrobe keepers in schools, and housekeepers in wealthy families or houses of business.

Women were employed as assistants in fancy shops, fish shops, glass and china businesses, music, book, stationery, confectionery and toy shops and in retail drapery stores: as dressmakers, milliners and confectioners: in steam laundries: and in the fruit-growing, goat- and poultry-keeping industries; and the report pointed out that though, as yet, women did not own or manage shops, there was no reason why they should not.

The first typewriter had been invented in 1873, the first public telephone exchange opened in London in 1878, and although as late as 1900 there were still only ten thousand telephones in the whole country, these two inventions helped to widen the scope of women's employment.

Yet in 1897 only 20,000 girls were receiving a secondary education. In 1899 a Board of Education was created and municipal and county secondary schools established, for both boys and girls, to which elementary school children were admitted if they passed the necessary examination, and in addition some of the high schools and endowed schools were given grants by the Board in order that they, too, could admit some of the scholarship children.

With the Education Act of 1902 the school boards were abolished and the control of schools was handed over to the county, borough and urban district councils, who became the local educational authorities, responsible for the provision of elementary and secondary education in their areas. It was shortly after this that the Girls' Public Day School Company, in order to remain eligible for the Board of Education grant, a point which had been queried because they were a private company, changed its organization and became the Girls' Public Day School Trust.

The Local Education Authorities established more secondary schools, as well as technical schools and training colleges for teachers, and by 1920 the number of girls receiving secondary education had risen to 185,000.

In 1926 the Hadow Report recommended that secondary education be made available to all children, by dividing the existing elementary schools into two sections—primary schools for the children between five and eleven, and post-primary or secondary schools for children between eleven and the school-leaving age, which was then fourteen and is now sixteen.

This arrangement was amended in the 1944 Act, when the Board of Education became a Ministry of Education. The aim of the Act, planned during World War II, was 'to secure for children a happier childhood and a better start in life, and ensure a fuller measure of education opportunity for young people and to provide means for all of developing the various talents with which they are endowed and so enriching the inheritance of the country whose citizens they are'. It is the legal duty of every parent to see that his child receives 'efficient, full-time education suitable to his age, ability and aptitude, either by regular attendance at school or otherwise, between the ages of 5 and 15'.[1]

The leaving age has now been raised to sixteen and education for both boys and girls is compulsory to this age. Secondary education was reorganized to include grammar, secondary technical and secondary modern schools, all maintained by local education authorities, and since that time some of the secondary schools have been amalgamated with grammar schools or with technical secondary schools and are known as bilateral, while others, embracing all three forms of second-ary education, have amalgamated to form the controversial 'comprehensive' schools. Up until the last year or two the grammar schools have been taking those who appear to be most intellectually promising and here they can stay until they are eighteen years of age and try for a place at a university, although most of the children, particularly the girls, leave at sixteen. The curriculum includes English, history, Classical and modern languages, mathematics and science, with hand-work for the boys and domestic science for the girls.

As well as these fully maintained grammar schools there are the 'direct grant' schools, which include the schools of the Girls' Public Day School Trust and some of the public schools, which are helped by a grant from the Ministry and in return must take a certain proportion of non-fee-paying pupils, while charging fees for the rest.

The secondary technical schools are similar to the grammar schools in many respects, taking children of about the same intellectual level and providing a similar curriculum, but in their last school years their education is directed towards the kind of work they intend to do on leaving school.

The largest number of children attend the secondary modern schools, where only a few are prepared for the general cer-tificate or advanced level certificate of education, but it has been possible for children to move from a secondary school to a grammar school, or, if in a comprehensive school, from one

[1] Education Act, 1944.

stream to another, at the age of thirteen or even at fifteen, if they are considered to have been wrongly placed.

In 1975 the Ministry is working to phase out the direct-grant schools by 1976 and make all the schools under their control comprehensive, a system which has as many, if not more antagonists than protagonists among educationists. The idea in support of them is to make things fair for all children, but fairness is a word capable of an infinity of interpretations: and against the system are the arguments, repeated again and again by experienced teachers, that they are far too large and impersonal for many young children and that since children of all levels of intelligence are brought together, the standard is inevitably lowered to suit the pace and capacity of the slowest and dullest, while the bright ones become frustrated and bored, though admittedly a dull child mixing with clever ones might sometimes benefit intellectually.

Yet in the battle for an equal opportunity with boys for education, the girls can now claim a hard-won victory. The battle for all boys and all girls, of all classes and degrees of wealth, to attend the same types of schools is another matter and an altogether different problem, but today every child entering a primary school has an opportunity, with financial support, of reaching a university, provided it has the mental equipment and the capacity for sustained effort which reading for a degree entails, and these are qualities for which no government can legislate. Their possession is a matter of luck, fate, the will of God—call it what you will—which ultimately orders our lives.

Just as the number of men and women of genius born in any generation is limited, so is the number who are potentially academic, and although no education which is assimilated can ever be wasted, it is futile to try to educate children beyond their mental capacity.

The universities which have been established throughout the country during the last twenty years are all co-educational and the indomitable Emily Davies would have marched happily into the controversy at Oxford over the admission of women to the old-established men's colleges. Four years ago Cambridge opened the doors of three of its men's colleges to women, and in October, 1974, at Oxford, where the numbers of men candidates applying for admission has fallen during the last year or two and the number of women candidates risen, five colleges—Brasenose, Hertford, Jesus, St. Catherine's and Wadham—admitted between them a hundred students for a three-year trial period.

While some of the girls feel they have a perfect right of entry, as part of the present trend towards co-education, and others are looking forward to the more relaxed and l ss competitive atmosphere of a men's college—which it will no longer be, of course—others are opposed to the idea, feeling that while there is still discrimination against women in the world at large, they would do better to cling to their colleges so that, if more of Oxford becomes co-resident, and there is a danger of their losing their identity as women in the generality of student, they will have strongholds from which to do battle for further privileges.

This argument applies equally to the men, and although a number accept the situation of women in their midst as inevitable, many of the dons, particularly the traditionalists, are understandably unhappy at the prospect.

The ancient prejudice that learning ill-becomes a woman has nearly disappeared, but women students have admitted that they are more competitive than men and anxious to prove themselves.

On purely social grounds, it would seem better to leave the men and women in their separate colleges, for that way, since they will meet freely whenever they have the inclination, both sexes will retain the best of both worlds. Yet the number of co-educational boarding schools is growing. In 1922 the King Edward's Girls' School in St. George's Fields was closed as numbers were declining and maintenance becoming unduly expensive. From their endowment, the Governors paid the fees of a number of girls at other schools, but in 1952, in fulfilment of their Charter obligations, they prepared the boys' school at Witley for the reception of girls and the school became co-educational. Roedean made history a few years ago by appointing a headmaster for its girls, after generations of headmistresses, and in January, 1975, Felixstowe College, Suffolk reversed the usual order by inviting boys to join the A-level courses with their Sixth-Form girls. 'They may not become boarders, but they may join in the games and sport' says the headmistress, and she feels they will be a 'civilizing influence'.

Chapter Seventeen

AND NOW?

As well as shedding the stigma that academically-minded women are sexually unattractive, women have shown that they are the intellectual equals of men and established that proved intelligence is more attractive than the tiresome boasting of the feather-brained woman that she knows nothing. Whether the same amount of brains has been distributed equally between the sexes as a whole and there are the same number of men and women of equal intelligence throughout the world is a problem for some future statistician to decide.

Amongst the population as a whole there seems to be an upper limit to those who can, or wish, to absorb a university education. In 1974 the universities throughout the country reported six thousand unfilled places, which suggests that the thirst for higher education has been slaked by the current generation.

Of the 124,634 candidates who sought admission, 61,963 were eventually accepted. Nearly 50,000 of those who were rejected withdrew their applications. There remained 13,000, of whom more than 6,000 showed qualifications abysmally below university standard. Empty places in science subjects rose in twelve months from 930 to nearly 3,200 and vacancies in engineering and technology to almost 2,000; and for the first time there were also 1,570 empty places in the more favourite arts subjects.[1]

[1] These figures are taken from the report of the University Central Council on Admissions.

Some of the withdrawals may have been for economic reasons, for it is only the students from the poorest families who receive full maintenance at a university, and during the recent years of uncertainty and inflation, middle-class parents may not have felt able to give financial help to a son or daughter for three or four years. Alternatively, children of university quality may have preferred to go straight from school into apprenticeship or some other form of training or into one of the highly-paid if unproductive jobs now open to young people in their middle teens.

It is the existence of these openings which is causing so much resentment amongst young people and their parents at the raising of the school-leaving age to sixteen, yet there are many subjects they can learn during their last school years of which they can make good use in later life, particularly if they end up in the kind of routine, technological job which is little more than slavery during working hours, but promises ever-increasing hours of leisure.

Another reason for not wishing to go to a university may, of course, be a dislike to being associated with the extraordinary antics of many of the present day students, who seem to prefer to live in turmoil where, as in Roman times, 'both sexes alike trample on their modesty' and 'the grand maxim of their religion' is 'that nothing is lawful'. Students who 'go on strike', which presumably means 'withdrawing their mental labour', since that is the purpose of their being at the university, are withdrawing a commodity which many have not yet given any proof of possessing. But, to be fair, the mood is changing, and today the majority of students are serious minded, hard-working and extremely intelligent.

There has been a marked decline also in the number of students studying the Classics. Learning for learning's sake is no longer fashionable and most students choose courses which will lead directly to one of the professions, such as education, medicine, dentistry, business studies or architecture.

Today it is the woman's magazines and the advertisers of

clothes, cosmetics and all the rest who breed girls up to regard marriage as the ultimate goal in life. Biologically, of course, it is, and for most girls in their late teens it is their principal concern, although today, as there is a surplus of men over women throughout the country, they have no need to worry about being left on the shelf. At the same time, there are now ample opportunities for girls and women, whether they are single or married, and there are hardly any professions, trades or businesses not open to them.

In a recent survey, *Social Trends*, published by the Central Statistical Office, it is asserted that women still remain the underdogs in work and marriage, despite legislative changes, and that because of differences in educational training and their special role as child bearers they continue to occupy less skilled, less responsible and therefore lower paid jobs. Although the situation of women in home and work has been substantially modified in recent years, it has not fundamentally changed. The husband is still responsible for maintaining his wife and the tax system is based on the family as a single unit with the husband responsible for paying the tax.

It refers to 'traditional attitudes which keep women in a subordinate role and which lead to different patterns of life only indirectly related to biological difference'. These attitudes, it says, began to be formed in the home, were reinforced in schools and left most girls ill-equipped to find jobs outside a narrow range. Boys and girls took different subjects and examinations at school because of complex and subtle social pressures and expectations. Thus, although girls generally achieved better examination results than boys, fewer stayed on beyond the minimum leaving age and markedly fewer girls went on to university.

The result, in spite of the advances in opening up educational advantages for girls in recent years, was that for every young woman with a degree there were nearly four men.

The Department of Employment booklet *Women at Work*, published in International Women's Year, says much the same thing, deploring the fact that although an increasing number of women are at work there is little widening of the range of work they are undertaking.

There are few women in agriculture, forestry or fishing, says the booklet, virtually none in mining, construction or engineering, and they form less than 2 per cent of professions such as shipbroking, accountancy, chartered surveying and banking.

But this surely implies a lack of initiative or, more likely, a disinclination for the job, on the part of women, than any prejudice against their being employed in them.

Despite the claims of the Women's Liberation Movement, women have reached the state of liberation where the minorities who are intent on gaining further privileges for themselves can make a stand, without the absurdity and indignity of mass demonstrations.

Compared with conditions at the turn of the century, they now have the vote, they are able to enter Parliament and take high office, the learned professions are open to them, they have equal rights with their husband over their children and equal rights of divorce. To attempt to control the division of duties between a husband and wife in the home is absurd, for no one can legislate for the human emotions and the conduct of one's personal and private life.

All too often, women are their own worst enemies and submit to becoming slaves of their husbands and families. Some prefer it that way and find in it a personal fulfilment. Those who don't can always take a stand from the outset. If they choose to walk out, they do so with the confidence that they can quickly become economically independent by taking a job. There is no legal obligation to submit to conduct and conditions which have become intolerable to them. Moreover, married women can now choose whether or not they will have children, and if they and their husbands are honest they will decide the question before they marry.

The real problem for women is how to combine a job or profession with marriage and a young family. To expect a young woman to look after a home, produce and care for a family of young children, share a social life with her husband

and do a full-time job is asking the impossible. Something must go, and if a child or husband falls sick, it is the job which suffers.

Even if a woman has no economic need or any wish to earn her own living after marriage, a sound education must be regarded as a necessity. Over and over again, throughout the centuries, people have urged that properly educated women make not only better and more understanding wives, but mothers infinitely better able to fulfil the most important function of their existence—the proper training of their children.

Home training and discipline are vital, particularly today, when from the time they can sit up and take notice, children are indoctrinated through the mass media with every form of violence and incitement to amorality. In common humanity, they need firm guidance in this bewildering, harsh world of unstable values, for however intelligent they may be, the one vital thing they lack, by virtue of their youth, is experience. And to leave them to learn by trial and error all too often means paying far too high a price.

In the training and discipline of young children, the voice of common sense is now winning over the dangerous precepts of the psychologists, which may be well enough for those who are truly mentally deranged, but not for the mass of ordinary human beings.

Dr. Spock himself has recently confessed that he must partly take the blame for some of today's 'difficult' children and has admitted that some of their trouble is due to over-attention on the part of parents to 'the child psychiatrists, psychologists, teachers, social workers and paediatricians like myself'.

It is also dangerous to assume that children are not adversely influenced, as some would have us believe, by what they see on the television screen. Some are not, but a great many are, and no research by elaborate commissions of enquiry can alter the fact.

At no time in our history have educated women had a more important part to play than today, in the training of their children.

In regard to their employment outside the home, there is the employer's viewpoint also to be considered. If he wants reasonable continuity of employment in a job which can be filled equally well by a man or a woman, it is hardly surprising if he chooses a man instead of a young housewife who is likely to be involved in family cares. This is surely sound business sense rather than discrimination.

There are plenty of ways of solving the problem. Women teachers are often accused of taking a training course, using it for only a year or two and then leaving the profession to marry. But a large number of them return in their late thirties, when their children are growing up and their home responsibilities are not so exacting. In other professions it may not be so easy to leave for a period and then return, nor can a woman expect to re-enter on an equal footing with men and women who have not had to interrupt their professional life in this way, but she has had her compensations, and a woman of ability and good sense will soon find her own level again.

It is ridiculous to try to deny the physiological differences between men and women, and a unisex world, apart from leading to the total extinction of the human race, would be deadly boring and spoil a lot of fun.

Having achieved so much, women's best plan now is to consolidate their gains and make better use of them, for despite a century of education for all, there are still thousands of women throughout the country who have not progressed much farther than Dudley Ryder's female relations who, more than two hundred and fifty years ago, irritated him so much with their mindless preoccupation with tittle-tattle.

Never before has the world had such need of intelligent and educated women and never before have women had such opportunities to use their abilities to their full extent.

BOOKS CONSULTED

Adamson, J. W., *A Short History of Education*, C.U.P., 1922.

Adamson, J. W., *The Illiterate Anglo-Saxon and Other Essays*, C.U.P., 1946.

Aubrey, John, *Brief Lives*.

Ayling, Stanley, *George The Third*, Collins, 1972.

Bayne-Powell, R., *The English Child In The Eighteenth Century*, Murray, 1939.

Bell, E. Moberly, *Francis Holland School*, 1939.

Binder, Pearl, *Muffs and Morals*, Harrap, 1953.

Boswell, James, *The Life of Samuel Johnson*.

Brittain, Vera, *The Women at Oxford*, Harrap, 1960.

Bruce, Maurice, *The Coming of the Welfare State*, Batsford, 1961.

Chapman, Hester, *Lady Jane Grey*, Cape, 1962.

Clarke, Benjamin, *Glimpses of Ancient Hackney*, A. T. Roberts, N.D.

Cobbe, Frances Power, *Life—by Herself*, Bentley, 1894.

Cole, G. D. H. and Postgate, R., *The Common People* (1746–1946), Methuen, 1938.

Cunnington, C. W., *The Art of English Costume*, Collins, 1948.

Cunnington, C. W., *The Perfect Lady*, Max Parrish, 1948.

D'Arblay, Mme (Fanny Burney), *Diary and Letters*, Vol. 1, Macmillan, 1904.

Day, E. S., *An Old Westminster Endowment*, Reed, 1902.

Doran, John, *A Lady of the Last Century*, Bentley, 1873.

Drake, Mrs., *An Essay in Defence of the Female Sex*, London, 1697.

Dunning, Beatrix (Ed.), *Graham Street Memories*, Hazell, Watson and Viney, 1931.

Encyclopaedia of English Literature, Chambers, 1901.

Epton, Nina, *Victoria and Her Daughters*, Weidenfeld and Nicolson, 1971.

Evelyn John, *Diary*.

Falk, Bernard, *Old Q's Daughters*, Hutchinson, 1951.

Firth, Sir Charles, *Oliver Cromwell*, O.U.P., 1900.

Gardiner, Dorothy, *English Girlhood at School*, O.U.P., 1929.

Gérin, Winifred, *Emily Brontë*, Clarendon Press, 1971.

Gilchrist, Isabella, *The Life of Mrs. Sherwood*, Sutton, 1971.

Green, David, *Queen Anne*, Collins, 1970.

Green, J. R., *A Short History of the English People*, Macmillan, 1921.

Harrison, William, *A Description of England*, 1577.

Hibbert, Christopher, *Charles I*, Weidenfeld and Nicolson, 1968.

Hodge, Jane A., *The Double Life of Jane Austen*, Hodder and Stoughton, 1962.

Humphreys, Gordon, *Shared Heritage*, 1972.

Hutchinson, Lucy, *Memoirs of Colonel Hutchinson*, 3rd Edn., 1810.

Jones, M. G., *The Charity School Movement*, C.U.P., 1938.

Kamm, Josephine, *Hope Deferred*, Methuen, 1965.

Kamm, Josephine, *How Different From Us*, Bodley Head, 1958.

Kamm, Josephine, *Indicative Past*, Allen and Unwin, 1971.

Laver, James, *A Concise History of Costume*, Thames and Hudson, 1969.

Law, William, *A Serious Call to a Devout and Holy Life*, 1729.

Lemprière, William, *History of the Girls' School of Christ's Hospital*, C.U.P., 1924.

L'Estrange, A. G., *Mary Russell Mitford*, Bentley, 1870.

Lutyens, Mary, *Millais and the Ruskins*, Murray, 1967.

Masterman, C. F. G., *The Condition of England*, Methuen, 1909.

Mavor, Elizabeth, *The Ladies of Llangollen*, Michael Joseph, 1971.

Mitford, Mary Russell, *Our Village*, Paris, 1839.

Morrison, M. N. B., *Haworth Harvest*, Dent, 1969.

Nesbitt, E., *Long Ago When I Was Young*, Whiting and Wheaton, 1966.

Ogg, David, *England in the Reign of Charles II*, Oxford Paperback.

Overton, J. H., *Life of William Law*, Longman, 1881.

Paston, George, *Lady Mary Wortley Montagu*, Methuen, 1907.

Pearce, E. R., *Annals of Christ's Hospital*, C.U.P., 1946.

Pepys, Samuel, *Diary*.

Phillips, M. and Tomkinson, W. S., *English Women in Life and Letters*, O.U.P., 1926.

Power, Eileen, *Medieval People*, Methuen, 1925.

Reich, Emil, *Woman Through The Ages*, Methuen, 1908.

Roberts, A. T., *Glimpses of Ancient Hackney*, Clarke, 1895.

Roberts, David, *Victorian Origins of the Welfare State*, Yale U.P., 1960.

Robinson, Mary (Perdita), *Memoirs*, Lippincott, 1894.

Ryder, Dudley, *Diary 1715–1716*, Methuen, 1939.

Seaborne, Malcolm, *The English School, Its Architecture and Organisation*, Routledge and Kegan Paul, 1971.

Sewell, Elizabeth, *Autobiography*, Longmans, Green, 1907.

Simon, Joan, *Education and Society in Tudor England*, C.U.P., 1966.

Sophie in London, 1786, Diary (Sophie v. La Roche), Cape, 1933.

Stewart, Campbell, W. A., *Quakers and Education*, Epworth Press, 1953.

Thompson, Craig R., *Schools in Tudor England*, Cornell Univ. Press, 1962.

Trevelyan, G. M., *English Social History*, Longmans, 1944.

Tuke, Margaret, *A History of Bedford College for Women*, O.U.P., 1939.

Wallas, Ada, *Before The Bluestockings*, Allen and Unwin, 1929.

Walters, John, *The Royal Griffin*, Jarrolds, 1972.

Watson, Foster, *Vives on Education*, C.U.P., 1913.
Watson, Foster, *The Old Grammar Schools*, O.U.P., 1916.
White, R. J., *The Age of George III*, Heinemann, 1968.
Wollstonecraft, Mary, *A Vindication of the Rights of Woman*, Fisher Unwin, 1891.
Young, Arthur, *Diary*, Smith Elder, 1898.

Index

Louise, Princess, 287
Luther, Martin, 70, 71
Lyttleton, Lord, 211, 213

Magazines for Women, 284
Magna Carta, 39
Makin, Bathsua, 91, 99, 100
Mandeville, Bernard de, 151
Mangnall, Richmal, 23, 235, 260
Map, Walter de, 33
Margaret of Anjou, 47
  of York, 47
  Queen of Scotland, 28, 29
Markham, Mrs., 260
Marshall, John, 162
Martineau, Harriet, 265
Maurice, Professor, 264
Mary I, Queen, 52, 53, 58, 62
  II, Queen, 95, 96
  Virgin, 18
    Legends of, 19
Mass, 22, 32
  Priest, 39
Mathilda, Queen, 29
Mercers' School, 65
Merchant Taylors' School, 65, 71, 269
Mercia, 21, 27
Merton Hall, Cambridge, 289
Messalina, 17
Millais, John, 237
Milner, Esther, 186ff
Milton, John, 80, 81
Mines, Children in, 249
Ministry of Education, 296
Mitford, Dr., 194
  Mary Russell, 135, 196–200
Monasteries, 22, 31, 35
  Dissolution of, 55ff
Monks, 22, 34
Monsey, Dr., 213
Montagu, Edward, 209
  Elizabeth, 136, 184, 209ff, 221
  Lady Mary Wortley, 119–123

More, Hannah, 162–164, 195ff, 198, 213
  school at Bristol, 178
  schools near Cheddar, 163
More, Sir Thomas, 51, 52, 54, 62, 73
  d. Margaret Roper, 52
Mulcaster, Richard, 71, 72
Murray, Hon. Miss, 263, 264
Mytilene, 11

National Society, 159, 251
  Union for the Education of Girls of all Classes above the Elementary, 287
Needlework, 87
  (see also Embroidery)
Nesbitt, E., 278
Newberry (Publisher), 160, 161
Newcastle, Duke of, 101
  Margaret, Duchess of, 101, 102
Newman, Francis, 265
Newnham College, Cambridge, 289
Nonconformists, 94
Normans, 20, 30ff
  Position of Women, 31
North London Collegiate School for Ladies, 269, 271, 274
  (Later renamed N.L.C. School for Girls, 287)
Northumbria, 21, 27
  Earldom of, 30
Nunneries, 26, 35, 37, 38, 39, 48
  Dissolution of, 55
Nunnery Schools, 27, 48
Nuns, 22, 23, 34, 37

Octavia, 17
Osborne, Dorothy, 92
Orinda (Mrs. Phillips), 85
Oundle School, 131
Owen, Robert, 253
Oxford University, 35, 100, 259, 265, 273, 289